An A.B.C. of
ENGLISH USAGE

SOME OXFORD DICTIONARIES

A Dictionary of Modern English Usage. By
H. W. FOWLER. 1926. Pp. 750.

The Concise Oxford Dictionary of Current
English. Adapted by H. W. FOWLER and
F. G. FOWLER from *The Oxford English
Dictionary*. Third Edition, revised by
H. W. FOWLER and H. G. LE MESURIER.
1934. Pp. 1524.

The Pocket Oxford Dictionary of Current
English. Compiled by F. G. FOWLER and
H. W. FOWLER. New Edition, revised by
H. W. FOWLER and H. G. LE MESURIER.
1934. Pp. 1040.

The Little Oxford Dictionary of Current
English. Compiled by G. OSTLER. 1930.
Pp. 640.

An A.B.C. of
ENGLISH USAGE

BY

H. A. TREBLE

AND

G. H. VALLINS

OXFORD
AT THE CLARENDON PRESS

Oxford University Press, Amen House, London E.C. 4

GLASGOW NEW YORK TORONTO MELBOURNE WELLINGTON
BOMBAY CALCUTTA MADRAS KARACHI CAPE TOWN IBADAN

Geoffrey Cumberlege, Publisher to the University

FIRST PUBLISHED, MAY 1936
REPRINTED WITH CORRECTIONS, AUGUST 1936;
1937; 1946; 1950; 1954
PRINTED IN GREAT BRITAIN

PREFACE

In this book an attempt has been made to present in dictionary form the main elements in the accidence and syntax of the English language, both spoken and written. Spelling, punctuation, pronunciation, and idiom have their place in the scheme of what is intended to be a dictionary of grammar and usage—an alphabetical companion to English composition. The definitions and rules have been presented in their simplest and most concise terms. This presentation assumes a knowledge of what may be called the axioms of grammar, and involves a frequency of cross reference that will, it is hoped, be as interesting and profitable in the limited spaces of this book as in the wider fields of Fowler's *Modern English Usage*, that prince of reference books for the connoisseur in language. To *M.E.U.* our debt is deep and gladly acknowledged, not only for an idea that we have tried to translate into the terms of the class-room or the office, but for its guidance on all points of which we have been doubtful or ignorant. We are much indebted, also, to various other commentaries on language and grammar, especially Mr. Logan Pearsall Smith's *Words and Idioms* and Prof. Sonnenschein's *New English Grammar*; and to innumerable pupils of our own who have often helped us to a great right by doing a little wrong. Our special thanks are due to Mrs. Jessie Coulson, lately of the staff of the *Oxford English Dictionary*, who read the manuscript from end to end and made a large number of invaluable suggestions. We also owe much to the criticisms and suggestions of our publishers. Besides *M.E.U.* and *The King's English*, our chief courts of appeal have been the various Oxford Dictionaries, the *Report on Grammatical Terminology* (which seems to survive only in such prefaces as this), *Authors' and Printers' Dictionary* (F. H. Collins), and *Rules for Compositors and Readers* (Horace Hart).

Croydon,
February 1936

H. A. T.
G. H. V.

CHIEF CONTRACTIONS USED

>	becomes.
<	is derived from.
OED	*Oxford English Dictionary.*
SOED	*Shorter Oxford English Dictionary.*
COD	*Concise Oxford Dictionary.*
KE	*King's English.*
MEU	*Modern English Usage.*
RCR	*Rules for Compositors and Readers* (Hart).
RGT	*Report on Grammatical Terminology.*
Mod.E.	*Modern English.*
ME.	*Middle English.*
OE.	*Old English.*
AV	*Authorised Version,* 1611.

Small capitals refer the reader to the article so indicated, for further information.

A.B.C. OF ENGLISH USAGE

a. (i) The indefinite article. See AN.

(ii) In 'I go a fishing', 'A hunting we will go' the *a* is a weak form of OE. *on*.

ablaut. See GRADATION.

-able, -ible. Our blurred pronunciation makes it difficult to decide between the two suffixes; and in spelling all but the commonest words there is often an uneasy doubt in the mind of the speller. The OED helps a little—but only a little: 'In English there is a prevalent feeling for retaining -*ible* wherever there was or might be a Latin -*ibilis*, while -*able* is used for words of distinctly French or English origin.' Examples, however, will be worth all attempts at generalization. They are taken, with a few omissions, from the lists in RCR:

-ABLE

actionable
adorable
advisable
agreeable
amenable
amiable
analysable
arguable
believable
blam(e)able
changeable
chargeable
comfortable
conceivable
conversable
debatable
definable
delineable
demonstrable
detestable
dissolvable
drinkable
dutiable
eatable
endorsable
excisable
forgettable

forgivable
immovable
immutable
impassable (i.e. that cannot be passed; cf. impassible, i.e. incapable of feeling)
impenetrable
impressionable
improvable
inalienable
incalculable
inconceivable
incurable
indispensable
inestimable
inflatable
inviolable
irreconcilable
lik(e)able
lovable
malleable
manageable
movable
nam(e)able
notable
noticeable

palatable
peaceable
personable
preferable
probable
provable
rat(e)able
reasonable
regrettable
removable
sal(e)able
serviceable
tam(e)able
teachable
tenable
tolerable
translatable
treasonable
tun(e)able
uncontrollable
undeniable
unendurable
ungovernable
unmistakable
unpronounceable
unquenchable
unshakable

-IBLE

accessible
adducible
admissible
audible
avertible
collapsible
comprehensible
compressible
contemptible
controvertible

credible
deducible
dirigible
discernible
divisible
edible
eligible
expressible
fallible
feasible

fencible
flexible
forcible
gullible
impressible
incomprehensible
incorruptible
incredible
indefeasible
indefensible

-IBLE (*contd.*)

indelible
indestructible
indigestible
inexhaustible
inflexible
intangible
intelligible
irascible
irresistible
legible

negligible
ostensible
perceptible
permissible
persuasible
plausible
reducible
reprehensible
repressible
responsible

reversible
submersible
suggestible
suppressible
susceptible
tangible
transmissible
vendible
visible

abridgement, abridgment. The first is preferable. See under MUTE E.

absolute. For nominative absolute see NOMINATIVE CASE.

abstract. *Abstract* is an epithet sometimes applied in grammar to nouns which are the names of intangible things—*love, thought, opinion,* and the rest.

accent. In English *accent* is a matter of stress, i.e. it depends on force of utterance; and the contrast between accented and unaccented syllables is very marked, whereas in French it is slight. Hence English verse depends primarily on alternation of stressed and unstressed syllables, rather than on quantity, as in Latin, or strict numbering of syllables, as in French.

In English words the accent falls as a rule on the first syllable or on the root syllable; and the comparative weakness of the end syllables is the main reason for the confusion or loss of inflexions, which is marked if we compare King Alfred's English with Chaucer's, or Chaucer's with Shakespeare's.

Some words that have the same spelling but different accentuation according to their grammatical function are included in the following list. In such pairs the noun usually has the accent on the first syllable, the verb on the second:

ábsent (adj.) / absént (v.)
ábstract (n. or adj.) / abstráct (v.)
áccent (n.) / accént (v.)
Aúgust (n.) / augúst (adj.)
cóllect (n.) / colléct (v.)
cómpound (n.) / compoúnd (v.)
cómpress (n.) / compréss (v.)
cóncert (n.) / concért (v.)
cónduct (n.) / condúct (v.)
cónflict (n.) / conflíct (v.)
cónsort (n.) / consórt (v.)
consúmmate (adj.) / cónsummate (v.)
cóntract (n.) / contráct (v.)
cóntest (n.) / contést (v.)
cónvert (n.) / convért (v.)
cónvict (n.) / convíct (v.)
cónvoy (n.) / convóy (v.)
déscant (n.) / descánt (v.)
désert (n.) / desért (v.)
détail (n.) / detaíl (v.)
díctate (n.) / dictáte (v.)
dígest (n.) / digést (v.)
díscount (n.) / discoúnt (v.)
éscort (n.) / escórt (v.)
éssay (n.) / essáy (v.)
éxpert (n.) / expért (adj.)

éxploit (n.) / exploít (v.)
éxport (n.) / expórt (v.)
éxtract (n.) / extráct (v.)
férment (n.) / fermént (v.)
fréquent (adj.) / frequént (v.)
ímport (n.) / impórt (v.)
ímpress (n.) / impréss (v.)
ímprint (n.) / imprínt (v.)
íncense (n.) / incénse (v.)
íncrease (n.) / incréase (v.)
ínstinct (n.) / instínct (adj.)
ínsult (n.) / insúlt (v.)
ínterdict (n.) / interdíct (v.)
ínvalid (n. or adj.) / inválid (adj.)
[ínvaleed] / [inválid]
mínute (n.) / minúte (adj.)
[mínit]
miscónduct (n.) / miscondúct (v.)
Natál (n.) / nátal (adj.)
óbject (n.) / objéct (v.)
pérfect (adj.) / perféct (v.)
rébel (n.) / rebél (v.)
súspect (n.) / suspéct (v.)
tránsport (n.) / transpórt (v.)
tránsfer (n.) / transfér (v.)

access, accession. The general distinction between the two words is well illustrated by examples given in MEU. *Accession* means actual coming to, *access* the possibility of coming to; so *accession to the throne*= coming to the throne, i.e. becoming sovereign; and *access to the throne* = the opportunity of coming to the throne, i.e. approaching the sovereign (with a petition). *Accession* is generally restricted in use to the idea of rising to a state, a rank.

accusative case. The case of (1) the direct object of a verb, (2) the object of a preposition.

The accusative case occurs in the following special and idiomatic constructions:

(*a*) *Accusative and infinitive*: the accusative of a noun or pronoun used with the verb infinitive, making a noun phrase as object of a verb of *knowing, thinking, believing*:

'I know *that virtue to be* in you, Brutus.'
'Behind the man was a girl in a silvery grey robe, *whom* Graham perceived *to be* beautiful.'

(*b*) *Adverbial accusative*: (i) the idiomatic accusative of extent of place and duration of time, making an adverbial phrase of place, time:

We walked *ten miles*.
He had lived *three years* in London.

(ii) the adverbial accusative of cost: The book cost *six shillings*.

(iii) adverbial accusative of respect: *heart* broken; *tongue* tied; *foot* sore; *conscience* stricken.

(*c*) *Cognate accusative*: a noun of the same significance as the verb to which it becomes an 'emphasizing' object. Thus in the sentence 'I have fought the good fight', the verb is intransitive, the noun *fight* being a cognate (Lat. *cognatus*, 'born with') object, not suffering but emphasizing the action:

　　　　　　　'Such a *sleep* they sleep,
　　　The men I loved.'
'Let us run with patience the *race* that is set before us.'
　　　　　　　'ere the bat hath flown
　　　His cloister'd *flight*.'

(*d*) *Retained accusative*: the direct object that is kept or 'retained' in the sentence when a verb with a direct and an indirect object is made passive. Thus:

	Subject	Active verb	Indirect obj.	Direct object
Active sentence .	He	gave	me	a book

	Subject	Passive verb	Retained obj.	Instrument or agent
Passive sentence .	I	was given	a book (accusative)	by him

See also DATIVE CASE.

(*e*) *Accusative with factitive verbs*: verbs of 'making' (*factitive* < Latin *facio*, 'I make') sometimes have two direct objects, one in apposition to the other:

　　　　　'Then the King made *Daniel* a great *man*.'

acknowledgement, acknowledgment. The first is preferable. See under MUTE E.

active voice. See PASSIVE VOICE.

addicted. *Addicted* cannot be followed by the infinitive. The idiom is *addicted to* + noun, or noun equivalent. A gerund, therefore, may legitimately follow the preposition: 'He is addicted to betting on horse-races' (not 'to bet').

adjective. The adjective (Lat. *ad* + *jactum*, 'put near', 'added to') quali-fies a noun or pronoun. Syntactically adjectives may be either:

(*a*) *attributive*—the adjective that stands with (usually before) its noun as in 'the *blue* sky', 'the *angry* sea', 'He was a friar of orders *grey*', and
(*b*) *predicative*—the adjective that stands in the predicate as complement to the verb: 'The sky is *blue*', 'He seems *angry*'

For possessive adjective see POSSESSIVE.

adjective clause. The adjective clause is always introduced by a rela-tive pronoun, or by a word that plays the part of a relative pronoun, whose antecedent the clause qualifies: 'At one period Swift was acting as secretary and adviser to a distinguished lady *who often required him to read to her aloud.*' The adjective clause (italicized) qualifies the an-tecedent of the relative pronoun, *lady.*
The relative pronoun introducing an adjective clause may be

(*a*) governed by a preposition: 'Far away, down a long declivity, was the opening of the tunnel *up which we had fled.*'
(*b*) adjectival: 'And you, good yeomen, *whose limbs were made in Eng-land.*'
(*c*) replaced by the relative conjunctions *when, where, whither, whence, why.* For examples see under the words concerned.
(*d*) represented by *as*, especially after *same, such*; see AS.
(*e*) represented by *but* (= who, which [do not]) after a negative or in-terrogative; see BUT.

In modern idiom the relative pronoun may be omitted ('understood') when it is not the subject of its own clause: 'Almost every sentence ⌃ we speak has a natural rhythm or form of its own'; 'That is the room ⌃ I slept in.'

The following two sentences illustrate the difference between *defining* (or *restrictive*) and *non-defining* (or *non-restrictive*) adjective clauses:
The man *who broke the bank at Monte Carlo* was a lucky fellow. (defining clause).
The Prime Minister, *who had just returned from Switzerland*, was met at Victoria by an enthusiastic crowd. (non-defining clause).

In the first sentence the subject is *defined* by the clause; if the clause were removed we should not know *who* was the lucky fellow. In the second sentence the clause is almost parenthetical (and as such is enclosed within commas), and merely adds a fact to the sentence, the subject of which is sufficiently defined without it.

For a further note on this see under COMMA.

adjective phrase. The adjective phrase qualifies a noun or pronoun in the sentence and has the following forms:

(a) containing an adjective, or adjectives, separated by a comma from the noun (or pronoun) qualified:

'*Unstable as water*, thou shalt not survive.'
Tall, strong and intellectual, he seemed to be the darling of the gods.

(b) preposition and noun. The chief prepositions in this construction are *of* (introducing the genitive phrase), *with*, and *for* : 'the top *of the table*'; 'the man *with the white hat*'; 'the Society *for the Propagation of the Gospel*'.

(c) phrase containing an infinitive. See INFINITIVE (d).

(d) phrase containing a participle. See PARTICIPLE.

Since there is the minimum of inflexion in English, the position of the adjective phrase in the sentence is all important. It must be so placed as to qualify without ambiguity the noun it is intended to qualify. The familiar advertisement quoted long ago in *Punch* will point the moral: 'Wanted easy chair by gentleman *with sliding back and oak legs*.' Other examples of misplacement of the adjective phrase are given under PARTICIPLE.

admit. (a) When it has a personal subject *admit* is not followed by *of*: 'I admit being in the wrong' (not 'admit of'). But with a non-personal subject (e.g. *it* or an abstract noun) *admit of*, meaning 'present an opening for' or 'leave room for', is the verb: 'His conduct admits of no other interpretation.'

(b) The noun from *admit* in all senses, concrete and abstract, is *admission*: 'His admission of guilt caused great surprise'; 'admission sixpence'. The noun *admittance* survives idiomatically only in 'No admittance except on business' and similar phrases—e.g. 'They knocked, but could not gain admittance'—when *admission* is rather less likely to be used.

adverb. (a) *Form.* The OE. normal inflexion for the adverb was -*e* added to the adjective form. That inflexion has disappeared; but the few adverbs, like *fast* and *hard*, which have the same form as the adjective in Mod.E., are a reminder of the inflexion. *Fast* was originally *fæste* and *hard* was *hearde*. Our modern characteristic ending -*ly* arises out of the adjectival form -*lic*, which was common in OE. (e.g. *manlic*, Mod.E. *manly*; *godlic*, Mod.E. *godly*), and which had the normal OE. adverb termination in -*e*: *manlic* (adj.), *manlice* (adv.). These terminations (-*lic* and -*lice*) have both become -*ly* in Mod.E., which therefore contains both adjectives and adverbs ending in -*ly*. It is important to remember that the adjectives ending in -*ly* cannot always act as adverbs. The adverb corresponding with *godly* is *godlily* (though the Prayer Book has 'that under him we may be *godly* and quietly governed'), with *manly* is *manlily* and with *lonely* is *lonelily*. But *early*, *likely* (in the phrase 'very likely'), *daily*, and *hourly*, with some others, may be both adjectives and adverbs.

(b) *Classification.* The conventional classification of adverbs into adverbs of *time, place, manner, degree*, &c., is a matter of logic rather than of grammar. It is worth noting, however, that adverbs of degree (e.g. *too*, *very*) do not modify verbs (except their adjectival forms, i.e. participles), but adjectives and adverbs. See also VERY.

(c) Function. The adverb modifies:

(i) a verb:

'And Agag came unto him *delicately*.'
'*There* lay Duncan.'
'*Now* sleeps the crimson petal.'

(ii) an adjective:

'*Too* deep for tears.'
'You are *very* kind.'
'I am *sincerely* glad.'

(iii) an adverb:

'Yours *very* faithfully.'
'Her sceptre *so* fantastically borne.'
'He behaved *extraordinarily* badly towards me.'

In such sentences as 'The train ran *right* through the station', 'I shall help you *only* when you deserve it' the adverbs modify the adverb phrase and the adverb clause respectively rather than the preposition ('through') and the conjunction ('when'). Often (especially in sentences containing verbs of incomplete predication) the adverb modifies the whole predicate: '*Now* the time is ripe for action.' In compound prepositions and conjunctions an adverb is the modifying element: '*up* to', '*out* of', '*even* if', '*as well* as'.

For the idiomatic use of *there* see THERE, and for comparison of adverbs see DEGREES OF COMPARISON.

adverb clause. The following classification of adverb clauses is based on that given in RGT, from which one or two of the examples are quoted.

Type	Conjunctions	Examples and Notes
(i) Time	when, before, after, while, since, till, until, as, as soon as	'*When most I wink*, then do my eyes best see.' '*As they pass by*, pluck Casca by the sleeve.'
(ii) Place	where	'*Where Claribel low lieth* The breezes pause and die.'
(iii) Cause	because, for, since, as	'I do but sing *because I must*.' '*Since there's no help*, come let us kiss and part.'
(iv) Purpose	that, so that, in order that, lest (negative)	'And wretches hang *that jurymen may dine*' (RGT).
(v) Result	so . . . that	He runs so quickly *that I cannot keep up with him*. (Note that here the adverb clause strictly modifies not the verb but the notion implied in the adverb *quickly*; the adverb clause of result is therefore often a kind of clause of degree; e.g. it answers here the question 'how quickly?'.)

Type	Conjunctions	Examples and Notes
(vi) Condition	if, unless (negative) whether . . . or, BUT (idiomatic) in case, PROVIDED, so long as	Pigs might fly *if they had wings.* Take an umbrella, *in case it rains.* (Note the conditional construction with the 'inverted subjunctive': *Should you be passing,* call in to see me. *Had I been there,* it would not have happened.)
(vii) Concession	though, although, even if	'*Though I give my body to be burned* . . . it profiteth me nothing.' (Note the construction of concession with *whatever, whichever,* &c. *Whatever you do,* you will not be right; and with *let: Let him be the best man possible,* he is still too old for the appointment. See WHATEVER and LET.)
(viii) Comparison: (*a*) Manner (*b*) Degree	as, as if, as though as, than	'Heaven does with us *as we with torches do*' (RGT). 'She is as wise *as she is beautiful.*' He is taller *than his brother was at his age.*

adverbial accusative. See ACCUSATIVE CASE.

adverb phrase. The adverb phrase has the following main forms:
  (*a*) Two or more adverbs joined together: '*Slowly and sadly* we laid him down.'
  (*b*) Preposition + noun: the most familiar form of adverb phrase. It most frequently indicates time and place—as in 'after tea', 'before noon', 'until the evening', 'in the sky', 'along the road', 'over the hills'. Many adverb phrases with prepositions (e.g. 'at last', 'for luck', 'in time') are idiomatic (see IDIOM). The preposition + gerund may make an adverb phrase:
    After waiting two hours, we decided to go home.
  (*c*) Infinitive of purpose: 'I come *to bury Caesar,* not *to praise him.*' See INFINITIVE MOOD.
  (*d*) Adverbial accusative (duration, extent, cost): 'And Jacob served *seven years* for Rachel'; He walked *ten miles* a day during his holiday; The book costs *six shillings.* See ACCUSATIVE CASE.
  (*c*) Nominative absolute: 'And (she), *her attendants absent,* swallowed fire.' See NOMINATIVE CASE.

adverse, averse. *Adverse* is always followed by *to*; *averse* is followed by *from* or *to*. MEU quotes examples to show that 'averse *to*' is the common usage.
  The following, from *The Observer,* may be of interest:
  'Sir,—I have an aversion for "writing to the papers" lest some one holding an opinion adverse to my own and not averse from writing should reply. But I should

like to ask why we so frequently meet with a misuse of the word *averse*? In a letter in your latest issue . . . we read "I have been averse to receiving personal letters typed" . . . Surely well educated people ought to recognize the distinction between the two words *averse* and *adverse*.'

OED says, in one of its extremely rare discourses on syntax, s.v. AVERSE:

'The use of the prep. *to*, rather than *from*, after *averse* and its derivations, although condemned by Johnson as etymologically improper, is justified by the consideration that these words express a mental relation analogous to that indicated by *hostile, contrary, repugnant* . . . and naturally take the same construction. *Aversion* in the sense of an action, which would properly be followed by *from*, is now obsolete.'

advice, advise. See PRACTICE.

advocate. *Advocate* (verb) is followed by a noun or verbal noun as object, not by a noun (*that* . . .) clause: 'advocate his being', not 'advocate that he should be'.

aerate. Pronounce as three syllables 'ay-er-ate'. The diaeresis is not usually placed on the *e* (aërate) in writing or printing: 'The Aerated Bread Company'; 'aerated waters'. To call the bread made by the A.B.C. *aereated*, as the uneducated so frequently do, is to slander the Company (Latin *āēr, āĕris* = air; *āes, āeris* = copper).

aeroplane. *Aeroplane*, with the Greek prefix *aero-*, is the normal English word. Attempts to popularize the anglicized form *airplane* have not been successful; but they have unfortunately encouraged the extraordinary spelling *airoplane*. The contraction, which is better avoided in view of the many functions of the word *plane*, should be spelt with an apostrophe—*'plane*.

affect, effect. (*a*) There are two distinct verbs *to affect*: one means 'to assume', 'to make a pretence of' ('affect the pessimist', 'affect enthusiasm'), and from it are derived the (participial) adjective *affected* and the noun *affectation*: the other means 'to influence', 'to have an effect on'. Its related noun is *affection*. The noun *affect* is used only in psychology, and means the emotional antecedents or accompaniments of an act.

(*b*) *Effect*, as a verb, means 'to make, bring about, produce, result in' in such phrases as 'effect an entry, an escape'. As a noun it means

(i) result, consequence—'The effect of his speech was to gain twenty converts'.

(ii) power, efficacy—'of no effect'.

(iii) 'combination of colour or form in picture, &c.' (COD).

The plural *effects* is used in the concrete sense of personal property—'furniture and effects'.

The four adjectives from the Latin *efficio, effectum*, are troublesome; the principal facts about them are set out in the table below:

Word	Meaning	Example
efficacious	'sure to have the desired effect'—used of things, principally medicines.	The doctor prescribed an efficacious tonic.
efficient	'capable of producing the desired effect'—used of persons and things.	She was an efficient teacher. The engine was efficient for the work it had to do.

Word	Meaning	Example
effectual	applies to action apart from the agent, and means 'not falling short of the complete effect aimed at' (MEU).	effectual measures.
effective	'having a high degree of effect' (MEU).	effective acting, actor; an effective picture.

affinity. Affinity *between* two things, persons; affinity *with* a thing, person. MEU condemns both *to* and *for*.

affixes. The particles or words affixed to a root word are of two kinds— *prefixes*, 'fixed before', and *suffixes*, 'fixed after'. Prefixes are adverbial in effect; that is, they modify the idea suggested in the root, e.g. for *time* (*pre-*, *post-*), for *place* (*in-*, *ad-*, *ab-*), for *negation* (*un-*, *dis-*). Suffixes are either grammatical inflexions, e.g. the *'s* of the genitive and the *-ed* of the weak past tenses and participles, or endings indicative of various parts of speech, e.g. *-ness*, as the suffix of abstract nouns, *-ible* and *-able* of adjectives, *-ly* of adverbs.

afflict, inflict. The idioms are: '*afflict* a person *with* a thing', '*inflict* a thing (*up*)*on* a person'. In the passive (where the confusion of the two words is more common than in the active), a person is afflicted *with* a thing, and a thing is inflicted *on* a person. Cf. INCULCATE.

aged. As an attributive adjective and as a collective noun (e.g. in 'the poor and the aged') *aged* has two syllables (cf. *learned*). In other uses (e.g. 'aged twenty') it is a monosyllable.

aggravate. *Aggravate* is a verb meaning to *increase, to make heavier.* Thus you *aggravate* an offence, a grievance, a sorrow. The use of *aggravate* with a personal object (= tease or irritate) is purely colloquial: 'I *aggravate* him purposely'; 'She is an *aggravating* person'. It should never appear in written English.

ago. *Ago* should not be followed by the conjunction *since*, but by the conjunction *that* or *when*: 'It was a hundred years ago *that* (*when*) Coleridge died' (not 'a hundred years ago *since* . . .'). *Ago since* is tautological, the two words being parallel in meaning. Thus, adverbially, *since* = *ago* in such a phrase as 'ten years since'.

agreement. 1. *Subject and Verb.* The verb agrees with its subject in number and person. The subject when *double* (i.e. consisting of two nouns or noun equivalents) or *multiple* (i.e. consisting of more than two nouns or noun equivalents) is always plural. When a multiple subject consists of a third, second, and first person pronoun, the verb is in the *first* person. Note that in such sentences as 'The bread and butter is on the table', where the two nouns of the subject are so closely related in thought as to make a unit, the subject is singular, not double. In 'The tumult and the shouting dies' the apparently double subject may be considered as an example of HENDIADYS (the tumult and the shouting = the tumultuous shouting), and therefore legitimately singular.

Difficulties arise only when the number and person of the subject are for some reason disguised, as:

(a) when the subject is a collective noun. See COLLECTIVE NOUNS.

(b) when the verb is so placed in the sentence as to be 'attracted' into the number and person of a noun or pronoun which is not the subject (see ATTRACTION). Thus 'Each of us were willing to pay our own fares.' The subject is the distributive *each* [3rd person singular]; the verb is attracted into the plural and the possessive adjective [relating to *each*] into the 1st person by the pronoun *us* in the partitive genitive phrase. Since the verb has a tendency to be 'attracted' to the noun nearest to it, this error is likely to occur when a noun differing in number and person from the subject stands between the subject and the verb, or when the noun (in a multiple subject) that stands nearest the verb is singular, and so attracts the verb into the singular: 'Ten boys, a handkerchief, and a piece of stout rope *is* needed for a tug of war.'

(c) when the subject is alternative. The two parts of a subject linked by *or, either . . . or, neither . . . nor* agree separately with the verb. If both parts are *of the same number and person* the verb may be common to both; if not, the verb cannot be common, and, in correct writing, the sentence must be expanded so that each part of the alternative subject has its appropriate form of verb. Thus:

> Neither the driver
>   (3rd singular)   } was hurt.
> nor the dog   } (3rd singular)
>   (3rd singular)
>
> Either the time-tables
>   (3rd plural)   } are wrong.
> or the clocks   } (3rd plural)
>   (3rd plural)

But in the sentence 'Neither the men nor the dog was hurt' the verb cannot possibly be common to *men* and *dog*; and in 'Neither you nor I am eligible' the verb (1st singular) cannot agree with both *you* (2nd singular) and *I* (1st singular). The only remedy is to recast the sentences. Colloquial English, however, allows considerable latitude to the verb with an alternative subject. It is noteworthy that since there is no inflexion for person in the plural of verb tenses in English, a plural verb will agree with any two pronouns without any question of person.

(d) when the subject follows the introductory *there*. Shakespeare's 'There is pansies, that's for thoughts' is an example, if faulty grammar may be attributed to Shakespeare. But the construction is so common in colloquial English as to become almost an idiom. For all that, it should not be admitted in writing.

(e) in such sentences as 'The Prime Minister, with (= accompanied by) the Chancellor of the Exchequer, *are* to attend the funeral' the verb has become plural through confusion with the construction 'The Prime Minister and the Chancellor of the Exchequer are . . .'. *With* is a preposition, not a conjunction, and introduces an adjectival phrase qualifying *Prime Minister*. The verb should therefore be singular agreeing with the true subject.

2. *Adjective and Noun.* Since there is no inflexion in English adjectives

there can be no visible agreement of adjective and noun as in Frenc
Latin. There is one exception: the demonstrative adjectives *this*
inflect for number (pl. *these, those*) and agree in number with the n
they qualify. *A, an* has a quasi-plural in *some*. The cardinal nume
above *one* can qualify only plural nouns or pronouns. Such a sente
as 'Three American, two British, and one French airship have n
with disaster since the war' presents a problem in agreement (*three a*
two cannot qualify *airship*) that can be solved only by rearranging th
ellipsis. 'Three American and two British airships, as well as on
French [airship]' is better.

3. *Relative Pronoun and Antecedent.* The relative pronoun agrees with
its antecedent in number and person when it is subject of its own clause.
Since the relative pronoun itself inflects for neither number nor person,
such agreement is distinguishable only in the verb: 'They that *go* down
to the sea in ships'; 'It is not I who *am* to blame.'

aim. Used metaphorically, the verb is followed by *at* + the gerund: 'I
aim at making (not 'to make') a hundred in the match to-morrow.'
American usage, however, admits the infinitive after *aim* used metaphorically. 'Aim to make' is good American.

ain't, an't. MEU justifies these forms as contractions for *am not* but not
for *is not*, at any rate in speech. They have not yet been promoted to
writing, though a contraction for *am not* is badly needed.

Alexandrine. The iambic line of six feet, common in French verse, but
occurring in English usually as a deliberate variation of the normal
iambic pentameter. The last line of a SPENSERIAN STANZA is an alexandrine. Pope's couplet both defines and illustrates the term:

> 'A needless Alexandrine ends the song,
> *That like a wounded snake drags its slow length along.*'

allegory. 'Narrative description of a subject under guise of another
suggestively similar' (COD). An allegory is usually a piece of sustained
personification. The two greatest examples of allegory in English are
Spenser's *Faerie Queene* and Bunyan's *Pilgrim's Progress*, in both of
which various virtues and vices are personified and introduced into a
metaphorical scene: thus, in *The Pilgrim's Progress, Christian* falls into
the *Slough of Despond*; *Christian* and *Hopeful* come to *Doubting Castle*
and are set upon by *Giant Despair*; *Mr. Talkative, Mr. By-ends, Mr.
Ready-to-Halt* are other pilgrims they see on the way. It is in its greater
length, and in this element of personification, that the allegory differs
from the *parable* and the *fable*.

alliteration. The recurrence of a consonantal (or more rarely a vowel)
sound, especially in a line of verse. Alliteration of stressed syllables was
the chief metrical device of OE. verse before the predominance of rhyme
about the 13th century; but in Mod.E. verse it is a device used for effect:

> 'The *f*air *b*reeze *b*lew, the white *f*oam *f*lew,
>   The *f*urrow *f*ollowed *f*ree.'
>
> '*A*pt *a*lliteration's *a*rtful *a*id.'
>
> '*A*fter life's *f*itful *f*ever he sleeps well.'

all right. So written: not *all-right, allright,* or *alright.* See IRREGULAR
UNIONS.

all together, altogether. The divided form means 'all in one place' or 'at one time'; the compound word *altogether* is an adverb, meaning 'entirely': 'They are going *all together* to the fair'; 'He has *altogether* mistaken my meaning'. It is a commoner mistake to write *altogether* for *all together* than to write *all together* for *altogether*.

allusion. *Allusion* is one of a number of words derived from the Latin verb *ludo*, 'I play'; most of them have departed considerably from the original Latin meaning. A list for reference, with brief comments, is given below:

allusion (verb: allude, adj.: allusive)	an indirect reference, in speech or writing, to a person, character, legend, book, &c.
collusion (verb: collude, adj.: collusive)	in law, secret 'play' or understanding, especially between guilty persons.
delusion (verb: delude, adj.: delusive)	a false or deceiving impression on the mind. 'Under the (or a) delusion' is the phrase. MEU has a witty column on the difference between *delusion* and *illusion*. The gist of it is: a delusion is a false impression accepted by the whole mind as the truth; an illusion is also a false belief, but being based upon imagination it 'awaits full acceptance' by the mind. We speak of the *delusions* of lunacy, but the *illusions* of childhood. 'That the sun moves round the earth was once a delusion, and still is an illusion' (i.e. it seems to the senses to go round; but the mind, on stronger evidence, rejects the belief). So the thing that deludes is a delusion; the thing falsely supposed to exist is an illusion. 'What a conjuror actually does—is a *delusion*; what he seems to do is an *illusion*.'
elusion (verb: elude, adj.: elusive)	a rare word, meaning an escape from, or avoidance of. The adjective is sometimes used concretely, as in 'an elusive criminal', but more often in a more abstract sense—'an elusive word, quotation, reference': i.e. one that escapes or baffles the mind.
illusion (adj.: illusive, illusory)	a deception of the mind. See above for the distinction between *delusion* and *illusion*. The adjectives *illusive* and *delusive* are distinguished in the same way.

ally. The COD puts the accent on the second syllable in both verb and noun; but nowadays in the noun the first syllable is universally stressed, whereas in the verb the second syllable is generally stressed.

also. 1. The safest way with *also* is to banish it entirely from the beginning of sentences, clauses, and phrases. Its best place is between subject and verb, but it may stand legitimately at the end of a sentence. In other words, *also* should always have purely adverbial force (= 'as well', 'too'), and should never trespass on the function of the conjunction *and*. 'And also' is usually, if not always, tautological.

2. Granted that *also* is a true adverb, there remains the question of its position in the sentence. It resembles words like *only* in being apt to stray from its proper place. The rule is simple: Let it be as near as possible to the word it is intended to modify. The following sentences illustrate the point:

(*a*) You also are concerned in this business.
(*b*) You are also concerned in this business.
(*c*) You are concerned in this business also.

The position of *also*, which in each sentence may be said to modify the whole predicate, determines the emphasis. In (*a*) the stressed word is *you* (i.e. as apart from somebody else); in (*b*) the stress is on *also* itself and on *this* (i.e. you are concerned in *this* business as well as *that*); and in (*c*) the stress is more definitely on *this*, inferring that this business is the last of many that have been mentioned.

alternate(ly), alternative(ly). The COD definition for *alternate* is: '(of things of two kinds) coming each after one of the other kind'. Thus 'Boys and girls will step forward *alternately*'; i.e. a boy, then a girl, then a boy, &c. But the definition is inadequate. SOED admits the familiar use, dating from 1697, in the sense of 'turn and turn about', 'He and I go on *alternate* days' (i.e. one one day and the other the next). *Alternative*, as adjective, implies 'one or the other'—i.e. 'mutually exclusive' (COD). The word is, however, more often a noun than an adjective; and the following examples of its use, all taken from MEU, will be helpful:

> We have no alternative in the matter.
> We need not do it. But what is the alternative?
> If we decline, what are the alternatives?

The last sentence suggests a question that is often raised whether there can be more than two alternatives. The etymology of the word says no; but sound usage says yes. The often acrid disputes in newspaper correspondences on this point illustrate the tendency of would-be grammatical pundits and purists to stress etymology at the expense of good English usage.

alternative subject. See AGREEMENT.

ambiguity. Ambiguity is 'double (and therefore doubtful) meaning' in a sentence. It arises in four main ways: (*a*) through the incorrect position of a word, phrase, or clause; (*b*) through confusion of pronouns, especially in indirect speech; (*c*) through double meaning in words themselves; (*d*) through faulty punctuation. Thus:

(*a*) 'I *only* lent him one book'. (Does this sentence mean (i) 'I only *lent*, I did not *give*', or (ii) 'I *only* (i.e. I alone) lent him', or (iii) 'I lent him only *one* book (not two or three books)'? See ONLY.

'He came to tell me you had been to see him *after tea*.' (Does the italicized adverb phrase modify *came* or modify *to see*?)

'Choose the poems from the green book *which I told you to read*.' (What does the adjective clause qualify—*poems* or *book*?)

'In the course of an interesting survey of the question of copyright in books *published in a recent number of* "*Economica*".' The adjective phrase (italicized) seems to qualify *books*; it should qualify *survey*. A simple remedy for this particular ambiguity would be the insertion of a comma after *books*. (See also under ONLY, ADJECTIVE PHRASE, and ADJECTIVE CLAUSE.)

(*b*) 'And when *they* (i.e. the Israelites) arose in the morning, behold, *they* (i.e. the Syrians) were all dead corpses.'

'He told him *he* was selected to play.' (Who was selected—the speaker or the person spoken to?)

(*c*) All words with the same spelling but of different etymology and meaning should be rigorously tested for ambiguity. Sometimes ambiguity of meaning in a word is deliberate (e.g. in puns). The BBC once arranged a series of talks called 'Mind the doctor', where the word *mind* was deliberately ambiguous (either noun or verb).

(*d*) There is a beautiful example in MEU: 'He wants to give workmen more interest in their work and vulgarity, sloth and luxury less scope.'

The subject is dealt with indirectly in many of the articles in this book, since the whole business of correct and idiomatic writing is to express one's meaning without ambiguity.

among, amongst. (*a*) Euphony, and euphony alone, decides which of the two shall be used. There is no real syntactical or idiomatic difference between them. MEU suggests that '*amongst* is more usual before vowels'.

(*b*) *Among, amongst* must be followed by a plural (cf. BETWEEN); beware of such phrases as 'among the number of his friends', where the correct preposition is *in*. The actual plural should follow *among*: 'among his friends', 'among the people (plural, not collective) present'.

ampersand. The symbol *&* for *and*. It was once the custom to print at the end of the alphabet the two signs &c. and &, with explanations:

&c. = *et cetera*.
& (*per se*) = *and*.

The word *ampersand* is a corruption of *and per se and*. OED gives *ampassyand, ampussyand, ampusand* as corruptions of *ampersand* itself, and quotes *Adam Bede*: 'He thought it (*z*) had only been put there to finish off th' alphabet like, though *ampersand* would ha' done as well.'

The sign should be used only in the writing of business addresses, formulae, etc.; it is better avoided in ordinary literary writing.

amphibrach. See FOOT.

an. The simple rule is that *an* is used for *a* before vowels and before an unaspirated *h*: *an* actor, *an* elm-tree, *an* hour, *an* honourable man. There are two special cases: (i) before consonantal *u*, *a*, not *an*, is customary: 'a union', 'a unicorn'. (ii) before stressed aspirated *h*: 'a history book' is certainly the spelling and pronunciation, but where, through the throwing forward of the accent, the *h* becomes unstressed as in *historical*, there is some justification for *an*. But, like most matters connected with pronunciation, the question can only be decided personally. Probably the modern tendency is to use *a* in the two positions noted.

anachronism. An anachronism is a reference, in speech or writing, that is 'out of time'. When Shakespeare refers in *Julius Caesar* to the striking of a clock, he is guilty of anachronism. The anachronism is often used with humorous effect, especially in caricature. Mark Twain's *A Yankee at the Court of King Arthur* is a good example of sustained literary anachronism. In drawing, Mr. Arthur Morland's *Humours of History* provides some excellently funny examples. Anachronism usually has the effect, often ludicrous, of grafting a bit of the present on to the past; e.g. causing an aeroplane to drop bombs at the Battle of Hastings.

anacoluthon (Greek = 'not following') is the name given to a break in the grammatical construction of a sentence the latter part of which does not accord with the former. Such a figure is frequently employed to indicate that the speaker is labouring under some deep emotion. Thus King Henry before the Battle of Agincourt says:

'Rather proclaim it, Westmoreland, through my host,
That he which hath no stomach to this fight,
Let him depart.'

On this passage Dr. Abbott remarks: 'Henry begins by dictating a proclamation, and then passes into the imperative of the proclamation itself.'

anagram. The rearrangement of the letters in a word to make another
word, or words, sometimes (but not always) related in meaning or significance to the original. *Caliban* (in *The Tempest*) is an anagram of
can(n)ibal (often spelt with one *n* in Elizabethan times). The popularity
of crossword puzzles has given a new lease of life to the anagram. Here
is an example from *The Times*: 'Mince Fido in a tin' is the clue: it
turns out to be an anagram of *indemnification.*

analogy (grammatical). 'Imitation of inflexion or construction of existing
words in forming inflexions or constructions of others, without interven-
tion of the formative steps through which these at first arose' (SOED).
Thus the etymological plural of the word *book* would be *beech* (<OE.
bec—an I-MUTATION plural; the *k* becomes soft *ch* by another law of
language); the actual plural *books* is formed by analogy with the vast
majority of English nouns, which form their plural by adding *s*. In
the same way many strong verbs have become weak, by imitation of
the majority (e.g. *sleep*, *help*). The adjective is *analogous*. Thus the *'s*
inflexion in the genitive of all nouns other than those derived from OE.
masculine nouns is *analogous*, i.e. it is an inflexion made by analogy with the
OE. singular genitive ending -*es* (> Mod.E. *'s*). Examples of the workings
of analogy in idiom will be found under IDIOM and PREPOSITIONAL IDIOM,
and (e.g.) the words PURPOSE, VIEW.

analysis. For method of analysis into clauses see CLAUSE.

anapaest. See FOOT.

and + relative pronoun.
  (i) 'Among the letters which formed Major Pendennis's budget for that morn-
      ing there was only one unread, *and which* lay solitary and apart from all the
      fashionable London letters.'
  (ii) 'I saw a Jewish lady, only yesterday, with a child at her knee, *and from whose*
      face towards the child there shone a sweetness so angelical that it seemed
      to form a sort of glory round both.'

Both sentences (which are from Thackeray) illustrate the incorrect use
of *and* before the relative pronoun. The simple rule is: a co-ordinating
conjunction (*but, and, or*) should stand before a relative pronoun only
when it is joining two co-ordinate adjective clauses. If only one adjective
clause is qualifying an antecedent the *and, but, or* is obviously intrusive,
since the relative pronoun introducing the clause itself acts as a conjunction. The mistake arises when the antecedent is already qualified by,
e.g., a participle, as in sentence (i), or an adjective phrase, as in sentence
(ii). It is important to remember that the misconstruction may occur with
where and *when* used as relative pronouns:

   'It was a pleasant road, fringed with elms, *and where* I often walked in the
   evening.'

Sentence (ii) illustrates the error with the possessive form of the pronoun
used adjectivally.

anomalous, defective, irregular. A *defective* verb is one whose con-jugation is not full or complete: e.g. *shall*, *may*, and *can*, which have no in-finitive or participle forms. An *irregular* verb is one whose conjugation, though complete, is not of the ordinary weak or strong type: e.g. *to be*, *to go*. The term *anomalous* is used of both defective and irregular verbs.

antecedent. A word grammatically related to another word that (normally) follows it in the sentence; but especially the noun or pro-noun of the main clause to which the relative pronoun in an adjective clause is related: 'What shall be done unto the *man* whom the king delighteth to honour?'; 'And the three mighty men drew water out of the *well* of Bethlehem, that was by the gate.'

anticipatory subject. For sentences constructed on the plan *Noun phrase or clause as subject + verb of incomplete predication + complement*, we commonly substitute sentences in which the real subject is placed after the verb and an impersonal *it* stands before the verb as anticipatory subject. Thus:

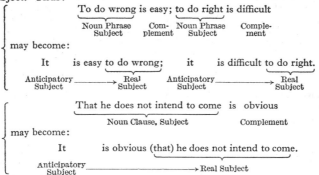

anti-climax (or BATHOS), a descent from the more impressive to the less impressive, often with a ludicrous result which is not always intentional. Thus Macaulay speaks of the Chief Justice as being 'rich, quiet, and infamous'. Pope is very fond of this figure, sometimes in a combination of the literal and the metaphorical, e.g.

> 'She sees, and trembles at th' approaching ill,
> Just in the jaws of ruin, and codille.'

A striking example occurs in De Quincey's *Murder considered as one of the Fine Arts*: 'If once a man indulges himself in murder, very soon he comes to think nothing of robbing; and from robbing he comes next to drinking and Sabbath-breaking, and from that to incivility and procrastination.' The examples quoted are all witty, intended to heighten effect by an unexpected descent or deviation. Ordinary anti-climax is an unskilful descent, which may be unintentionally humorous, but only uninten-tionally. A newspaper, commenting on a terrible explosion, said in its opening descriptive sentence that the explosion laid waste the country for miles around, and then went on to say that 'typewriters were knocked off tables'.

antistrophe. See ODE.

antithesis is a figure of speech in which words or ideas are brought into contrast by being balanced one against another. Bacon is especially fond of antithesis, e.g. 'Reading maketh a full man; conference (i.e. conversation) a ready man; and writing (i.e. taking notes) an exact man.'

antonym. Antonyms are words of opposite meaning: thus *blunt* is the antonym of *sharp*, *fall* of *rise*, *top* of *bottom*, *to* of *from*. The negative form of a word, indicated by a prefix or a suffix, is an antonym of the positive form: *valueless—valuable*; *unnecessary—necessary*; *immortal—mortal*; *non-luminous—luminous*.

anybody else. The genitive form is *anybody else's*. See ELSE.

anyone, any one. The distinction between the two is important; *anyone* is an indefinite pronoun, and is not followed by a partitive genitive; in *any one*, *any* is an adjective and *one* is the numeral. The following sentences illustrate the point: '*Anyone* is liable to fall ill'; '*Any one* of us is liable to fall ill.'

aorist (Greek = 'without limit', 'undefined'). This Greek term is sometimes given to the past simple tense, i.e. the tense denoting no more than that something happened at some moment in the past.

aphorism. A short pithy sentence into which much thought or observation is compressed. Bacon's *Essays* will supply countless examples, e.g. 'Some books are to be tasted, others to be swallowed, and some few to be chewed and digested.' The adjective is *aphoristic*.

apodosis. (Greek = 'giving back') is the name given to the main or consequent clause of a conditional sentence:

> If you think this, *you are wrong*.
> *Do not come* unless you want to see me.

See PROTASIS.

apophthegm. Much the same as APHORISM.

apostrophe. 1. A mark (represented in print by a raised comma) to indicate the omission of a letter or letters from a word. It is used

(*a*) in the contractions that are commonly employed in speech and reproduced in writing: *doesn't*, *'tis*, *thro'*, *o'er*; and

(*b*) especially in the genitive case of nouns and certain indefinite pronouns.

It originally represented the *e* in the *-es* of the normal masculine genitive ending in OE.; but is now, by analogy, used with all nouns, whatever their origin. The rule for the genitive apostrophe in nouns may be summarized thus:

SINGULAR: Singular noun + *'s*.

The only exceptions are classical names like *Mars* and *Venus* which make genitive *Mars'*, *Venus'*; the name Jesus, with genitive *Jesu's*; and the genitives in such phrases as 'for *goodness*' sake', 'for *conscience*' sake'.

PLURAL:

(*a*) If the noun ends with *s* in the plural: Plural noun + an apostrophe after the final *s*.

(*b*) If the noun does not end with *s* in the plural: Plural noun + *'s*.

It is a good working rule not to use the apostrophe form of the genitive when the resultant word would be ugly or cacophonous. Use instead the genitive phrase (of + noun); thus *of a rhinoceros*, not *rhinoceros's*. The genitive of the personal and demonstrative ('third person') pronouns has no apostrophe: *ours, yours, hers, its, theirs*.

2. A figure of speech; words addressed in parenthesis to a person in the course of speech or narrative:

> 'No, that's the World's way: (*keep the mountain-side,*
> *Make for the city!*)
> He knew the signal, and stepped on with pride
> Over men's pity.'

apposition. (Lat. *ad + positum* = 'placed alongside of'). The placing of one noun or noun-equivalent beside or against another in the sentence, to add description or explanation. The nouns (or noun-equivalents) in apposition are in the same case, are equal in function, and bear the same relation to the rest of the sentence. It is important to remember that nouns used attributively as adjectives are not in apposition; in the phrase 'a street accident', *street* is in function an adjective qualifying, not a noun in apposition with, *accident*. Here are some representative examples.

'Alexander *the coppersmith* did me much evil' (subject in apposition).
'You and I and honest Casca, *we* have the falling sickness' (subject in apposition).
'*All* that served Brutus, I will entertain them' (object in apposition).

> 'Happy in this, *she is not yet so old*
> *That she may learn*'

(noun clause in apposition to *this*).
'It is true *we are in great danger*' (noun clause in apposition to *it*).

Note especially the construction with the genitive of nouns in apposition: 'I come at the King my master's bidding' not 'the King's my master's'; that is, the genitive is expressed only in the second of the nouns.

archaism. In writing, an *archaism* is a word, spelling, construction, &c., that has become old-fashioned or out of date. The only legitimate place for archaisms is verse or prose in which an old-fashioned atmosphere is relevant and deliberately aimed at. Examples are: *anent* (= 'concerning'), *burthen* (for 'burden'), *certes, peradventure, quoth he, save* as a preposition (= 'except'), *albeit, natheless*. It is a safe rule that no word that is not in current English usage should appear in normal prose writing.

arise, rise. *Arise*, except in poetical use (e.g. 'Arethusa arose from her couch of snows'; 'I arise from dreams of thee') is the metaphorical word, *rise* the literal: a question, a situation, a doubt *arises*; soldiers *rise* at six o'clock; the river *rises*; the sun *rises*.

arouse, rouse. Like *arise*, *arouse* is the metaphorical word; and like *rise*, *rouse* is the literal: suspicions, fears are *aroused*; the alarm clock *roused* him.

artificial distinction. Distinction between related words, or between two functions or meanings of the same word, is sometimes made artificially. There are four main methods of making the distinction:

(*a*) *through grammatical form*: examples are nouns that have two plurals (like BROTHER and GENIUS), each plural form having its own meaning; and the verb HANG with two separate past forms *hung* and *hanged*.

(b) *in spelling*: examples are URBAN, HUMAN, SUIT, ARTIST, and MORAL, where *urbane, humane, suite, artiste,* and *morale* are the respective artificially distinguished forms.

(c) *with a hyphen*: after the prefix *re-*. Thus *re-cover* (e.g. an umbrella) is differentiated from *recover*; *re-create* from *recreate*.

(d) *by accent*: the difference between noun and verb, verb and adjective, noun and adjective, is often indicated by difference of stress; *absént* (verb), *ábsent* (adjective); *objéct* (verb), *óbject* (noun) are examples. See ACCENT.

The following distinctions are also interesting:

{ abuse (-*ūz*): verb;
{ abuse (-*ūs*): noun.
{ aerial (ā-*er*): adjective;
{ aerial (*air*-): noun (in wireless).
{ annéx: verb;
{ ánnexe or annéxe: noun (the *-e* is in imitation of the French).
{ cleanly (-*ěn*-): adjective;
{ cleanly (-*ēn*-): adverb.
{ conjure (*kŭnjer*): juggle, produce magical effects;
{ conjure (*konjoor*): charge solemnly.
{ excuse (-*ūz*): verb;
{ excuse (-*ūs*): noun.
{ house (-*z*): verb;
{ house (-*s*): noun.
{ minute (*mĭnūte*): adjective = small, little;
{ minute (*mĭnĭt*): noun = sixty seconds.
{ put (*poŏt*): verb = to place, set, &c.;
{ putt (*pŭt*): verb or noun, in golf.
{ refúse (-*ūz*): verb;
{ réfuse (-*ūs*): noun (= waste).
{ slough (-*ow*) = quagmire;
{ slough (-*ŭf*) = skin (of snake).
{ used (*ūzd*) = employed;
{ used (*ūst*) = accustomed.

artist, artiste. The first is the general word; the second is restricted to the meaning 'professional (or amateur) performer in singing, dancing, &c.'. There is no question of differentiation of sex in the use of the words; *artiste* means performer, either male or female.

as. The word *as* has the following main uses in English:

(*a*) Conjunction introducing an adverb clause of (i) Time: 'What was it that so fascinated the young student, as he stood by the river shore?' (ii) Reason: 'As I knew him to be a harmless amusing little thing, I could not return his smiles with any degree of severity.' (iii) Parenthesis: 'Without it, as I have said, I could scarcely have sustained my thraldom.' (iv) Manner: 'As the whirlwind passeth, so is the wicked no more.' See also under LIKE.

(*b*) The conjunction of comparison, with the correlative adverb *as* modifying an adjective or an adverb: 'as tall as'; 'as fast as'; 'as easily as'. The second *as* is always a conjunction, not a preposition; therefore it is not automatically followed by the accusative case. The *as* clause of comparison is usually elliptical. Thus, 'He is as tall as I' = 'He is as tall as I (am tall)'. 'He is as tall as me' is a common colloquialism, not grammatically, but perhaps idiomatically, defensible (see under DISJUNCTIVE

PRONOUNS). The sentence 'You have offended me as deeply as him' is elliptical for 'You have offended me as deeply as (you have offended) him'. *Him* is object of *offended*, not of *as*. Note that *as soon as, as well as* are often compound conjunctions.

(*c*) A relative pronoun (i) after *same, such*: 'It was such a day *as* I have rarely seen in England'; 'You saw the same places *as* we saw last year'; (ii) standing for an antecedent not definitely expressed: 'There is no way of getting the information, *as* there ought to be.' See also under SUCH, SAME.

(*d*) A conjunction compounded with *if* and *though*, introducing usually an adverb clause of manner: 'It seems *as* if the difficulty once mastered naturally resolved itself into ease and grace, and *as* if, to be overcome at all, it must be overcome without an effort.' In archaic English *as* is used in this sense without *if* or *though*:

> 'Which made his horse's flanks to smoke
> *As* they had basted been.' (*John Gilpin*)

There is also an exclamatory use of *as if, as though*, corresponding with the use of *if* without APODOSIS (see IF): '*As if* you meant it!'; '*As though* that were true!'

(*e*) An adverbial element in certain elliptical phrases: 'as before', 'as usual', 'as now', 'as to the second matter', 'as for me'.

as follows. The verb, having an impersonal subject 'understood', is invariable in number; never 'as *follow*': 'The rules, conditions, results, are as *follows*.'

aside. OED definition: 'Words spoken aside, or in an undertone, so as to be inaudible to some person present; words spoken by an actor, which the other performers on the stage are supposed not to hear.'

aside, a side. *Aside* is the adverb (= 'apart', 'away from'), as in 'We turned, spoke, were taken *aside*'; *a side* is an adverbial phrase meaning 'on each side', as in the sentences 'The teams played twelve *a side*'; 'We were sitting six *a side* in the train.'

assembly, nouns of. We speak of 'a *flock* of sheep', 'a *herd* of buffaloes', 'a *swarm* of bees'. *Flock, herd*, and *swarm* are some of the most common nouns of assembly in ordinary use to-day. Some of the more uncommon and certainly more picturesque ones, dating from the great days of hunting and hawking, are enumerated in the following interesting passage from Conan Doyle's *Sir Nigel*:

'It is sooth, Nigel, that for every collection of beasts of the forests, and for every gathering of birds of the air, there is their own private name, so that none may be confused with another. Answer me now, lad, how would you say if you saw ten badgers together in the forest?'

'A *cete* of badgers, fair sir.'

'Good, Nigel—good, by my faith! And if you walk in Woolmer Forest and see a swarm of foxes, how would you call it?'

'A *skulk* of foxes.'

'And if they be lions?'

Nigel scratched his head. 'Surely, fair sir, I would be content to say that I had seen a number of lions.'

'Nay, Nigel, a huntsman would have said that he had seen a *pride* of lions, and so proved that he knew the language of the chase. Now, had it been boars instead of lions?'

'One says a *singular* of boars.'

'And if they be swine?'

'Surely it is a herd of swine.'

'Nay, nay, lad, it is indeed sad to see how little you know. One talks of a *sounder* of swine. Hark ye! only last week that jack fool, the young Lord of Brocas, was here talking of having seen a covey of pheasants in the wood. How would you have said it, Nigel?'

'Surely, fair sir, it should be a *nye* of pheasants.'

'Good, Nigel—a *nye* of pheasants, even as it is a *gaggle* of geese or a *badling* of ducks, a *fall* of woodcock or a *wisp* of snipe.'

Though a large number of such terms are recorded from the Middle Ages, many of them were purely artificial inventions and there is no evidence that they were ever in actual use.

Some years ago Sir John Squire invited readers of a literary magazine to invent new nouns of assembly. Here are half a dozen of the happiest inventions: a *squirt* of chauffeurs, a *tattoo* of typists, a *budget* of politicians, a *cue* of actors, a *fleece* of income-tax collectors, a *chuckle* of charwomen.

assets. *Assets* (<Fr. *assez*) is properly a singular noun with a plural form, meaning the money or property of a person that may be used to pay his debts. Cf. *riches* from French *richesse*. MEU frowns on the modern use of the singular form (*asset*) as a synonym for *possession, gain, advantage*, in such sentences as: 'In batting, his height was his greatest *asset*, since it enabled him to smother the breaking ball'; 'There is no doubt that a good appearance is a valuable *asset* in life.' But false forms are not uncommon in English; and the history of *assets* is, after all, a natural one. There are sentences where *asset* is useful, and will perhaps become legitimate, even in the false meaning that MEU condemns. When Fowler substitutes *stroke* for *asset* in the phrase 'Her forehand drive—her most trenchant *asset*', he is only begging the question. The writer (in spite of his confused ideas concerning *trenchant*) did not mean *stroke*; he meant something like *possession* or *advantage*. Could he, after all, have found a better word than *asset*? If not, *asset* is filling a want and should (like many other words in the past) take its place in English against all etymological prejudice.

assimilation. (*ad* + *similis*, like). The changing of a sound by the influence of an adjacent sound. Thus in the word *cupboard*, the *p* takes the sound of the adjacent *b*. Usually, however, the change takes place in spelling as well as in pronunciation, as when the final consonant of a prefix is changed into the initial consonant of the root word: in + legal >illegal; in + mortal>immortal; Latin *sub* + *fero*>English suffer.

assonance. In verse, the correspondence of vowel sounds in two syllables without the identity of consonant sounds which would make a RHYME: *drown—crowd*; *clean—dream*; *ride—write*. It is common in proverbial expressions, where the jingle of vowels without perfect rhyme is a natural and spontaneous characteristic—e.g. 'A stitch in *time* saves *nine*'. So in simple ballad, especially Scottish, verse, assonance frequently occurs. There are examples of assonance in the first and the last stanzas quoted under BALLAD.

assure, ensure, insure. The constructions are:

    (i) *assure*: (*a*) assure life, the future.
            (*b*) assure a person *of* a fact, &c., or *that* a thing is so.

(ii) *ensure*: (*a*) ensure a person, thing, *against* or *from* risks, &c.
   (*b*) ensure *that* something shall happen; ensure something *for* or *to* a person.

(iii) *insure*: *insure* is the legal and commercial variant of *ensure*, used particularly in the construction (*a*): to insure a house or person, or (used absolutely) to insure *against* fire, burglary, death.

In commercial idiom the noun *assurance* is used of life (though you *insure* against death—see above) and *insurance* of property, &c.

as to. The chief function of *as to* is 'to bring into prominence at the beginning of a sentence something that without it would have to stand later' (MEU): '*As to the natives*, there is no doubt that they will be happier under English rule; '*As to whether he will consent*, it is too early to say'. All other uses are doubtful and better avoided. See QUESTION AS TO.

as well as. *As well as* is a conjunction, not a preposition. In sentences like 'He is anxious to go as well as me' the question of case arises. If *me* (accusative) is to stand, *as well as* must be replaced by a preposition (*besides*); but if he and I are linked together as anxious to go, i.e. if *as well as* is meant to be a conjunction, then *me* must become *I* ('as well as I [am]'). The sentence as it stands is too ambiguous to claim for *me* the indulgence suggested under DISJUNCTIVE PRONOUNS. But the difficulty of case is not the only one. A sentence from MEU will illustrate another:

'A German control of the Baltic must vitally affect the lives of all the Scandinavian Powers as well as *influencing* the interests of a maritime country like England.'

As well as is a conjunction joining the infinitive *affect* to—what? A gerund. The author has suddenly given to *as well as* the syntactical power of *besides*, which could be substituted for *as well as* to make the sentence correct. If *as well as* is to stand it must be followed by the infinitive we were expecting after it: 'as well as *influence* the interests.'

at any rate. Three words: not *at anyrate*.

attraction. The grammatical influence of one word upon another in the sentence; as, particularly, when a plural noun draws or 'attracts' into the plural a verb that should properly agree with a singular subject: 'A large supply of guns, projectiles, gun-shields, marine articles, and other parts of ships *are* produced here.' So also when a singular indefinite pronoun is the subject: 'Each of us *have* decided to discontinue *our* membership.' See AGREEMENT.

augmentatives are affixes that express increase in the meaning of the word from which they are formed. Thus a ball-*oon* is a large ball; a milli-*on* is a large thousand; a drunk-*ard* is a person often drunk.

auxiliary verbs. Auxiliary (Lat. *auxilium* help) verbs are those which help other verbs to form their voice, mood, or tense. When the different parts of *be, have, shall, will, may, do* are used as substitutes for inflexions in the conjugation of a verb, they are auxiliaries. But when these verbs possess full meaning of their own and are not merely substitutes for inflexions they are called NOTIONAL. Thus in:

I *have* my own room.
He *shall* (= *must*) not go.
May I go to town to-day? } the verbs in italics are notional.
We *do* our best for our children.
How do you *do*?

But in
I *have* tidied up my own room.
We *shall* not go.
We work that we *may* live. } the verbs in italics are auxiliaries.
We *do* try hard.
How *do* you do?

averse. See ADVERSE.

await, wait. *Await* is followed by a noun, pronoun, or gerund, not by an infinitive: *wait* may have the infinitive construction, as well as the normally transitive construction of *await*, and an intransitive use with *for*. The following sentences are correct:

I *await* (or *wait*) your decision.
I *wait* for you to decide (not *await*).
They found him *awaiting* them.
They found him *waiting* for them.
I shall *wait* to bring him home (not *await*).
I *await* (or *wait*) his ruling on the matter with some impatience.

awake, awaken, wake, waken. The following table is compiled from the article in MEU:

	Past simple tense	*Past participle*	*Remarks*
awake	*awoke*, rarely *awaked*	*awaked*, rarely *awoke*	with *awaken*, 'usually preferred in figurative senses'.
awaken	*awakened*	*awakened*	(i) 'usually preferred in figurative senses'; (ii) tends to be transitive rather than intransitive, and therefore (iii) is preferred to *awake* and *wake* in the passive uses.
wake	*woke*, rarely *waked* (and that always in transitive sense)	*waked*, rarely *woke* or *woken*	'the ordinary working verb', whose use is only restricted in the cases mentioned in this table under the other three.
waken	*wakened*	*wakened*	in form and use is merely a variant of *awaken*.

MEU adds the note that '*up* is very commonly appended to *wake*, rarely to *waken*, and hardly at all to *awake* and *awaken*'.

ay, aye. *Ay* means 'yes' and is pronounced *ī* (as in *mice*); *aye* means 'ever' and is pronounced *ā* (as in *mace*).

bacillus. Pl. *bacilli* (see FOREIGN PLURALS).

back-formation. Back-formation is a reversal of the normal order of things in the development of words. Thus in English an agent noun is usually formed by means of a suffix from a verb stem: *act—actor*; *preach—preacher*; *love—lover*. But a few agent nouns existed first, and have had verbs 'formed back' from them. The noun *pedlar* is a good example; it is not derived from the verb 'to peddle', but the verb is a back-formation from the noun. Under STAFFS is given an example of what may be called grammatical back-formation.

bale. There is strictly no verb *bale* in English; SOED and MEU give *bale* as an 'erroneous spelling' for *bail* in the phrase 'bail water out of a boat'; but COD recognizes it as an alternative spelling, and that spelling is now so usual that it may be accepted, especially as *bail* has so many other uses.

ballad. The word is used technically for the ancient and simple folk poems like *Chevy Chase*, *Thomas the Rhymer*, and *Binnorie*, or for more modern poems written in imitation of the style and spirit of such originals —e.g. *Rosabelle* and others by Scott, and, greatest of all, *The Ancient Mariner* by Coleridge. The ballad stanza is the simplest of all English stanzas. In its normal form it consists of four lines with only one rhyming pair (abcb), written (as Peter Quince would say) in eight and six, and in iambic rhythm. But this four-lined stanza was sometimes varied with stanzas of six or eight lines. There were, too, other types of simple iambic stanzas. The true old ballads—representing the songs of the bards or minstrels—were nearly always sad poems of love and war, sorrow and death, told with suggestive omissions of detail that stir the imagination. Repetition of word or phrase, sometimes developing (as in *Binnorie*) into a definite refrain, was an outstanding characteristic of the ballad. The following stanzas from *Sir Patrick Spens* (describing the wreck of the ship on its return from Norway) illustrate the stanza form and chief characteristics of the ballad, and remind us that most of the ancient ballads are Northern in origin:

> 'Mak ready, mak ready, my merry men a',
>   Our gude ship sails the morn.'
> 'Now ever alack, my master dear,
>   I fear a deadly storm.
>
> 'I saw the new moon late yestreen
>   Wi' the auld moon in her arm;
> And if we gang to sea, master,
>   I fear we'll come to harm.'
>
> They hadna sail'd a league, a league,
>   A league but barely three,
> When the lift grew dark, and the wind blew loud,
>   And gurly grew the sea.
>
> The ankers brak, and the topmast lap,
>   It was sic a deadly storm:
> And the waves came owre the broken ship
>   Till a' her sides were torn.
>
> 'Go fetch a web o' the silken claith,
>   Another o' the twine,
> And wap them into our ship's side,
>   And let nae the sea come in.'

They fetch'd a web o' the silken claith,
    Another o' the twine,
And they wapp'd them round that gude ship's side,
    But still the sea came in.

O laith, laith were our gude Scots lords
    To wet their cork-heel'd shoon;
But lang or a' the play was play'd
    They wat their hats aboon.

And mony was the feather bed
    That flatter'd on the faem;
And mony was the gude lord's son
    That never mair cam hame.

O lang, lang may the ladies sit,
    Wi' their fans into their hand,
Before they see Sir Patrick Spens
    Come sailing to the strand!

And lang, lang may the maidens sit
    Wi' their gowd kames in their hair,
A-waiting for their ain dear loves!
    For them they'll see nae mair.

Half-owre, half-owre to Aberdour,
    'Tis fifty fathoms deep;
And there lies gude Sir Patrick Spens,
    Wi' the Scots lords at his feet!

It is interesting to note that later poets have imitated the ballad theme
and spirit in modified stanza forms. Notable examples are Tennyson's
The Lady of Shalott, Kingsley's *The Sands of Dee*, and Keats's *La Belle
Dame sans Merci*, where the last line of the normal stanza is deliberately
shortened for effect.

ballade. Not to be confused with BALLAD. An artificial verse form
borrowed from the French, consisting (usually) of three eight-lined
stanzas and a four-lined envoi. The rhyme scheme is the same in each
of the stanzas—ababbcbc; and the envoy rhymes bcbc. The same line
occurs, as a refrain, at the end of each stanza and the envoy. This form
was popular at the end of the 19th century, and has attained a revived
popularity to-day, though not among serious poets.

'You will remember—when I called a spade,
    And, like a shot, she put me up to three?
A miniature she was, in blue brocade,
    And eyes as blue—what is the simile?—
Well, well, for rhyme's sake let us say the sea,
    And half a hundred Helens in her face,
That caused at least a ten hours' war in me—
    I liked my partner, but she trumped my ace.

Do you remember now?—She looked afraid
    To bid, so kind and unaffected she;
Was it for wantonness her plots she laid
    To lead me unsuspecting up a tree?
No! No!—for heartless could she never be;
    I'm certain those bright eyes could bear no trace
Of guile—and that from tricks her hand was free—
    I liked my partner, but she trumped my ace.

Oh! surely you remember—how she made
  The cards—a gentle shuffle?—and how we
Watched in a kind of wonder as she played
  With simple art and feigned duplicity
Each vain finesse; but then, with artless glee,
  Formed with her witching lips a sweet grimace,
And made for my locked heart a golden key—
  I liked my partner, but she trumped my ace.

Prince! on her lovely charms we both agree,
  The wavy hair, the sweet attractive grace;
Yet firm against such fair I hold a plea—
  I liked my partner, but she trumped my ace.'

bandits, banditti. The Italian form is the collective, the English form the distributive plural: '*Banditti* are still found in the mountains'; '*Two bandits* were executed this morning.' But the distinction is artificial, and the Italian plural is rarely found except in rather pretentious writing.

barbarous. The various adjectives and nouns of this root, with their differences in meaning and use, are tabulated below:

barbarian, as adj.	'an attributive use of the noun barbarian' (MEU).	a barbarian king = a king of barbarians. a barbarian custom = a custom among barbarians.
barbaric	used in a favourable sense (= unsophisticated, rough, rude, unchastened).	barbaric finery, simplicity, gold.
barbarous	used in an unfavourable sense (= cruel).	barbarous treatment, custom, words.
barbarism	(*a*) 'uncivilized condition'; (*b*) 'grossly uncultivated taste'; (*c*) 'illiterate expression' (MEU).	to live in barbarism; to offend with barbarisms of speech.
barbarity	cruel conduct	The barbarity of the victors is terrible to relate.
barbarousness		may usually be substituted for either *barbarism* or *barbarity*.

bathos. See ANTI-CLIMAX.

beat. In *dead-beat* the shortened form of the passive participle remains; but it is used in other connexions only as a deliberate archaism, or as a colloquialism.

beeves, beefs. *Beeves* is an archaic plural meaning 'bulls' (<Fr. *bœuf*); the plural *beefs* (very rarely used) means different types or qualities of beef.

begin, commence, start. *Begin* is the familiar and usual word in speech and writing; *commence* is the word of official and formal language; *start*, which is of the same root as *startle*, is best restricted to the idea of actual physical motion. Exercises and operations *commence* in the army; a train *starts*; a runner *starts* from scratch. In all other uses and for all other senses use *begin*. MEU has the additional note, '*Begin* has, owing to its greater commonness, more nearly passed into a mere auxiliary than *commence*, and from this it follows that *begin*, not *commence*, is even in formal style the right word before an infinitive.' To sum up, use *start* for motion, *commence* only in formal language and never before an infinitive, *begin* on all other occasions.

beholden. *Beholden* is the old passive participle of the verb *behold*, and survives in the phrase '*beholden* to a person'. By confusion of forms *beholding* is sometimes used for *beholden* in this phrase. SOED marks *beholding* obsolete, and says it was 'originally an error for *beholden*'. The error occurs in Shakespeare ('Well, Shylock, shall we be *beholding* to you?') and in many writers since his time.

beloved. Two syllables as past participle; three as attributive adjective or noun.

benedick. The word is *benedick* (= a newly married man), from the name Benedick, the character in *Much Ado about Nothing*. The user of the common *benedict* obscures the immediate origin of the term in order to stress its connexion with Latin *benedictus* 'blessed'. SOED erroneously gives *benedict* as the term, 'from the character of that name [in *Much Ado*]'. But after all *-ict* and *-ick* are only variants.

beside, besides. *Beside* is always a preposition, in the sense of 'by the side of':

> 'There came in a spider
> And sat down *beside* her,
> And frightened Miss Muffet away.'

Besides is

(*a*) an adverb = 'moreover', 'also', 'as well':

> 'It is late; *besides*, I am too tired to go out';
> 'An ignorant man; and one who does not wish to learn *besides*.'

(*b*) a preposition = 'in addition to', 'except': 'No one knows it, *besides* me'; 'The Jews for ever unsainting all the world *besides* themselves' (SOED).

between. There are two correct constructions: (*a*) *between* + plural noun, (*b*) *between* + noun *and* noun. Normally the noun that follows *between* is 'dual'—i.e. it represents two persons, things, or ideas: 'There was a passage *between* the two houses'; '*between* two evils'. But in certain constructions the noun may represent more than two: 'The choice lay *between* the three candidates.' Note, however, the difference in use between *among* and *between*: 'He liked to spend his evenings *among* his friends'; 'There was an agreement *between* the two friends that they should help him in every way.' Construction (*b*) is illustrated in the sentences: 'He came *between* six *and* half-past'; '*Between* us *and* you is a great gulf fixed'; 'There is a big difference *between* doing good *and* refraining from doing evil'. The following sentences illustrate common faults:

(*a*) making *between* govern a singular noun;
(*b*) treating a distributive pronoun, *each*, *every*, as a plural after *between*;
(*c*) using the nominative for the accusative after *between*;

4084   C

(*d*) forgetting that only *and* can follow *between* in construction (*b*);
(*e*) repeating *between*:

(*a*) 'The house stood between the junction of the two streams' ('between the two streams').
(*b*) 'Distinguish between each of the following pairs of words' ('between the words in each of the following pairs').
'There will be an interval of ten minutes between each act' ('between the acts').
'Between every joke there was a burst of laughter' ('after each joke').
(*c*) 'All debts are cleared between you and I' ('you and me').
(*d*) 'We have in that substance the link between organic or inorganic matter' ('organic and inorganic').
(*e*) 'Between his daily work and between his conjuring in the evening he could not find enough time even to eat his tea.' (Second *between* superfluous.)

See also under AMONG.

blank verse. Blank verse is any unrhymed verse, but especially the unrhymed iambic pentameter, which was introduced into England from Italy in the sixteenth century, used by the dramatists (e.g. Marlowe, Ben Jonson, Beaumont and Fletcher) who slightly preceded, or were contemporary with, Shakespeare, and perfected for dramatic writing by Shakespeare himself. It was found suitable for the drama as an escape from the jigging artificiality of rhymed verse. In its earliest form the lines tended to be the units of the thought; that is, they were syntactical wholes, the sense of one line not running over into the next. To put it more concretely, most lines ended with an actual mark of punctuation—a comma, a semicolon, or a full-stop. For that reason the convenient and expressive epithet 'end-stopped' is often applied to them. It is easy to see that a succession of end-stopped lines would have a monotonous regularity far from suitable to the drama. The problem, then, was to make the blank verse more flexible; since, once granted the convention of blank verse in play-writing, its style and rhythm had to approximate as far as possible to the naturalness of elevated prose speech. Shakespeare's greatest contribution to our prosody was the 'naturalizing' of blank verse by replacing the rigidity of the end-stopped line with the flexibility of the 'overflow' line—that is the line whose sense ran on into the next. In other words, he made his lines fit the sentences, not his sentences fit the lines. And to this he added an irregularity in regularity, that is, he deliberately broke the monotony of the iambic pentameter, by sometimes introducing a trochee, especially in the first foot; by cunningly varying the position of the caesura; and by the occasional use of the feminine ending, that is, the unstressed eleventh syllable 'overhanging' after the final stressed tenth (contrast *weak ending*, below). In his later blank verse (especially that of *The Tempest*, *Antony and Cleopatra*, *The Winter's Tale*, and *Cymbeline*) Shakespeare, while retaining the prevailing iambic pentameter, indulged in greater and more frequent irregularities in the interest of naturalness. Especially, he introduced what is known as the weak ending, that is, the unstressed *tenth* syllable at the end of a line—e.g. an auxiliary with its verb, a preposition with its noun, or a conjunction with its clause in the next line. The following passages, all from Shakespeare, illustrate the three steps in the development of blank verse:

(i) Early.

'The ox hath therefore stretch'd his yoke in vain,
The ploughman lost his sweat, and the green corn
Hath rotted ere his youth attain'd a beard;
The fold stands empty in the drownèd field,
And crows are fatted with the murrion flock;
The nine men's morris is fill'd up with mud,
And the quaint mazes in the wanton green,
For lack of tread, are undistinguishable:
The human mortals want their winter here;
No night is now with hymn or carol blest:
Therefore the moon, the governess of floods,
Pale in her anger, washes all the air,
That rhéumatic diseases do abound:
And thorough this distemperature we see
The seasons alter: hoary-headed frosts
Fall in the fresh lap of the crimson rose,
And on old Hiems' thin and icy crown
An odorous chaplet of sweet summer buds
Is, as in mockery, set: the spring, the summer,
The childing autumn, angry winter, change
Their wonted liveries, and the mazèd world,
By their incréase, now knows not which is which
And this same progeny of evils comes
From our debate, from our dissension;
We are their parents and original.'

[From *A Midsummer Night's Dream*. Most of the lines are end-stopped, but line 2 has 'overflow' or 'enjambment'. In lines 15 and 19 there is internal caesura—after *alter* and *set*.]

(ii) Middle.

'I have possess'd your grace of what I purpose,
And by our holy Sabbath have I sworn
To have the due and forfeit of my bond:
If you deny it, let the danger light
Upon your charter and your city's freedom.
You'll ask me, why I rather choose to have
A weight of carrion flesh than to receive
Three thousand ducats: I'll not answer that:
But, say, it is my humour: is it answer'd?
What if my house be troubled with a rat,
And I be pleased to give ten thousand ducats
To have it ban'd? What, are you answer'd yet?
Some men there are love not a gaping pig;
Some, that are mad if they behold a cat;
Some, when they hear the bag-pipe: for affection,
Mistress of passion, sways it to the mood
Of what it likes or loathes.'

[From *The Merchant of Venice*. Note the number of 'overflow' lines; the variation of caesura; and the feminine endings in lines 5, 11, and 15.]

(iii) Late.

'Well demanded, wench;
My tale provokes that question. Dear, they durst not,
So dear the love my people bore me, nor set
A mark so bloody on the business; but
With colours fairer painted their foul ends.
In few, they hurried us aboard a bark;
Bore us some leagues to sea; where they prepared
A rotten carcass of a boat, not rigg'd,

> Nor tackle, sail, nor mast; the very rats
> Instinctively had quit it: there they hoist us,
> To cry to the sea that roared to us; to sigh
> To the winds, whose pity, sighing back again,
> Did us but loving wrong.'

[From *The Tempest*. Notice the feminine ending in line 2, and the weak ending in line 4.]

In non-dramatic writing the greatest exponents of the unrhymed iambic pentameter have been Milton (in *Paradise Lost* and *Paradise Regained*), Wordsworth (in *The Prelude*, &c.), Tennyson (chiefly in *The Idylls of the King*), Keats (in *Hyperion*), Browning (in *The Ring and the Book*), and Arnold (in *Sohrab and Rustum* and *Balder Dead*).

both . . . and. The chief point to be remembered is that any word or words common to both the items joined by these conjunctions must *either* be repeated after each *or* taken outside and put in front of the 'both'. Thus you can say *both* for eating *and* for drinking or for *both* eating *and* drinking, but NOT *both* for eating *and* drinking. To take another simple example: 'Both the hall and kitchen were brilliantly lighted.' Here the two items differ in form; one is qualified by the article and the other is not. As the sentence stands 'hall and kitchen' must be taken together after the article; hence the *and* is an ordinary linking conjunction and not correlative with *both*. The construction would therefore postulate another item, as, for example: '*Both* the hall and kitchen *and* the drawing-room were brilliantly lighted.' Amend the original sentence: '*Both* the hall *and* the kitchen were brilliantly lighted' or '*both* hall *and* kitchen'. One or two other examples will help to make the construction clear:

(*a*) 'He both uses his head and feet well in front of the goal' ('uses *both* his head *and* his feet').

(*b*) 'There is no page of this work which does not deserve quotation, both because of the strangeness of the facts recorded and the eloquence and quiet humour of the prose' ('*both* because of the strangeness &c. *and* because of the eloquence &c.').

(*c*) 'Broadcasting and the cinema have also brought new possibilities of propaganda, both in its good and its bad sense' ('*both* in its good *and* in its bad sense' or 'in *both* its good *and* its bad sense').

(*d*) 'How does J. B. Priestley distinguish humour, wit, and parody? Illustrate your answer by reference both to the writers and writings mentioned by him'. (The sentence is from a London University Examination paper in English. Correct: '*both* to the writers *and* to the writings'. The examiners probably hesitated (rightly) at 'to both the writers and the writings'; but in avoiding that ambiguity fell into the sin of misplaced correlatives.)

(*e*) 'I shall help him both for his own sake and because he knew my father.' Sentence (*e*) exemplifies the fact that the items introduced by the correlatives may be of different construction though of the same type: in this sentence *both* introduces an adverb phrase and *and* an adverb clause of reason.

Remember, as a working rule, that *both* and *and* are usually followed by the same part of speech.

brackets. See PARENTHESIS.

broadcast. Since the verb is formed from the adverb *broadcast*, not from the verb *cast* + the adverb *abroad*, the past tense demanded by analogy, grammar, and common sense is *broadcasted*. But it seems likely that the false analogy with the past tense of *cast*, verb, and the influence of *broadcast*, adjective, wrongly regarded as a past participle, will make the erroneous form *broadcast* victorious.

broke. This is the slang term (in 'stony-broke'). It is only a misguided desire for grammatical correctness that drives people to say they are 'broken'; cf. *swollen* (for *swelled*) head.

brothers, brethren. 1. Forms: See -EN PLURALS.

2. Use: *Brothers* is used

(*a*) to express the family relationship 'My brothers are both married'; 'He works for the firm of Smith Brothers'. 'And when his brethren saw that their father loved Joseph more than all his brethren . . .' (AV, 1611) is a reminder that the form *brothers* and its use are comparatively modern.

(*b*) usually, though not always, in the extended meaning of friends, sympathizers, equals. Thus to-day 'All men are brothers' is commoner than 'All men are brethren'.

The old plural *brethren* survives in two main usages:

(*a*) in ecclesiastical language: 'Dearly beloved brethren'; the brethren of a church or of a monastic order; Plymouth Brethren; and

(*b*) to indicate the members of a society or club: 'The brethren have contributed generously to the Relief Fund'.

bull. 'A self-contradictory proposition; in modern use, an expression containing a manifest contradiction in terms or involving a ludicrous inconsistency unperceived by the speaker. Now often with epithet *Irish*; but the word had been long in use before it came to be associated with Irishmen' (OED). Examples:

'Don't come down the ladder, Mike, for I've just taken it away.'
'Just you go the way I've come,' replied an Irish cattle-drover who had been asked the way to Carlisle.
'I arranged to meet my brother at 4 o'clock; but when I met him he wasn't there.'
'Salt is what makes potatoes so nasty if you don't eat it with them.'

burlesque is a word used generally of a play or scene in a play which sets out to ridicule by exaggerated imitation a serious play or scene. (Cf. *caricature* in art and PARODY in literature.) Thus the interlude 'Pyramus and Thisbe' in *A Midsummer-Night's Dream* is a burlesque of some types of popular Elizabethan tragedy; Beaumont and Fletcher's comedy, *The Knight of the Burning Pestle*, is a burlesque of knight-errantry; *Don Quixote* burlesques the romances of chivalry popular in Spain.

bus. The full form *omnibus* has been superseded by *bus* (without an apostrophe) as the name of the vehicle; *Punch* ridiculed the 'O'bus' (which at one time appeared on London buses) thus:

> To stop o'bus
> Ring o'bell.

Omnibus has had a new lease of life in recent times in the phrase 'an *omnibus* volume'.

but. *But* is

(*a*) a disjunctive co-ordinating conjunction:

'Naaman was a mighty man in valour, *but* he was a leper.'
I waited a long time, *but* nobody came.

(*b*) an adverb = only:

'Have you seen *but* a white lily grow
Before rude hands have touched it?'
He is *but* young.
'*But* yesterday the word of Caesar might
Have stood against the world.'

(*c*) a negative relative pronoun after a negative or quasi-negative, e.g. *few* (cf. Latin *quin* = *quine*, *qui*+*ne*):

There are few of us *but* I love and honour him
(= 'who do not');
'No mind that's honest
But in it shares some woe'
(= 'that does not share').

(*d*) a preposition = except; other than:

'Nothing *but* leaves';
He had nothing *but* contempt for my proposal;
'There is none *but* he
Whose being I do fear.'

The third example is from *Macbeth*. Mod.E. (as well as Shakespearian) idiom allows a nominative after *but* in this construction, as if *but* were conjunctive = other *than*. See CASE.

(*e*) a preposition or conjunction in certain idiomatic phrases, representative examples of which are given with comments:

(i) What can he do *but* refuse?
(ii) 'He cannot choose *but* hear.'
(iii) Nothing would content him *but* I must come.
(iv) 'It never rains *but* it pours.'
(v) Justice was never done *but* someone complained.
(vi) 'It shall go hard *but* I will better the instruction.'
(vii) I am not such a fool *but* I can see through that manœuvre.
(viii) 'It is impossible *but* that offences will come.'

Examples (i) and (ii) illustrate a special form of the prepositional use noted under (*d*), the *but* governing an infinitive (*refuse*, *hear*) instead of a noun or pronoun. In examples (iii), (iv), (v) there are varying forms of the conjunctive use to express condition, where *but* = (approximately) *unless*, *except that*; or the whole construction may be replaced by *without*+gerund ('without my coming', &c.). Example (vi) illustrates another type of conditional conjunctive use: *but* = 'if I do not'. In (vii) *but* = 'that not' after *such*, and introduces an adverb clause of consequence. Similarly in sentence (viii) the *but* supplies in itself the negative after the negative *impossible*: 'It is impossible that offences will *not* come'. Cf. *but* as relative pronoun, under (*c*) above. It is noteworthy that in its idiomatic uses *but* usually has a negative force. As the first word in a sentence *but* is generally adverbial (= *however*, *nevertheless*).

This use is particularly common in interrogative, imperative, and exclamatory sentences:

> *But* why did you go?
> *But* send your luggage in advance.
> *But* you told me you would play!

but, than, when. The types of words followed respectively by *but*, *than*, and *when* may be defined briefly as follows:

(a) *but* (= except): the uncompromising negatives *nothing, no, not,* or the diminutive *little*: 'nothing but leaves'; 'There was little in the play but the usual feeble wit' (for case after *but* in this sense see CASE);

(b) *than*: only a comparative adjective or adverb: 'Rather than', 'other than', '(no) sooner than' are especially to be noted. ELSE is the only true non-comparative to be idiomatically followed by *than*;

(c) *when*: 'HARDLY had, was, &c. . . . *when*'; 'SCARCELY had, was, &c. . . . *when*', not '*than*'.

by, bye. The recommended spellings are:

(a) *by* in all normal prepositional and adverbial meanings.

(b) *by* in combinations, with or without hyphen: *by-path, by-road, by-election, by-word* (in which *by-* is adjectival), *bystander, bygone* (in which *by* is adverbial).

Note that the adjectival *by-* is written with a following hyphen, and the adverbial *by* without.

(c) *bye* in terms connected with sport—cricket, golf, tennis.

(d) *by and by*; *by the by,* or *by the bye.*

(e) *bye-law* or *by-law* (where *bye* is OE. *by,* a town—as in *Derby*).

(f) good*bye* (= God *be with ye*).

c and g. *C* and *g* are normally soft before the 'front' vowels *e, i, (y),* and hard before the 'back' vowels *a, o, u*. When a suffix beginning with *a, o,* or *u* is added to a word ending in *-ce, -ge,* the *e* is retained in spelling to indicate the 'soft' pronunciation of the *c* or *g*: *peaceable, outrageous, noticeable, changeable.* (See MUTE E.) In a few words *g* is doubtful before *i*; thus the *g* is hard in *girl* owing to the tendency of *i* to the 'back' (*u*) sound under the influence of *r*. Other examples with *i* are:

(a) *g* soft: *gibber, gibe, gill* (the measure), *gilly-flower, gimcrack, gist, gyves.*

(b) *g* hard: *gibberish, gibbous, gig, gill* (= ravine), *gillie* (= shooting or fishing attendant), *gimlet, gimp.*

caddie, the golf-attendant; **caddy,** the tea-box.

caesura (Latin *caedere, caesum,* to cut) is the break between words within a metrical foot in the quantitative verse of Greek and Latin. In modern English prosody it is the natural pause in the rhythm of most lines, particularly in pentameters and long metres generally. Variation of the caesura produces metrical subtlety and is the secret of good blank verse. Four successive lines from *Hamlet* are quoted to show how Shakespeare varied the position of the caesura:

> 'Beware
> Of entrance to a quarrel; | but being in,
> Bear't, | that the opposed may beware of thee.
> Give every man thine ear | but few thy voice:
> Take each man's censure, | but reserve thy judgment.'

can is derived from AS. *cunnan* = to know (cf. cunning), past participle *cūth* (cf. uncouth). The modern past tense, indicative and subjunctive, is *could*, the *l* of which is intrusive on analogy of *should* and *would*, where the *l* belongs to the stem. Care must be taken not to confuse *can* and *may*. *Can* implies ability, *may* permission.

capital letters. In English the initial letter of a word is a capital:

(*a*) at the beginning of a sentence; that is, always following a full-stop, and following a question mark and exclamation mark when they end a completed sentence, but not after an exclamation mark when it follows a single word or a phrase: 'I never heard of such a thing! He must be mad', but 'Alas! it was I who leapt at the sun'.

(*b*) at the beginning of a passage or sentence of direct speech, whether it is the actual beginning of the sentence or no: 'I said, "Ask him to come in".'

(*c*) usually at the beginning of each line of verse; though the modern tendency is to eliminate capitals in this position unless they are demanded by the syntax.

(*d*) when the word is a proper noun—e.g. the name of a place or a person. The names of the months and of the days of the week are spelt with capitals. In designation of streets or roads the actual name is always written with a capital; the words *street*, *road*, *avenue*, &c., may or may not be: 'George Street', 'George street', 'George-street'. Where a proper name is used adjectivally it has a capital: 'Bunsen burner', 'buff Orpington (chicken)', 'Bramley seedling'. Adjectives of nationality begin with capitals (*French*, *English*), but other derivatives from proper names do not : *jovial* (from Jove), *macadamized* road (from Macadam), *frenchified*. Names of trains, aeroplanes, ships begin with capitals: *Royal Scot*; *Skylark*; *Lusitania*; but nouns indicating types of things or creatures are considered common, and therefore written without the capital: *sparrow*, *author*, *apple*(-*tree*), *dog*.

(*e*) in titles (of books, music, plays, poems). The first word of the title always begins with a capital, and the other chief words in the title (e.g. nouns, verbs, descriptive adjectives): *A Tale of Two Cities*; *The Ring and the Book*; *It is Never too Late to Mend*; *Much Ado about Nothing*.

(*f*) in personified words:

> 'There *Honour* comes, a pilgrim grey,
> To bless the turf that wraps their clay,
> And *Freedom* shall awhile repair
> To dwell, a weeping hermit, there.'

case (in grammar). 1. In inflected languages the form of a noun, adjective, or pronoun expressing its relation to some other word or words in the sentence is called its case. English is largely an uninflected language, having inflected forms for case only

(*a*) in the genitive singular and plural of some nouns (chiefly those that denote persons);

(*b*) in the accusative, genitive, and dative of the personal, the third person demonstrative, the interrogative, and the relative pronouns.

Thus *man's* is the genitive singular form of *man*; *me* the accusative and the dative form of the first person pronoun; *whom* the accusative and the dative form of the interrogative or the relative pronoun (denoting persons). In nouns the forms for the nominative (the case of the subject), accusative (the case of the object), and dative (the case of the indirect object) are the same. The case of a noun (except where it is the inflected genitive with apostrophe *s*) can be deduced only from the relationship of the noun to the rest of the sentence. Thus in 'The Lion beat the Unicorn', *Lion* is subject and therefore in the nominative case; *Unicorn* is direct object of the verb *beat*, and therefore in the accusative case. For the genitive, dative, and ablative cases, which are expressed by inflected forms in Latin, English often uses a case-phrase, preposition + noun, the noun itself being in the accusative after a preposition. Thus in the sentence 'The quickness *of the hand* deceives the eye', *of the hand* is a genitive case-phrase, but *hand* itself is a noun in the accusative, governed by the preposition *of*; and in the sentence 'The *hand's* quickness deceives the eye', *hand's* is the genitive of the noun *hand*. Similarly, in the sentence 'He gave a letter *to the king*', *to the king* is a dative case-phrase, whereas in the sentence 'He gave *the king* a letter', *king* is in the dative case, indirect object of the verb *gave*.

2. Forms and Syntax: see under NOMINATIVE, ACCUSATIVE, GENITIVE, DATIVE.

3. Common Errors:

(i) *Errors of word-form.* Sometimes the nominative form of a pronoun is used when the pronoun is objective in function, or the accusative is used when the pronoun is subjective:

(*a*) after the verb *to be*: 'It's *me*'; 'Regardless of grammar they all cried "That's *him*"' (for *I*, *he*). But this is common usage and may be justified by universal practice. It may be said that our accusative forms correspond with the French disjunctive pronouns in 'C'est *moi*', 'c'est *lui*'. Jespersen says: 'On the whole, the natural tendency in English has been towards a state in which the nominative of pronouns is used only where it is clearly the subject, and where this is shown by close proximity to (generally position immediately before) a verb, while the objective [accusative] is used everywhere else.'

(*b*) after *as*, *than*: In 'He is as tall as me', 'Her sister is a little older than her', *as* and *than* are conjunctions, not prepositions; and the sentences quoted are elliptical for 'He is as tall as I am', 'Her sister is a little older than she is'. Hence 'as *I*', 'than *she*'—nominative, not accusative. Again, however, the French disjunctive 'que *moi*', 'que *lui*' may be cited as some explanation, if not justification, of the English usage. In the sentence 'Luck favoured you more than me' the accusative is correct. The sentence is elliptical for 'Luck favoured you more than it did me'. When in doubt of the case supply mentally the words understood. (For *whom* after *than* see THAN.)

(*c*) after *let*: 'Let you and I go' is an ungrammatical sentence frequently used because it is believed to be grammatical. *Let* is a transitive verb (= allow), of which both pronouns are objects, and therefore accusative, *you* and *me*.

(*d*) after *between* and *but* (= except): 'Between you and I' has become a stock phrase—again in the belief that 'you and I' is more grammatical (and more genteel) than 'you and me'. *Between* governs both pronouns: therefore both are accusative. In the same way *but* is often followed by the nominative. The following examples, all from Shakespeare, will illustrate the faults referred to:

'All debts are cleared between you and *I*.'

'There is none but *he*
Whose being I do fear.'

'I never saw a woman
But only Sycorax my dam and *she*.'

MEU, however, from common usage both past and present, justifies and even prefers the conjunctive use of *but* in this construction: in other words, 'Whence all but *he* had fled' is correct Mod.E. idiom.

(*e*) in relative (adjective) clauses: When an adjective clause is broken by a parenthesis like 'I said', 'I remarked', 'I know', the tendency is to make accusative a relative pronoun that is properly subject of its own clause. Thus, in 'He is a man whom I know is trustworthy', the relative pronoun is subject of the adjective clause, and 'I know' is an adverb clause of parenthesis: 'He is a man who (I know) is trustworthy'. Probably the mind suspects that *whom* is object of *know*: hence the mistake. The following example is from *The Times*:

'Irmin is resolved to discover the murderer, whom he realizes from the start is almost certainly a Jew, not an Arab.'

There may be, too, some confusion with the accusative and infinitive construction: 'He is a man whom I know to be trustworthy.' A similar mistake arises with the interrogative pronoun: 'Whom did you say he was?' Correct: 'Who did you say he was?' Here 'who he was' is a noun clause, object of 'did you say'; *who* is complement of the finite verb *was*, and therefore nominative.

(ii) *Errors in the construction of a sentence.* A word (e.g. a noun) which has no inflexion for case in the nominative and accusative may be so placed in the sentence that it is compelled to act as subject and object at the same time—a bit of double-dealing that cannot be condoned. Thus in the sentence (from KE.):

'The occupation of the mouths of the Yalu, however, his Majesty considered undesirable, and should only be carried out in the last resort',

the noun *occupation* is first object of the verb *considered* and then subject of the subordinate clause 'and should only be carried out in the last resort'.

case. (= Lat. *casus*, 'that which befalls'). The word *case* is used legitimately when it has a 'semi-concrete' meaning: 'The *case* of the miners was discussed' (i.e. the whole state or matter); 'a hospital *case*' = a case (i.e. a matter) for hospital treatment, the word being applied by a natural transference of thought to the patient himself; 'We were in bad *case*' (= circumstances); 'He stated his *case*' well' (= argument, statement of position or affairs); 'The flowers that bloom in the spring Have nothing to do with the *case*' (= business, affair); 'The magistrate said it was a bad *case* of careless driving' (= instance); 'There were four *cases* of drunkenness before the court' (in legal sense); 'In *case* of fire, ring the bell' ('in case of' is an idiomatic conditional phrase, in which *case* has its root meaning of a 'befalling', a chance).

It is used illegitimately whenever it has no meaning or significance of its own—i.e. when it relies for its interpretation on the context in which it appears. The evil resulting from such use is long-windedness and ugly PERIPHRASIS. 'In the case of' is the chief sinner. Sir Arthur Quiller-Couch gives an amusing example: 'In the case of John Jenkins deceased, the coffin was of the usual nature', where the somewhat grim pun (on *case* and *coffin*) helps to point the moral and encourage the simple statement 'John J's coffin was . . .'. Here are four examples selected from MEU, with suggested improvements:

In the case of *Pericles*, the play is omitted.	*Pericles* (or the play *Pericles*) is omitted.
In Mr. Baring Gould's case he was, like Miss Hesba Stretton, mistaken for a relative.	Mr. Baring Gould was, like Miss Hesba Stretton, mistaken for a relative.
In many cases the answers lacked care.	Many answers lacked care.
In no one case did the Liberals win a seat.	The Liberals did not win a seat.

MEU also gives a warning against the use of the phrase 'be (was, &c.) the case' to avoid the repetition of a verb: 'Some people enjoy listening to the band, but this is not the case with me' (for 'but I do not').

The general rule is therefore: If *case* has no recognizable meaning of its own as illustrated in the first paragraph of this article, do not use it, but find a simpler and more direct construction. See also INSTANCE.

causative verbs. Certain native verbs of the same etymological origin exist side by side, one being intransitive and the other transitive. The transitive verbs are called 'causative', since they signify the causing of the action indicated in the intransitive verbs. All the intransitive verbs, except *fare*, are strong, and all the transitive (causative) verbs are weak.

Intransitive	*Transitive (Causative)*	
To lie	To lay	= To cause to lie
To rise	To raise	= To cause to rise
To fall	To fell	= To cause to fall
To sit	To set	= To cause to sit
To drink	To drench	= To cause to drink
To fare (= to go)	To ferry	= To cause to fare

centre and middle. *Centre* is the mathematical and metaphorical word: the *centre* of a circle, an arc, a line, the universe; the *centre* point; Dr. Johnson was the *centre* of the literary world of the eighteenth century; an unemployment, educational, ecclesiastical *centre*. *Middle* is the everyday term: to part your hair in the *middle*; the *middle* of the road; to live in the *middle* house. There is a tendency for *centre* (as what MEU calls a 'genteelism') to encroach upon the domain of *middle*. The barber is apt to say, 'Will you have your hair parted in the *centre*?', and the cricketer taking his guard will ask for *centre* rather than *middle*, though he will usually refer to the *middle* stump. Except in such mathematical and metaphorical uses as are outlined here *middle* is to be preferred.

change of meaning. In a living language the continual traffic of words over a number of centuries must inevitably occasion changes of meaning. Sometimes, with the progress of science and knowledge, words add to their original meaning or meanings a new significance. We have examples of this in such words as *railway*, which just over a century ago meant nothing but the rude rails over which trucks were drawn by ponies in a coal-mine, and *broadcast*, up to a few years ago an agricultural term for the sowing of seed. But there are many words which have actually changed their old meaning for a new one. Such changes may be roughly classified thus:

(*a*) *elevation*—the process by which a word of colloquial or slang origin becomes part of the standard or literary language;

(*b*) *degradation*—the process by which a word once dignified and literary loses, by misuse or too familiar use, its original and true significance;

(*c*) *narrowing*—by which a word that was once general in meaning becomes particularized;

(*d*) *association*—by which a word loses its original meaning for one associated with it; and

(*e*) *popularizing*—by which a word, usually of Latin derivation, takes in English a meaning only half related to that in the original language.

Some representative changes are set out in the following table:

	Original	*Modern*
(*a*)	*elevation*:	
	religious and political nicknames like *Christian* (Acts xi. 26), *Methodist* (a nickname given to the members of the 'Holy Club' founded by the Wesleys at Oxford), *Quaker* (a nickname for the Friends, with reference to 'quaking at the word of the Lord'), *Tory* (a derisive name given to the opponents of the Exclusion Bill in the reign of Charles II).	Such words have now a literary and official meaning.
	pioneer—a soldier set apart for repair and entrenchment work.	a preparer of the way in any department of life.
	chamberlain—the servant in charge of the room (chamber) of his master.	a high official—e.g. the Lord Chamberlain.
(*b*)	*degradation*:	
	knave, a boy, particularly a servant, e.g. 'the knave of hearts'.	a rascal.
	churl, a countryman, a yokel, an ignorant fellow.	a rude, bad-tempered man (hence adjective *churlish*)
	gossip, a godparent.	a talker.
	silly, happy, blessed.	innocent > simple > foolish.
	clown, a country fellow. The artisans in *A Midsummer Night's Dream* are called 'clowns'. Keats uses the word in the original sense: 'The song I hear this passing night was heard In ancient days by emperor and clown.'	a fool, particularly a professional fool in a circus.
(*c*)	*narrowing*:	
	deer—in OE. and ME., any animal. Shakespeare has 'mice and rats and such small deer'.	a particular animal.
	fowl—in OE. and ME. any bird. The word is connected with the OE. word for *to fly*. AV has 'Behold the fowls of the air'.	the domesticated, farmyard bird.

	Original	*Modern*
(c)	*narrowing* (contd.):	
	husband—the master of a house.	a married man considered in relation to his wife.
	wife—originally a woman in the general sense—a sense which survives in *housewife*.	applied particularly to a married woman; a married woman considered in relation to her husband.
	gate—originally 'a way': 'Strait is the gate and narrow the way which leadeth unto life.' ME. has adverb *algates* = always.	the actual structure at the opening or beginning of a way.
(d)	*association*:	
	tell—originally 'to count' as in 'every shepherd *tells* his *tale*'. This sense survives in 'to tell the time', 'to tell one's beads', and in the noun *tally* (a measure, or reckoning).	to narrate, speak news.
	spinster—the feminine form of *spinner*. Shakespeare has 'The spinsters and the knitters in the sun'.	an unmarried woman: 'spinster of this parish'.
	cunning—originally 'knowing' (cunnan = to know; cf. Northern *ken*). Hence 'a *cunning* workman'.	'knowing' in the wrong sense; that is, using knowledge to evil ends.
	crafty—'full of craft or skill'.	turning skill to wrong purposes; sly. The word has somewhat the same change as *cunning*.
(e)	*popularizing*:	
	prevent (Lat. *praevenire*, 'to come before'). 'Though rising thou prevent'st the sun'—Fletcher (17th c.), i.e. 'comest before the sun'. Prayer Book: 'Prevent us, O Lord, in all our doings' ('precede', 'come before').	stop, hinder.
	admire (Lat. *admirari*, 'to wonder at'). 'Let none admire that riches grow in Hell' (Milton).	to appreciate, to praise (transitive).
	minister (Lat. *minister*, a servant, attendant). AV : 'And when he had given the book to the minister' (i.e. the attendant in the synagogue).	a counsellor of the king; a clergyman.

character. The phrases 'the [adjective] character of' and 'of an [adjective] character' are to be looked upon with suspicion as examples of ugly and unnecessary periphrasis. 'Owing to the dusty character of the pitch' = 'owing to the dustiness of the pitch'; 'hymns of a sentimental character' = 'sentimental hymns'.

checks. See CONSONANTS.

cherub. The Hebrew plural form is *cherubim*, the anglicized plural *cherubs*; so also *seraph, seraphim, seraphs*.

chiasmus is a figure of speech by which the order of the words in the first of two parallel clauses is reversed in the second. If the two phrases

are written one below the other, and lines drawn between the corresponding terms, those lines make the Greek letter *chi*, a diagonal cross: e.g.

To stop╲ ╱too fearful
and too faint╱ ╲to go.

childish, childlike. 'When I became a man I put away *childish* things.'
Saint Paul meant the things (e.g. the dress, interests) of a child, not *foolish*
things. But when the word, as most frequently, is used in connexion
with adults, it has a derogatory twist of meaning in Mod.E. The
adjective with a good sense is *childlike*. A man acts with *childish* petu-
lance, but with *childlike* simplicity.

choice. 'Citizens of Portsmouth North have a clear choice to-day of
voting for a friend of the common people or a representative of the
"National" Union of Face-grinders.' This sentence illustrates a common
error in the use of the word *choice*. Apparently, the unfortunate citizens
of Portsmouth North had no *choice*; they merely had an *opportunity* of
doing one thing or the other. The permissible constructions with *choice*
are
(*a*) choice *of* one thing (out of many);
(*b*) choice *between* (two or more things);
(*c*) choice *between* one thing *and* another.
As far as (*a*) is concerned the idiom explains itself. The constructions
(*b*) and (*c*) follow the idiom with BETWEEN. The sentence should read
'choice to-day between voting for A and voting for B', or 'have in voting
a choice between A and B'.

choir, quire. The Prayer Book has 'In *quires* and places where they
sing'; but *choir* is the standard modern spelling, though *quire* still survives in poetry and deliberately archaic prose. It is noteworthy that
choir keeps the pronunciation of *quire*.
Quire (of paper) is quite a different word, connected with the French
cahier.

chord, cord. In musical harmony the word is *chord*. The word *cord*
meaning 'string', as in *whipcord*, is spelt after the Greek original (*chordē*)
with an *h* in certain phrases: 'touch the right *chord*' (probably by confusion with the harmonic chord); 'the *chord* of an arc'; 'the vocal *chords*';
'the spinal *c(h)ord*'.

circumstances. MEU warmly justifies '*under* the circumstances', and
is apt to be scornful of the people who insist on *in* for *under*. OED has
the somewhat cryptic note: 'Mere situation is expressed by "*in* the
circumstances", action affected is performed "*under* the circumstances".'
But such a distinction is difficult to follow; so the wiser way is to be thank-
ful that *under* will pass muster, and to make a personal choice between
under and *in*.

claim. MEU stigmatizes the use of *claim* in the sense of *assert, maintain,
represent* as a vulgarism. *Claim* may be followed by the infinitive only
when (*a*) it is in the active voice and (*b*) the infinitive represents an action
done by the subject: 'He claims to have discovered a new planet.' But
in the following sentences one or other of the words mentioned above
should have been used: 'He *claimed* his score to be the lowest for the

course'; 'The car was *claimed* to do fifty miles to the gallon'; 'The examination was *claimed* to be just and fair.'

classical. In literature (and music and other arts) *classical*, as opposed to *romantic*, means 'conforming in style or composition to the rules or models of Greek and Latin antiquity' (OED), i.e. attaching more importance to form than to content, intellectual rather than emotional, and characterized by clearness, symmetry, harmonious proportion, and precision. In English literature (and in other arts), the 18th century is commonly regarded as the age which approached the classical ideal most nearly; the term 'romantic' is always applied to the poets and prose writers of the early 19th century.

clause. A clause consists of a subject and a predicate (i.e. it is a sentence in construction); but is itself part of, and has a definite function in, a longer sentence. Clauses are of three types:

(a) *Main.* The main clause is the sentence itself in its simple form; the clause, that is, on which the rest of the construction depends in both syntax and meaning.

(b) *Subordinate.* The subordinate clause is equivalent to a noun, adjective, or adverb in the main clause. It is called subordinate ('of lower rank') because it is dependent on another clause, which may itself be main or subordinate, and cannot stand by itself as the main clause can.

(c) *Co-ordinate.* The co-ordinate clause is one 'of the same rank' as another. Thus a clause may be co-ordinate with a main clause or with a subordinate clause. Co-ordinate clauses are linked together by co-ordinating conjunctions—e.g. *and, but, or* (see under CONJUNCTION).

The following analysis of two sentences will illustrate each type of clause:

Sentences.

(i) Once, after the winter holidays, when he and his brother William had set off on horseback to return to school, they came back, because there had been a fall of snow; and William, who did not much like the journey, said it was too deep for them to venture on.

(ii) The pain which is felt when we are first transplanted from our native soil, when the living branch is cut from the parent tree, is one of the most poignant which we have to endure through life.

Clause	Type	Function
Sentence (i)		
1. Once, after the winter holidays, they came back	Main	—
2. when he and his brother William had set off on horseback to return to school	Subordinate adverb	of time, modifying the verb *came back* in 1.
3. because there had been a fall of snow	Subordinate adverb	of reason, modifying the verb *came back* in 1.
4. and William said [it was too deep for them to venture on]	Co-ordinate	with 1.

Clause	Type	Function
Sentence (i) (contd.) 5. it was too deep for them to venture on	Subordinate noun	object of the verb *said* in 4.
6. who did not much like the journey	Subordinate adjective	qualifying the noun *William* in 4.
Sentence (ii) 1. The pain is one of the most poignant	Main	—
2. which is felt	Subordinate adjective	qualifying the noun *pain* in 1.
3. when we are first transplanted from our native soil	Subordinate adverb	of time, modifying the verb *is felt* in 2.
4. when the living branch is cut from the parent tree	Co-ordinate	with 3.
5. which we have to endure through life	Subordinate adjective	qualifying the adjective (= noun) *poignant* in 1.

Notes.

(*a*) Clause 2 under sentence (i) may be considered also as a subordinate adjective clause qualifying the noun understood in *once* (= 'at one time'): 'at one time when . . .', where *when* is the equivalent of a relative pronoun (see WHEN). The analysis given in the table does not exactly reflect the meaning of the sentence.

(*b*) Clauses 2 and 3 under sentence (i) are both adverb clauses modifying the same verb; but they are not co-ordinate since they have different functions —one is of time, the other of reason. Contrast clauses 3 and 4 under sentence (ii).

cleave (*a*) (= split). There is a free choice of past simple tenses (*clove*, *cleft*, or *cleaved*) and of past participles (*cloven*, *cleft*, or *cleaved*), except in one or two phrases where idiom has fixed the form: '*cloven* tongues, hoof'; 'a *cleft* stick, palate'.

(*b*) (= cling, stick). The past tense is *cleaved* or *clave* (archaic), and the past participle *cleaved*.

cliché. The word means in French a 'stereotype block'; and is used in English of such phrases as have become fixed or stereotyped in the language. Some—particularly stock similes like 'as good as gold', 'as brown as a berry'—have a long and honourable history. Others belong to, and are noted under, JARGON. Speech or writing that is packed with clichés can never be fresh and original, since by its very nature a cliché must have the drabness of something second-hand; only rarely does it become precious as a true antique.

climax (Greek = ladder), the gradual ascent from the less impressive to the most impressive in the arrangement of a series of words or ideas, e.g. Shakespeare's

'Like the baseless fabric of this vision,
(1) The cloud-capped towers, (2) the gorgeous palaces,
(3) The solemn temples, (4) the great globe itself,
(5) Yea, all which it inherit, shall dissolve';

five progressive stages of impressiveness.

clothe. There are two forms of the past simple tense and the past participle—*clothed* and *clad*. *Clothed* is the form for all normal uses; *clad* is appropriate in the slightly archaic and the half metaphorical senses illustrated in '*clad* in armour' and 'with verdure *clad*'.

cockney rhyme. See RHYME.

coco-nut, cocoa-nut, cokernut. All three spellings are permissible. The first is certainly the best; the second is too closely linked with the beverage; and the third is a happy invention of the shops and stalls. With a lucky shot you win neither a coco-nut nor a cocoa-nut but a cokernut.

cognate accusative. See ACCUSATIVE CASE.

collective nouns. Collective nouns are those that denote a collection of persons or things. *Congregation, herd, people, multitude, number* are examples. Certain difficulties of number arise in connexion with them. Should a collective noun be considered singular or plural? In this matter, as in others, the fashion of grammar changes. The modern Recreation Ground Committee will announce 'The public is requested to keep off the grass'; twenty or thirty years ago it (or they) would have said 'are requested'. However, this is mercifully a question in which each may decide for himself; but once having decided, he must be consistent. If he treats his noun as a singular, singular it must be throughout—that is, all verbs agreeing with and pronouns agreeing with or relating to it must be singular; and if he makes it plural, it must be plural throughout. Though the modern prejudice tends to the choice of the singular, the singular collective does not always prove amenable to idiom or even sense. 'The congregation is requested to keep its seat' and 'The congregation is requested to keep their seats' are equally impossible. One way out is to treat *congregation* as a plural: 'The congregation are requested'; another way is to get round the difficulty by saying 'The members of the congregation are requested to keep their seats'. But in the following question set by a University of London examiner there is no excuse whatever for the inconsistency: '*Henry IV Part I* is to be performed before an audience that *has* not read the play. Give a synopsis of it, act by act, for *their* benefit.'

Many collective nouns may themselves have a plural (e.g. *congregations, heaps*); and a few may in their singular form be both collective and distributive. Thus in the sentence, 'My people doth not consider', *people* is collective; but in the sentence, 'Many people are unable to find work', it is distributive, and syntactically plural. A few nouns have two plural forms—one collective and the other distributive. They fall into the following main groups:

(*a*) names of animals—*fish* (which may also be distributive), *fishes*;

(*b*) numbers, weights, and measures—*score, scores; dozen, dozens; pound, pounds.*

(*c*) a few odd words: PENCE, PENNIES; DICE, DIES; cabbage, cabbages.

For the syntax of ordinary collective nouns see AGREEMENT; and for the general principle governing the use of those with a separate plural see NUMBERS, WEIGHTS, AND MEASURES.

Another difficulty arises with collective nouns that are followed by a partitive genitive. A number of people, books, towns *are* or *is*? Here the force of attraction is at work. If a plural noun follows the *of*, the verb is almost inevitably, and on the whole justly, made plural by attraction. In such an expression as 'A number of books is' there is ugly cacophony, at any rate; so it is better to satisfy grammar and euphony by treating the collective itself as a plural. Indeed, this whole discussion leads us back to the simple rule for collectives—Be consistent and you may do what you will, trusting your ear and your sense of idiom.

See also PEOPLE and ASSEMBLY, NOUNS OF.

collusion. See ALLUSION.

colon. MEU says that the colon is a stop used 'chiefly as one preferred by individuals, or in impressive contexts, to the semicolon'; but adds that it has 'acquired a special function, that of delivering the goods that have been invoiced in the preceding words; it is a substitute for such verbal harbingers as *viz., scil., that is to say, i.e.,* &c.' Thus:

'The usual relation between the two is that of abstract to concrete: gesticulation is the using of gestures, and a gesture is an act of gesticulation.'

> 'These I have loved:
>   White plates and cups, clean-gleaming,
> Ringed with blue lines; and feathery, faery dust;
> Wet roofs, beneath the lamp-light.'

The colon, too, often stands after *said*, in a substantial passage of direct speech. Thus 'The Prime Minister said:' is a usual formula for introducing a verbatim report.

Often the colon, especially in formal or technical English, is followed by a dash. The example is from the text of MEU itself: 'Actual quotations will be found under many of the words mentioned in their dictionary places:—' (the words are given in a list following).

comma. The following hints are quoted verbatim from RCR:

Commas should, as a rule, be inserted between adjectives preceding and qualifying substantives, as—

'An enterprising, ambitious man.'
'A gentle, amiable, harmless creature.'
'A cold, damp, badly lighted room.'

But where the last adjective is in closer relation to the substantive than the preceding ones, omit the comma, as—

'A distinguished foreign author.'
'The sailor was accompanied by a great rough Newfoundland dog.'

Where *and* joins two single words or phrases the comma is usually omitted; e.g.

'The honourable and learned member.'

But where more than two words or phrases occur together in a sequence a comma should precede the final *and*; e.g.

'A great, wise, and beneficent measure.'

The following sentence, containing two conjunctive *and*'s, needs no commas:

'God is wise and righteous and faithful.'

Such words as *moreover*, *however*, &c., are usually followed by a comma when used at the opening of a sentence, or preceded and followed by a comma when used in the middle of a sentence. For instance:

'In any case, however, the siphon may be filled.'

Commas are often used instead of parentheses, as in:

'Perhaps the most masterly, and certainly the easiest, presentation of the thought is in the *Prelude*.'

In such sentences as the following a comma should be used:

'Truth ennobles man, and learning adorns him.'
'The Parliament is not dissolved, but only prorogued.'
'The French having occupied Portugal, a British squadron, under Rear-Admiral Sir Samuel Hood, sailed for Madeira.'
'I believed, and therefore I spoke.'
'The question is, Can it be performed?'
'My son, give me thy heart.'
'The Armada being thus happily defeated, the nation resounded with shouts of joy.'
'Be assured, then, that order, frugality, and economy are the necessary supporters of every personal and private virtue.'
'Virtue is the highest proof of a superior understanding, and the only basis of greatness.'

When a preposition assumes the character of an adverb, a comma should follow it, to avoid awkwardness or ambiguity:

'In the valley below, the villages looked very small.'

Omit the comma in such phrases as 'my friend Jones', 'my friend the Chancellor of the Exchequer'.

To these must be added a note on the occasional syntactical significance of the comma:

(*a*) *after the absolute phrase.* Two of the sentences quoted above illustrate the correct use. Here they are with the incorrect punctuation:

'The French, having occupied Portugal, a British squadron, under Rear-Admiral Sir Thomas Hood, sailed for Madeira.'
'The Armada, being thus happily defeated, the nation resounded with shouts of joy.'

In each sentence the effect of that added comma is to eject the noun (the French, the Armada) from its phrase and leave it high and dry in the main sentence as a subject without a predicate.

(*b*) *separating verb from subject, complement, and object.* The first example of this erroneous usage is from MEU:

'The charm in Nelson's history, is, the unselfish greatness.' (First comma separates subject and verb; second separates verb and complement.) 'The chief difficulty from our point of view, lay in convincing him of his mistake.' (The comma parts subject from verb. If it must be put in, 'from our point of view' should be indicated clearly as a qualifying phrase—i.e. there should be a comma after *difficulty*; but this is unnecessary stopping.)

(*c*) *marking a non-defining relative*:

The professor who lives next door to me has discovered a new gas.
The professor, who lives next door to me, has discovered a new gas.

These two sentences illustrate the potency of the comma (or commas) in distinguishing between two meanings. In the first sentence the relative is defining; the adjective clause it introduces cannot be dissociated from its antecedent. In the second, the commas have made the adjective clause non-defining or parenthetic. Here is a more subtle example from MEU, as both illustration and warning:

'The Scot, who ignores such literature, does not deserve his name.' (It is only the *ignoring* Scot who does not deserve his name; 'who ignores such literature' is therefore a defining clause, and the commas should not be there.)

The following sentences are given as miscellaneous examples of careless or faulty use of commas. They come from the work of literary men—novelists, reviewers, and the like. In one or two of the sentences the misuse of the comma is probably deliberate. Some modern writers will sink to any level to be different from, or superior to, ordinary people:

(i) Dan would roll up two or three buckets of water from the well, they would both strip to the skin, the boy would kneel in the tub and dash the water about his body for a few moments.

(ii) A flavour of regret, of racial instinct thwarted by nobility, shows itself sometimes in the faces of north-country sheep-dogs, they bury themselves to save the crag-fast sheep, the feeble lambs, but a faint memory of the wolf glows regretfully in their eyes.

(iii) But, for all that the biographer is candid to downrightness, here as on other pages of the book, in statement of mere fact, he falls short of complete success in treating of the middle period, when Gosse was not merely become aware that his poetry as a whole would never tell with either the large public or the best judges but, in consequence of Churton Collins's savage exposure, was feeling, in his own phrase, that he had been flayed alive.

(iv) On that had followed, no very remarkable success of popularity, scandal, or esteem, but a fairly steady and quite easy progress.

(v) Nothing had ever been right, the hamlet itself was poor. There was an old milestone outside his cot, he was pleased with that, it gave the miles to London and the miles to Winchester, it was nice to have a milestone there like that—your very own.

commence. See BEGIN.

common. See MUTUAL.

common and proper. In grammar, the words are applied to two different types of noun. The common noun is one that does not, and the proper is one that does, name a *particular* thing or person: *boy* and *town* are common, *George* and *Brighton* are proper nouns. There is no hard-and-fast distinction; a common noun may become proper in certain contexts, and a proper noun may become common. Thus in letter-writing we often make the nouns *street* and *road* temporarily proper in the address heading, when they are qualified by another proper noun, used adjectivally; and, conversely, the proper noun *Jack* becomes common in such compounds as *cheap-jack, jack-of-all-trades*. It is note-worthy that names of plants, flowers, trees, and animals are common nouns in English: *strawberry, lily, oak, tiger*.

The normal sign of a proper noun is its beginning with a capital letter. For further notes see CAPITAL LETTERS.

common sense. Two words (see IRREGULAR UNIONS); used adjectivally they should be hyphened: 'a common-sense proposition'.

compare. See PREPOSITIONAL IDIOM.

comparison. See DEGREES OF COMPARISON.

compass, compasses. The instrument for drawing circles has two related parts—like scissors, shears, and trousers. Like these, too, it has a plural form, *compasses*. The singular form *compass* belongs to the ship's instrument (mariners' compass), and to the sense of 'circumference, extent, area' and the figurative use of this in 'The music was beyond the compass of his voice'.

complement. 1. *Function.* A complement is the 'completer' of the predicate after a verb of INCOMPLETE PREDICATION. It may be a noun equivalent or a predicate adjective. As part of the simple sentence it is always nominative, but in an accusative and infinitive phrase it is accusative. Examples:

> 'Brutus is an honourable *man*.'
> Seeing is *believing*.
> 'This is *he* (who) was great by land as thou by sea.'
> To err is *human*.
> The waves often seem *blue* owing to the reflection of the sky.
> This is *what I believe*.
> I know him to be a good *man*
> (accusative in accusative and infinitive phrase).

2. *Syntax.* (*a*) For case of pronouns after the verb *to be* (in e.g. 'It is I') see CASE.

(*b*) In simple sentences with the construction

Subject	Predicate	
	Verb	*Complement*
Noun	*to be*	Noun

the subject and the complement should not be of different number. Thus the sentence 'Songs are the chief part of the programme' is grammatical but not idiomatic. Recast 'Songs are the chief items in the programme' or 'Songs form the chief part . . .'.

(*c*) 'In the playground the subject of our conversation was *about* what we were going to do in school.'
'But Miss Evans's strong point is not her people; it is *in* drawing vivid, violent scenes.'
The prepositions *about* and *in* are superfluous, since the verb should be followed by a complement—in the first sentence a noun clause ('what we were going to do at school') and in the second a gerund phrase ('drawing vivid, violent scenes').

complex. For complex sentence see SENTENCE.

compound. For the term in grammar see SENTENCE.

compound nouns. See PLURAL OF COMPOUND NOUNS.

concession. For concessional clauses see ADVERB CLAUSE.

condition. For conditional clauses see ADVERB CLAUSE.

conjunction. The conjunction joins (*a*) words, (*b*) phrases, (*c*) clauses. Conjunctions joining words and phrases are *and*, with the compound *as well as* and the correlative *both . . . and*; *or, nor*, with the correlatives *either . . . or, neither . . . nor; but.* For their use and syntax see under the conjunctions concerned. All these conjunctions join co-ordinate clauses together. For conjunctions introducing subordinate clauses see ADJECTIVE CLAUSE, ADVERB CLAUSE, NOUN CLAUSE.

conjunctive adverb. Conjunctive adverbs are grammatically adverbs that have conjunctive force by reason of their meaning. *Therefore, however, then, so* are the chief examples. Syntactically they cannot do the work of a conjunction; but they have the effect of carrying on the sense or theme without actually attaching to the sentence the clause they introduce. For the punctuation with conjunctive adverbs see SEMICOLON.

connexion. (*a*) So spelt, not *-ction*.

(*b*) *In connexion with* is a periphrasis better avoided, except in its literal or concrete sense: 'The concert was held in connexion with the fete'; 'A coach runs in connexion with the train.'

conservative. MEU deplores the use of the word as an adjective with the meaning 'moderate', qualifying a noun like *figure* or *estimate*. But the use is well established colloquially; and perhaps within twenty years the natural extension of meaning will be justified even in literary English.

consider. See REGARD.

considering. *Considering*, with one or two other present participles (*concerning, regarding, respecting,* [*not*] *excepting, notwithstanding*) may be a preposition, and so used to is exempt from the rules that govern the relationship of the participle to the noun or pronoun it qualifies:

Considering the weather, the football was quite good.

'Now *concerning* the collection for the saints, as I have given order to the churches of Galatia, even so do ye.'

See also EXCEPT and ADJECTIVE PHRASE.

consist. 'Consist *of*' = 'is made of'; 'consist *in*' = 'is': 'The trifle consists *of* fruit, cream, and jelly'; 'Goodness consists *in* being honest, true, and kind'. It follows that (i) 'consist of' is always followed by the name of a stuff or material, and (ii) the substitution of 'is' or 'is made of' is an effective test. Thus in the first sentence 'is' would make sense, but would not be idiomatic; in the second sentence 'is made of' would scarcely make sense. In the following sentence (quoted from MEU) the 'is made of' test reveals the error: 'The most exceptional feature of Dr. Ward's book undoubtedly consists of the reproduction of photographs.'

consonants (Latin *con+sonantes* = 'sounding with', i.e. with vowels) are sounds which are formed by stopping the breath or by obstructing it in some part of the mouth or throat so that it passes with audible friction or vibration.

They may be classified in three ways:

(i) according to breath. (*a*) When the breath is entirely stopped and then released with an explosion we get Stops (Checks, Mutes, Explosives). These sounds are represented by p, b; t, d; k, g (as in *get*).

(*b*) (1) When the breath is obstructed we get sounds which can be prolonged merely by continuing the breath. These sounds are called Continuants or Spirants and are represented by f, v; s, z; sh, zh; th (as in *thin*), th (as in *thine*), and the Scottish ch (in *loch*).

(2) When the breath is stopped in the mouth but allowed to escape freely though the nostrils, we get Nasals, represented by m, n, ng.

(3) There is a sub-class of continuants called Liquids (or flowing letters), produced by a partial stoppage of the breath. They are represented by l, r, and sometimes m and n.

(4) Note the term Sibilant which is given to the sounds represented by s, z; sh and zh, on account of their hissing sound.

(ii) according to the organ of speech chiefly used in their production. Thus we get

(a) Labials (Lat. *labium* = lip) produced when the breath is stopped by closing the lips. They are p, b; f, v; m; w and wh.

(b) Dentals (Lat. *dens* = tooth) formed by stopping the breath at the upper teeth. They are t, d; th (in *thin*), th (in *thine*); s, z; sh, zh; n.

(c) Gutturals (Lat. *guttur* = throat) formed by raising the back of the tongue against the soft palate. They are k, g (in *get*); the Scottish ch (in *loch*); the nasal ng.

(d) Palatals (Lat. *palatum* = palate) formed by raising the tongue against the palate proper: y (in *yes*).

(iii) according as they are produced with vibration of the vocal chords, when they are called Voiced (or Sharp), or without, when they are called Voiceless (or Flat). Examples of the voiced consonants are b, d, g (in *get*), z, v, th (in *thine*), and the corresponding voiceless consonants are p, t, k, s, f, th (in *thin*).

Table of Consonantal Sounds

	Stops			Continuants	
	Voiced	Voiceless	Nasal	Voiced	Voiceless
Gutturals	g (in *get*)	k	ng		ch (in *loch*)
Palatals				y (in *yes*)	
Dentals	d	t	n	th (in *thine*) z zh	th (in *thin*) s sh
Labials	b	p	m	v w	f wh

In addition there are two trilled sounds, both continuants, represented by r and l, r being partially palatal and l partially dental: ch (in *church*) and j represent compound sounds, ch = t+sh and j = d+zh: w and y are best grouped as semi-vowels.

constructio ad sensum. See SYNESIS.

contemptible, contemptuous. *Contemptible* is passive—'able, fit to be *contemned* (i.e. 'despised')': a *contemptible* attitude, number, sum of money; *contemptuous* is active—despising, looking down upon. A *contemptible* person is one who lays himself open to the sneers of the *contemptuous* person.

content. The reflexive construction is 'content oneself *with*', not *by*.

continual, continuous. The difference between the two words is difficult to define, since in certain uses they may be synonymous. In general, however, *continual* describes that which goes on indefinitely in time; there is usually the suggestion of intermittency, i.e. continued action or being, with brief intervals: '*Continual* dropping wears away the stone', 'The dog kept up a *continual* barking'. *Continuous* suggests unbroken action or state between two fixed points of time or space: '*continuous* performance' (i.e. a performance in a theatre or cinema which goes on without interruption to a fixed time); 'a *continuous* line, of houses, of men' (i.e. 'unbroken'). The COD definitions of the two words are:

continual—always going on; very frequent.
continuous—(of material things) connected, unbroken; uninterrupted in line or sequence.

continuants. See CONSONANTS.

continuous. (i) See CONTINUAL.
(ii) (of tenses) representing action that goes on or continues, in the past, present, or future. The ordinary active continuous tenses in English are made up of the auxiliary *to be* + the present participle: I am, was, shall be going. In Latin and French there is only one continuous tense, the past, which is usually called the *Imperfect*: amabam, j'aimais. See TENSE.

copulative. In grammar, *copulative* verbs are such as 'link' the subject to the complement; i.e. all verbs of INCOMPLETE PREDICATION, and the passive of FACTITIVE verbs ('is considered', 'is made'). *Copulative* conjunctions are those (like *and*) which make a combination, not an alternative or a contrast. See DISJUNCTIVE.

cord. See CHORD.

correlatives. With co-ordinating correlatives special care should be taken that the items correlated are of the same type. Thus if the first correlative word is followed by an adjective, the second should normally be followed by an adjective; if the first is followed by an adverb phrase, consisting of preposition and noun, the second should normally be followed by the same form of adverb phrase. The working rule is: *each of the two correlatives is usually followed by the same part of speech—often by the same word*. For the working out of the general rule see the correlatives concerned, which are: BOTH . . . AND; EITHER . . . OR; NEITHER . . . NOR; NOT ONLY . . . BUT ALSO; WHETHER.

councillor, counsellor. A *councillor* is a man or woman who sits on a council (e.g. Privy, urban, parish, borough); a *counsellor* is a private adviser. It is obvious that the one does not exclude the other.

counsel. The legal term (= a barrister pleading in a lawsuit) was originally an abstract noun, meaning the actual 'advice' or 'pleading'. That is the reason why it has no plural form, although it is now the word signifying the adviser as well as his advice. 'Learned counsel' may mean one pleader or several pleaders in a lawsuit.

couplet. In prosody, two consecutive rhyming lines, as at the end of a Shakespearian (or English) SONNET. See also HEROIC COUPLET.

credence, credentials, credit. *Credence* means 'belief', simply: 'Do not give too much *credence* to his story.'

Credentials is used officially of a letter (or letters) of introduction, especially that given to an ambassador.

Credit has one sense ('belief, trust') which is much the same as that of *credence*, as in 'to give *credit* to a person's story'. But it has also many other senses, such as 'reputation', 'acknowledgement of merit' ('to get *credit* for one's action'), 'source of honour' ('to be a *credit* to one's side'). In business, it may mean 'trust in a person's ability and intention to pay' ('to give *credit*') or 'a sum of money at a person's disposal in books of a bank, &c.' ('to have a *credit* account'); while a 'letter of *credit*' is a document authorizing a person to draw money from the writer's correspondent in another place.

crow. The normal Mod.E. past form (tense and participle) is *crowed*; the form *crew* is, probably by association with the expression 'the cock crew' in the Bible story of Peter's denial, nearly always associated with cocks.

curb, kerb. In the physical sense of (*a*) a stone edging for a footpath or road, or (*b*) a fender, the usual spelling in Mod.E. is *kerb*. The verb meaning 'check' and its associated noun are spelt *curb*.

curtailed words are such as have been shortened in popular use. All established curtailed words are legitimate in speech, although some (e.g. *bike, photo, tec*) are generally regarded as vulgarisms; but most of them are better avoided in writing, except when the curtailed form (e.g. *dynamo, magneto*) has become so much the normal one as to make us forget that it is a curtailment. A few interesting examples are given:

bike, cycle (bicycle); *bus* (omnibus); *cinema* (cinematograph); *consols* (consolidated funds); *dynamo* (dynamo-electric machine); *magneto* (magneto-electric machine); *mob* (mobile vulgus); *phone* (telephone); *pram* (perambulator); *pro* (professional); *soccer* (association football); *tec* (detective); *Zoo* (Zoological Gardens).

dactyl. See FOOT.

dahlia. So spelt (< Dahl, an 18th-century Swedish botanist), but pronounced dā′lya.

dare. *Dare* is an OE. defective verb. Its normal modern inflexions are those of an ordinary weak verb; but there are two survivals of its original forms:

(*a*) 'He *dare* not do it', '*Dare* he go?', 'He *dare* do anything'. In negative and interrogative sentences and wherever the dependent infinitive has no 'to' *dare* is used for the normal *dares* in the third singular present tense—a reminder of the fact that OE. *dearr* was actually a past form. Cf. OUGHT.

(*b*) *Durst*, an OE. past form, survives fitfully, particularly in colloquial

English—'I *durst not* (or *durstn't*) do it'. But *dared* is the standard form in modern literary English.

dash. In punctuation the single dash is nothing but a kind of ornamental comma, occurring usually at the end of sentences to mark a break, often made for effect before a dénouement:

> 'Rome shall perish—write that word
> In the blood that she has spilt.'

'It came nearer and nearer—a low murmuring noise, but full of secret life.'

'How different from such a scene is a tropical noon—a noon in Guiana or Brazil, for example.'

The two separate *dashes* (— . . .—) are used as a mark of PARENTHESIS.

dative case. (*a*) *Form*. Neither nouns nor pronouns have any special dative inflexion, but the dative has the same form as the accusative. Thus, in pronouns, *me, him, whom* may be datives.

(*b*) *Syntax*. There is only one use of the dative in Mod.E., i.e. for the indirect object of a verb. Thus in the sentence 'He gave me the letter' *letter* is the direct object of the verb and *me* the indirect object. Only a few verbs in English are capable of this construction: *give* is the most important; *send, write, bequeath, pay* are others. Notice that in Mod.E. the case following a preposition is said to be the accusative; in the sentence 'He gave the letter to me' *me* is accusative, object of the preposition *to*.

(*c*) *Special Datives*.

(i) *Retained*. When a verb governing a dative and an accusative is made passive and the direct object becomes the subject, the indirect object (dative) is kept or 'retained' in the passive sentence. Thus the sentence given under ACCUSATIVE (*d*) might be made passive thus: 'A book was given *me* by him', where *me* is the retained dative.

(ii) *In apposition*. See APPOSITION.

(iii) *Ethic*. The emotional or expressive dative, 'in which a person no more than indirectly interested in the fact described in the sentence is introduced into it, usually by himself as the speaker, in the dative' (MEU). The construction is common in Greek and Latin, and was common in English. Honest Casca will supply a good example: 'He plucked *me* ope his doublet and offered them his throat to cut' (note here that *them* is a real dative after the verb *offered*); and the first Gravedigger a grim one: 'Here's a skull now; this skull hath lain *you* i' the earth three-and-twenty years.'

deal. 'A deal of', though an old idiom, is still a colloquialism; in writing always qualify *deal* with *good* or *great*.

decided, decisive. *Decided* means (*a*) 'unquestionable', (*b*) 'fixed in intention'; *decisive*, which is used rarely of persons, means 'bringing to an issue or decision'. Thus *decided*: (*a*) 'decided signs of weakness', (*b*) a decided person, attitude; *decisive*: a decisive battle, over (in cricket), goal (in football).

decimate. Though it originally meant to kill one in every ten (as a punishment), *decimate* is legitimately used in the general sense of 'cause great loss or slaughter' in an army. But such use must be general; if any particularization is made, a loss of one in ten must be stated or inferred. 'To decimate by 50 per cent.' is wrong. Above all, there should be no suggestion that *decimate* means to destroy nine in every ten, leaving one alive. Always think of *decimate* as a less drastic word than it seems at first sight or on first hearing.

declare, express. '*Declare* oneself satisfied'; '*express* oneself *as* satisfied'. Cf. CONSIDER.

defective, deficient. *Defective* implies faultiness or unsatisfactory quality; *deficient* implies insufficient quantity or total lack. A person's muscle or his knowledge of mathematics may be defective (or deficient, i.e. not sufficient or quite wanting), whereas he himself may be deficient in muscle or in the knowledge of mathematics. Note that both of these epithets may be applied to the same noun, but with a difference in meaning. Thus *defective water* implies impurity, *deficient water* lack of adequate quantity. For defective verbs see ANOMALOUS.

defining. For defining adjective clause see ADJECTIVE CLAUSE and COMMA.

definite, definitive. MEU makes the distinction thus: *definite* means 'defined', 'clear', 'precise', 'unmistakable', and *definitive* means 'having the character of finality'. A *definite* offer is one of which the terms are clear; a *definitive* offer is one that must be taken or left without 'chaffering'. The use of the words is outlined and illustrated in John o' London's *Is it good English*:

'A good many people have been puzzled in recent years by the use of the word *definitive* where they had expected the shorter and more familiar *definite*. An amusing instance of this feeling of uncertainty came to light during the railway strike of 1919. A party of Labour leaders was found at Unity House poring over dictionaries to find out what Sir Auckland Geddes meant by *definitive*. Mr. J. H. Thomas had asked the Government for a definite offer. When, in reply, he received a *definitive* offer, he asked himself in what the difference, if any, consisted. It became known afterwards that in the first draft of his important letter Sir Auckland had described the Government's offer as "definite", using the word which Mr. Thomas had invited him to use; but when the letter was brought to him for signature he altered "definite" to "definitive" as being closer to his meaning.'

degrees of comparison. 1. *Form.* Degree of comparison in adjectives is expressed

(*a*) by survivals of the OE. inflexions *-ra* (comparative) and *-esta*, *-osta* (superlative), which have become in Mod.E. *-er* and *-est*: kind*er*, kind*est*; happi*er*, happi*est*; wis*er*, wis*est*. Most short adjectives (monosyllabic and disyllabic) of whatever derivation are thus inflected. Local spelling adjustments ($Y > I$, loss of MUTE E, &c.) occur before the addition of the suffixes, and are dealt with under their appropriate headings. A few OE. irregularities have survived here and there. In for*mer*, fore*most* the suffixes represent OE. *-ma*, *-mest*, though *former* is actually a double comparative combining the two OE. suffixes *-ma* and *-ra*. Four adjectives have special forms:

Positive	Comparative	Superlative
good	better	best
bad	worse	worst
much	more	most
little	less	least

A few adjectives have two comparative forms with etymologically distinct origins. The chief ones are set out in the following table, with the necessary explanations:

old	older, oldest elder, eldest	*Elder, eldest* are the survivals of the OE. *i*-mutation forms.
near	next, nearer, nearest	The OE. forms were *neah, nearra, niehst*. *Near* itself, therefore, represents the OE. comparative, the positive *neah* surviving in Mod.E. *nigh*. *Niehst*>*next*; *Nearer* and *nearest* are modern analogous forms.
late	(i) latter, last (ii) later, latest	The first pair represent the OE. form: *later, latest* are more modern analogous formations.
far	(i) farther, farthest (ii) further, furthest	The normal comparative of *far* would be *farrer, farrest*. Chaucer has *ferre, ferrest*. Euphony, however, stepped in, and a new comparative easier to pronounce was made for *far* from the old positive *forth*. *Forth* itself gave *further, furthest*; *farther, farthest* were formations influenced by the vowel of *far*.

For the distinction between the forms in use and meaning see the words concerned.

(*b*) by the modifying adverb *more* for the comparative and *most* for the superlative: 'more beautiful'; 'most acceptable'. Some adjectives of two syllables and all of more than two form their degrees in this way. Euphony will generally decide whether the inflexion or the adverb should be used.

Degree of comparison in all adverbs except those which have the same form as the adjective is expressed by the adverbs *more, most*. Those with the adjective form have also the adjective degree formation. Thus *harder, faster, longer* are both adjectives and adverbs.

2. Syntax. The general syntax is treated under the headings: DOUBLE COMPARATIVE and SUPERLATIVE WITH ANY. Special points are dealt with in connexion with irregular forms—e.g. ELDER, OLDER; SUPERIOR.

delusion. See ALLUSION.

demonstratives. 1. *Form.* Demonstrative ('pointing out', 'showing') is a term applied to (*a*) pronouns; (*b*) adjectives; (*c*) adverbs. For the forms of demonstrative pronouns see PRONOUNS. The demonstrative adjectives are *this* and *that*, plural *these* and *those*; they are the only adjectives that show agreement with their nouns in number. Demonstrative adverbs are *there, hither, thither, then, thence, here,* and *hence*, corresponding with the relative adverbs or conjunctions *where, when, whither, whence.*

2. *Syntax.* 'The sheet was then soaked in water, hammered with some form of mallet, and allowed to dry. These sheets were fastened together to form a roll.' What sheets? Only one has been mentioned. The demonstrative (adjective) is plural, but is pointing back to a singular. A natural jump of thought occasions the construction, but it is none the less faulty. The guiding rule is: A demonstrative pronoun or adjective must always be of the same number as the noun or pronoun to which it is related.

dentals. See CONSONANTS.

depends. Except when used colloquially and elliptically in the sentence 'It all depends', *depends* is always followed by (*up*)*on*; that is, it can never have an indirect question immediately after it: 'It depends *on* what he said, *on* who is coming', not 'It depends what he said, who is coming'.

deprecate, depreciate : *deprecate* (Lat. *precari*, to pray; *prex*, a prayer), to try to ward off by prayer, to plead against or express disapproval of; *depreciate* (Lat. *pretium*, price), to belittle (transitive), to fall in value (intransitive).

The usual blunder with these words is the use of *deprecate* (or any of its derivatives) instead of *depreciate* (or any of its derivatives).

The English people are apt to *deprecate* themselves; their stocks and shares may *depreciate*; but we should *deprecate* their anger at such loss, and smile at their self-*depreciatory* (not *deprecatory*) mood.

device, devise. See PRACTICE.

diaeresis. The pronunciation as separate sounds of two vowels standing together in a word (*aërate*, *Chloë*); hence, the mark (¨) placed over the second vowel to indicate such pronunciation.

dice, dies. *Dice* is the plural of *die*, the 'cube with faces bearing 1–6 spots used in games of chance' (COD); *dies* is the plural of *die*, the printer's stamp and the engineer's tool.

digraph. (Greek = double-writing) is the name given to a group of two letters forming one sound; e.g. *ae* in *Caesar*; *ch* in *church*; *ea* in *each*.

diminish, minimize. *Diminish* means to 'make or become less', *minimize* is superlative (< Lat. *minimus*, 'least') and means 'to make least', i.e. to reduce to the lowest amount. So, when a man's income is reduced 10 per cent., it *diminishes*; but when you try to save a man from punishment you *minimize* his guilt.

diminutives are nouns that express smallness, either actual or imputed, in token of affection or contempt. The chief suffixes forming diminutives are:

-et: coron-*et*.	-(c)ule, -(u)le: mole-*cule*, glob*ule*, circ-*le*.
-let: stream-*let*.	
-en: chick-*en*.	-el, -elle: mors-*el*, bagat-*elle*.
-ock: hill-*ock*.	-et, -ette: bill-*et*, cigar-*ette*.
-ling: prince-*ling*, duck-*ling*.	-ie: Charl-*ie*.
-ing: farth-*ing* (= a small fourth part).	-kin: manni-*kin*, Peter-*kin*.
-(e)rel: cock-*erel*.	-aster: poet-*aster*.

diphthong (pronounced *dif-*, not *dip-*). When two simple vowel sounds are uttered so rapidly one after the other as to become practically one sound (and that differing from both the simple sounds), we have a diphthong. Lazy people disintegrate diphthongs in their speaking: thus they say na-is for *nice*. There are four true diphthongs in English:

$$i \text{ in } pine = a \text{ (in } father\text{)} + i \text{ (in } pin\text{)}.$$
$$ou \text{ in } mouse = a \text{ (} father\text{)} + oo \text{ (in } stood\text{)}.$$
$$oi \text{ in } noise = au \text{ (in } laud\text{)} + i \text{ (in } pin\text{)}.$$
$$u \text{ in } mute = i \text{ (in } pin\text{)} + oo \text{ (in } pool\text{)}.$$

The *a* in *gate* and the *o* in *go* are also diphthongs in southern (standard) English, though pure vowels in Scottish and northern; the first is represented in international phonetic script as (ei), the second as (ou). Then all English long vowels (except o) followed by vocalic *r* (i.e. *r* not immediately followed by a vowel) are pronounced as diphthongs: e.g. *fire, fare, fear, cure*; the second vowel of the diphthong is the obscure sound represented as (ə).

The term 'false diphthong' is sometimes applied to such DIGRAPHS as *ea* (in *each*), *ei* (in *receive*), *ie* (in *believe*); but these are no more diphthongs than the *ch* (in *choir*), *ph* (in *euphony*). It is, however, possible for a DIGRAPH to represent a diphthong as in *mouse* and *noise* above. The æ (in *Cæsar*), œ (in *fœtid*) are merely printers' ligatures.

direct question. See QUESTION.

direct speech. For the writing of direct speech see INVERTED COMMAS.

disinterested, uninterested. 'On account of his age and his own believed *disinterestedness* in Test Cricket, Freeman is unlikely to be considered either for the Trial or for the Test.' Our special correspondent is wrong. Freeman is *uninterested* not *disinterested* in Test Cricket. A *disinterested* person is one who has no axe to grind, no 'interest' in the sense of expectation of advantage; a *disinterested* action is one performed without hope of any return. But cricket may be *uninteresting* when the batsman takes an hour to score ten runs; and the poor spectator may be fairly called *uninterested*.

disjunctive. The term is used in French for the pronouns *moi, toi, lui,* &c. in their use after the verb *to be* ('c'est *moi*'; 'c'est *lui*') and after *que* (= 'than'): 'Il est plus grand que *moi*'. The pronoun in such construction might be expected to be nominative. The influence of the French idiom is seen in English in such sentences as 'It's *me*', 'It's *him*', 'He is taller than *me*', where *me, him* correspond with the French disjunctive pronouns. See CASE.

Disjunctive conjunctions are such as introduce an alternative or contrast; *or* and *but* are the chief examples. See COPULATIVE.

dispatch, despatch. The first spelling is preferable, for both noun and verb.

distinct, distinctive. *distinct* means well defined, separate in identity (*from*); *distinctive* means serving as a mark by which something may be known from others of its kind. Care must be taken not to use *distinctive* for *distinct*. The converse error is scarcely possible. An OED definition affords a good example of the correct use: 'Typhoid fever: a specific eruptive fever, characterized by intestinal inflammation and ulceration: more *distinctively*, and now more usually, called enteric fever.'

distributives. The MEU definition is: 'Those adjectives and pronouns are so called which expressly convey that what is said of a class is applicable to its individual members, not merely to it as a whole.' The chief examples are: *Neither, either* (of them); *each* (of them); *every one* (of them). All these except *every* may be used as pronouns or as adjectives. Distributives have a nasty habit of suggesting a plural which is not grammatically expressed. Special care must therefore be taken with them wherever in a sentence confusion of singular and plural would lead to a serious error in syntax. See under AGREEMENT (*b*), BETWEEN, IDENTICAL.

The term 'distributive' is applied to those plurals which, though normally collective, sometimes signify persons or things taken separately. Thus the word *people* may also be distributive. See PEOPLE.

do. This verb had originally only one primary meaning, expressing an action, as in the modern 'I *did* this'. It has now several auxiliary uses:

(*a*) It is used to avoid the repetition of another verb, e.g. 'In passing through the market-place one morning, which he seldom *did*..' (Disraeli), where *did* represents the verb 'pass';

(*b*) It is used intensively, as in 'We *did* do this', 'We *do* know . . .', where it serves merely for emphasis;

(*c*) It is used interrogatively in direct questions. The affirmative 'I know' becomes the interrogative '*Do* I know?', &c.

(*d*) It is now used regularly in negative sentences with *not*. Thus 'I *do* not know' replaces the older 'I know not'.

do so. See SO.

double. For double sentence see SENTENCE, and for double subject see AGREEMENT.

double comparatives and superlatives. The use of the double comparative and superlative for emphasis, once common, is not tolerated in modern English. Three examples are quoted from Shakespeare:

> 'How much *more elder* art thou than thy looks!'

> 'This was the *most unkindest* cut of all.'

> 'I am sure my love 's
> *More richer* than my tongue.'

double consonants. Double consonants form one of the chief difficulties in spelling. They may be

(*a*) natural—i.e. part of the stem or 'body' of a word;

(*b*) formed directly by the addition of a prefix (often with assimilation), or a suffix;

(*c*) the result of doubling a single consonant before a suffix beginning with a vowel.

Some difficult words follow under their respective headings:

(*a*)

abbot	parallel	abyss
abbess	callous	admission
desiccated	consummation	ambassador
tobacco	summary	assassinate
vaccinate		caress
coffee	Britannia	cessation
daffodil	[but note Brittany]	dismissal
giraffe	tyrannous	embassy
paraffin	barrel	harass
toffee	barricade	intercession
baggage	carriage	mattress
exaggerate	corridor	necessary
	embarrass	omission
	quarrel	tassel

(b) With prefixes:

ad-
- ac-**c**omplish
- ac-**c**ommodate
- ac-**c**ept
- ac-**c**idental
- ad-**d**ition
- ad-**d**ress
- as-**s**ent
- at-**t**raction
- an-**n**ouncement
- ap-**p**earance
- ap-**p**ointment
- ab-**b**reviation
- al-**l**iteration
- al-**l**usion
- ag-**g**ravate
- ag-**g**regate

in-
- im-**m**ovable
- im-**m**ediate
- im-**m**inent
- im-**m**oral
- im-**m**ortal
- ir-**r**eligious
- ir-**r**igation
- ir-**r**everent
- ir-**r**esponsible
- il-**l**egal
- il-**l**iterate
- il-**l**ogical
- il-**l**egible
- il-**l**egitimate
- in-**n**ocent
- in-**n**umerable

con-
- col-**l**apse
- col-**l**aborate
- col-**l**eague
- col-**l**ection
- col-**l**ision
- com-**m**and
- com-**m**issioner
- com-**m**emorate
- com-**m**ittee
- com-**m**odity
- con-**n**exion
- cor-**r**ection
- cor-**r**elate
- cor-**r**ugated
- cor-**r**uption

dis-
- dif-**f**erence
- dif-**f**iculty
- dif-**f**idence
- dis-**s**atisfied
- dis-**s**atisfaction
- dis-**s**ection
- dis-**s**ension
- dis-**s**enter
- dis-**s**imilar
- dis-**s**ipation
- dis-**s**olution
- dis-**s**uade

un-
- un-**n**atural
- un-**n**ecessary

sub-
- suf-**f**er
- sup-**p**osed
- sup-**p**ort
- sup-**p**lant

ob-
- oc-**c**asional
- oc-**c**ur

inter-
- inter-**r**upt

With suffixes:

green-**n**ess, clean-**n**ess, and other words ending in *n* followed by the suffix *-ness*.

natural-**l**y, general-**l**y, and other words ending in *l* followed by the adverbial suffix *-ly*. Note especially: fu**ll**y, du**ll**y, who**ll**y.

with-**h**old, soul-**l**ess.

(c) The rule is:

(i) When a suffix beginning with a vowel is added to a word of one syllable ending in a single vowel+a single consonant, the consonant is doubled.

(ii) When a suffix beginning with a vowel is added to words of more than one syllable ending in a single vowel+a single consonant, the consonant is doubled only if its syllable bears the stress.

The consonant *l* does not conform to the rule. It is *always* doubled before a suffix beginning with a vowel, except in the one word *unparallel-ed*. The consonant *p* does not conform to the rule *(a)* in words whose final syllable, though unstressed, retains the quality of a stressed syllable: *kidnap* and *handicap* are the most important of them; *(b)* in words compounded with monosyllables: e.g. *horsewhip*, *sideslip*. In such words, and in one isolated word *worship*, the *p* doubles before a suffix beginning with a vowel: *kidnapped, handicapped, horsewhipped, sideslipping, worshipper.* The few words in single vowel+*g* always double the *g* before a suffix beginning with a vowel, irrespective of accent: *zigzagging, peri-*

wigged. Apart from these there are no exceptions to the general rule. Here are a few representative examples:

(i) beggar	(ii) beginning	listening
starry	occurring	answered
sinning	regrettable	benefiting
robber	travelling	happening
getting	woollen	offered
	jeweller	
	referred	

double negative. Modern English has logically and mathematically decided that two negatives make a positive; so the old downright construction in which a second negative intensified the first has dropped out of use. With what effect it could be used is illustrated in the following extracts from Chaucer and Shakespeare:

> 'He never yet *no* vileinye *ne* sayde
> In al his lyf, un-to *no* maner wight.'
>
> 'And he *nas nat* right fat, I undertake.'
>
> (Chaucer)
>
> ''Tis no sinister *nor no* awkward claim.'
>
> (Shakespeare)

A double negative does, however, sometimes survive accidentally and incorrectly in Mod.E., especially in conversation. Thus 'I shouldn't be surprised if he didn't come' is often intended to mean 'I shouldn't be surprised if he did come'. Here is a good example from a speech quoted in a daily newspaper: 'Many people would like to see a reduction of sixpence on income tax. I should not be at all surprised if it were not reduced by threepence.' More frequent, because more disguised, is the use of a negative with the adverbs *hardly*, *scarcely*, which have themselves a negative force. The following example of the error is taken from MEU: 'It has been *impossible* to tell the public *scarcely* anything about American naval co-operation with the British.'

double plurals. A few nouns have two separate plurals, one being regularly derived from the etymological plural, and the other an analogous form with the normal English ending in -*s*. The two plurals survive usually to express two different and distinct meanings. In the following table the chief nouns concerned are given, with their plurals; notes on the difference between the two forms in meaning and use are given under the words themselves.

Noun	Derivative plural	Analogous plural
brother	brethren (OE.)	brothers
cow	kine (OE.)	cows
formula	formulae (Lat.)	formulas
fungus	fungi (Lat.)	funguses
index	indices (Lat.)	indexes
genius	genii (Lat.)	geniuses
bandit	banditti (Italian)	bandits
cherub	cherubim (Hebrew)	cherubs
seraph	seraphim (Hebrew)	seraphs

(For *fish*, *fishes*, &c., see NEUTER PLURALS; and for 'two-*foot* rule', &c., see NUMBERS, WEIGHTS, AND MEASURES.)

doubt. (*a*) The sense of *fear* is now archaic: 'I doubt he will not come' (= I fear, &c.) belongs now only to dialect.

(*b*) The clause after *doubt* in the positive is introduced by *whether*, not by *that*: 'I doubt whether Easter will be fine'; 'He doubts whether he will play again'. But after *doubt* in the negative or interrogative the conjunction is *that*: 'I do not doubt *that* . . .'; 'Who doubts *that* . . .?'

(*c*) The clause after *doubt* as noun, or the adjective *doubtful*, is in apposition, and the conjunction is according to the idiom for the verb under (*b*) above: 'There is a doubt *whether* . . .'; 'There is no doubt *that* . . .'; 'It is doubtful *whether* . . .'. *About* and *as to* cannot govern a clause but may govern a noun or gerund after *doubt*: 'There is a doubt as to his sanity, his going'; 'There is no doubt about it', but not 'There is a doubt about whether he is sane'; 'There is no doubt as to that it is so'.

draft, draught. The first is merely a phonetic spelling of the second (<verb *draw*); but in English usage the two forms have become fairly clearly differentiated. A few common uses are distinguished below:

draft	draught
Banker's draft	sit in a draught
draft of soldiers	draught-horse
draft a bill, &c.	draught of fishes
a rough draft	draught of ships (= displacement)
	beer on draught
	a draughtsman (= one who draws plans, &c.)
	game of draughts

dramatic irony. See IRONY.

dramatic unities. Three general principles of dramatic art were expanded from Aristotle's *Poetics* by sixteenth-century dramatic critics and by French Classical dramatists of the seventeenth century. They were the Unities of Action, Time, and Place. Aristotle mentions the unity of Time only as a general practice and not as a rule to be observed. He barely alludes to the unity of Place. But the unity of Action he insists upon as necessary: if the play is to be a *whole* it must be *one*, i.e. there must be unity of Action.

(*a*) The unity of *Action*—that a play should consist of one main action, to the carrying on of which everything in the play must be subservient. This unity, taken in its broadest sense, Shakespeare followed.

(*b*) The unity of *Time*—that the time occupied by the action represented in the play should be no longer than the time the play takes to perform, or at any rate should not exceed twenty-four hours.

(*c*) The unity of *Place*—that the action represented in the play should take place continuously in one place.

Shakespeare and other English dramatists have usually ignored (*b*) and (*c*), and in general the English stage tradition attaches very little importance to them. In this connexion *The Tempest* is of considerable interest, for in it the whole action is compressed within the span of three hours. At the opening of the play we have this conversation:

Pros.   What is the time o' the day?
Ariel   Past the mid season.

Pros.   At least two glasses. The time 'twixt six and now
     Must by us both be spent most preciously.'   (I. ii. 239 ff.)

At the beginning of Act V we have:

'*Pros.*   How's the day?
Ariel   On the sixth hour; at which time, my lord,
     You said our work should cease.'   (v. i. 3 ff.)

Here then the unity of time is definitely observed, and emphasis is laid on this strict observance by a threefold mention in Act V of three hours as the time limit for the play:

'*Alonso* (to *Prospero*):
   How thou hast met us here, who *three hours since*
   Were wrecked upon this shore.'   (v. i. 136–7.)

'*Alonso* (to *Ferdinand*):
   Your eld'st acquaintance cannot be *three hours*.'   (v. i. 186.)

'*Boatswain* (to *Gonzalo*):   Our ship
   Which but *three glasses since* we gave out split
   Is tight.'   (v. i. 222.)

This play is also a perfect instance of the unity of Place, and is often quoted as such.

drunk, drunken. *Drunk* (not *drank*) is
   (*a*) the participle form, e.g. in verb tenses and in adjective phrases: 'as if of hemlock I had *drunk*'; 'If *drunk* with sight of power, we loose Wild tongues that have not Thee in awe';
   (*b*) the predicate adjective: 'He was quite *drunk*.'
   Drunken is the original form of the participle, restricted now to the attributive adjective in such vehement phrases as 'a *drunken* sot'.

dry. The chief forms with suffixes are: *drier, driest, drily, dryish, dryness, drying.* Cf. SHY, SLY, SPRY, WRY. The adverb form (*drily*) is generally metaphorical.

due. Unlike OWING TO, *due* (*to*) has never become a compound preposition, that is, *due* retains its adjectival function and must be properly related to the noun or pronoun it qualifies. Thus in the sentence 'Due to the bad weather, he cannot come', *due* obviously does not qualify *he*, and therefore has nothing left to qualify. If *due* is to be used, the only way is to provide it with an actual noun: 'His inability to come was due to the bad weather', where *due* qualifies *inability*. But the obvious and idiomatic construction is, 'Owing to the bad weather, he cannot come'. It is a good rule to use *due* only as a predicative adjective (as in the sentence above)—that is, not like a participle, as the first word of a phrase. Of the three following examples the first illustrates the misuse of *due* and is quoted from MEU; the second, from a literary magazine, shows the correct use of *due* in a qualifying phrase; and the third, also from a magazine, illustrates the incorrect use:

   (i) 'Some articles have increased in price, due to the increasing demand.' (Say 'owing to'.)
   (ii) 'Lord Ellen is, presumably, Lord Ellenborough, Governor-General of India from 1841 until his recall in 1844, who was responsible for the annexation of Sindh, due to the brilliant campaign of Sir Charles Napier.' (Here *due* correctly qualifies *annexation*; but the more idiomatic, and therefore the better, construction is 'owing to'.)

    (iii) 'Suddenly a rook, having seen a bird fly off with a piece of food in its beak, will leave its post and chase the unfortunate creature until, due to its inferior size and flying skill, it is eventually forced to surrender its prize.' ('owing to . . .'; *due* can only qualify *it*.)

duration of time. For the accusative of duration of time see ACCUSATIVE CASE.

durst. See DARE.

dye. The present participle is *dyeing* (not *dying*). See Y>I.

each. (*a*) *Each* is a distributive pronoun or adjective: for syntax see DISTRIBUTIVES.

    (*b*) *Each other*.
    (i) The words are treated as a compound and may be object of a verb or a preposition: 'They hated each other' (= 'they hated each the other'); 'We laughed at each other' (= 'each at the other').
    (ii) The genitive form is always *each other's*, never *each others'*.
    (iii) MEU condemns the use of the compound when *other* would be nominative: 'We know what each other wants'. The correct form is: 'We each know what the other wants'.
    (iv) The belief that 'each other' is restricted to two persons and 'one another' refers to more than two is harmless but unnecessary.

eat. The past simple tense is spelt *ate* in Mod.E., though *eat* is a fitful survivor; and the pronunciation is *et*.

economic, economical. The first is the technical word associated with *economics*, and meaning 'based upon the principles of the production and distribution of wealth'. An *economic* arrangement, agreement, between two countries is one that is based upon their wealth and resources. The second is the popular word associated with *economy*; it means 'not extravagant': an *economical* day's outing, meal, purchase.

-ed, -t. The following list of weak verbs which have both the *-ed* and the *-t* endings in the past simple tense and the past participle is taken from MEU:

bereave	BEREAVED	BEREFT
burn	burned	burnt
dream	dreamed	dreamt
kneel	kneeled	knelt
lean	leaned	leant
leap	leaped	leapt
learn	learned	learnt
smell	smelled	smelt
spell	spelled	spelt
spill	spilled	spilt
spoil	SPOILED	SPOILT

MEU recommends for all verbal uses the form in *-t*, in spite of the fact that custom and usage have been against it. Forms like *tost* (= *tossed*), *exprest* (= *expressed*), *kist* (= *kissed*) are eccentricities in Mod.E. They have always had a place in poetry, chiefly because of the doubt concerning the pronunciation of the *-ed* ending. Has *kissed* one syllable or two? Mod.E. relies on the reader for the answer.

effect. See AFFECT.

either . . . or. (*a*) *Either* is never followed by *nor* as a correlative; and *neither* is never followed by *or*. RCR says: 'Never print: *Neither* one *or* the other; *neither* Peter *or* James.'

(*b*) For position in the sentence see the rule under CORRELATIVES. We quote a sentence from *The Times Educational Supplement* with comments: 'When many symbols were needed they would *either* be obtained ready-made and gummed for sticking to their place on the chart, *or* lino-blocks or stencils prepared perhaps by specially selected boys beforehand in the art room, were used.' [The writer began with the intention of using the correlative construction, and actually wrote the *either*, but by the time he reached the *or* he broke off into another construction altogether. The *or* is simply the co-ordinating *or* and *either* has nothing whatever to do with the business. By taking out the *either*, therefore, the sentence may be made correct, if not elegant.]

(*c*) In alternative subject: see under AGREEMENT.

(*d*) *Or . . . or* is an archaic form of *either . . . or*, familiar, but sometimes a little confusing, in Shakespeare:

> (i) 'When yellow leaves, *or* none, *or* few, do hang
>   Upon those boughs that shake against the cold.'

> (ii)   'I do not doubt,
>   As I will watch the aim, *or* to find both,
>   *Or* bring your latter hazard back again.'

ei. For *ei* in spelling see IE AND EI.

elder. See OLDER.

elicit, illicit. *Elicit* is a verb = to draw out, to educe: 'Cross-examination failed to *elicit* any cogent reason for his being present at the critical moment.'

Illicit is an adjective = unlawful. An *illicit* still is one of which the Inland Revenue authorities have no knowledge.

eligible, illegible. *Eligible* (Lat. *eligere*, to choose) means 'fit to be chosen'; *illegible* (Lat. *in* = not; *legere*, to read) means 'unable to be read'. A person might be *eligible* for a certain appointment despite his *illegible* handwriting.

ellipsis. Ellipsis is the syntactical shortening of the construction of a sentence by omitting a word or words that might readily be supplied from the context or from the experience or general knowledge of the reader or hearer. Thus, to take a simple example, when a subject has two predicates, we 'understand' the subject in the second clause: 'Jack fell down and (Jack) broke his crown.' Other familiar examples of ellipsis in English are:

(*a*) of infinite parts or auxiliaries in compound verbs;
(*b*) of the conjunction *that* in NOUN CLAUSES;
(*c*) of the RELATIVE PRONOUN;
(*d*) of the verb after THAN and AS;
(*e*) of a noun or pronoun after *same, such*;
(*f*) of prepositions or conjunctions.

Certain dangers arise, however. Under

(*a*) the infinite part must be appropriate to both auxiliaries (or quasi-auxiliaries): 'I can and will go' is right; 'I shall and have been' is wrong. MEU justifies the construction illustrated in 'The ringleader was hanged and his followers imprisoned', the auxiliary with *imprisoned* being 'understood' in its correct number, *were*. Under

(b) MEU gives a rule 'that when the contents of a clause are attached by part of *be* to such words as *opinion, decision, view,* or *declaration, that* must be inserted'; and a reminder that some verbs, notably *assert*, prefer to keep the *that*: 'I am of the opinion *that* he should be consulted' (not 'of the opinion he should be'); 'Do you assert that he is wrong?' (not 'assert he is'). The keeping or dropping of *that* becomes, therefore, a matter of idiom.

(c) The relative pronoun is not omitted in Mod.E. when it is the subject of its own clause, though this ellipsis is fairly common in Shakespeare: e.g. 'There be some sports are painful.' The ellipsis of the antecedent (seen in 'Who steals my purse steals trash') is now an affectation rather than an idiom, though we have the common use of *what*, where the antecedent is actually expressed in the word (= that which). See WHAT.

(d) The simplest examples give rise only to doubts and difficulties of case: 'He is as tall as *I* (am)'; 'You know him better than *I* (do)', but 'You know him better than (you know) *me*'. The tendency is to fall into AMBIGUITY by using the accusative form (*me, him*) in the ellipsis when the nominative is essential to the meaning. In more complicated examples there arises the doubt whether the ellipsis is justifiable. Here the judgement is personal; but if there is any doubt, the ellipsis should be avoided. The following example is taken from MEU and corrected according to its ruling:

> The proceedings were more humiliating to ourselves than I can recollect in the course of my political experience. ('than *any that* I can recollect'.)

(e) The familiar error of using the relative pronoun instead of *as* after SAME, SUCH is due to faulty ellipsis. The constructions 'the same which', 'such men who', are incorrectly elliptical, for 'the same *as that* which' and 'such men *as those* who'.

(f) 'He is as tall, if not taller than you'; 'The novel is equal, if not better than the last one he published'. In both sentences *than* is made to serve two masters—one rightly and the other wrongly. The ellipsis is faulty: add *as* after *tall* and *to* after *equal*.

For ellipsis of verb with alternative subject see AGREEMENT.

else. (a) *Else, other* and their compounds are the only non-comparatives followed by *than*.

(b) *Else* is so closely joined with its preceding pronoun as almost to make a compound with it: *anybody else, everybody else*. The genitive therefore becomes 'anybody, everybody *else's* (not 'anybody's, everybody's else'). The interrogative pronoun, however, has retained its right to inflexion when it is compounded with else: *whose else?* is more idiomatic than *who else's?*

elusion. See ALLUSION.

emphasis. In speech the inflexions of the voice place the emphasis on the appropriate words or parts of the sentence. Thus the stress can give to the question 'Is Mr. Jones over forty?' five different meanings, by falling successively on *Is, Mr., Jones, over, forty*. We can indicate the emphasized words in writing only by means of italics:

(i) *Is* Mr. Jones over forty? (Is it a fact that Mr. J. is —?)
(ii) Is *Mr.* Jones over forty? (as well as Mrs.?)
(iii) Is Mr. *Jones* over forty? (and not Mr. Smith?)
(iv) Is Mr. Jones *over* forty? (and not just under?)
(v) Is Mr. Jones over *forty*? (as old as that?)

It is a legitimate use of italics to show the stress on a word when there is no other convenient method in writing or print of doing so—e.g. to point a contrast: 'He cannot *hear* and I cannot *see*'; or to introduce a surprise: 'It would be an ultimate benefit to the cause of morality to prove that honesty was the *worst* policy' (where you are expecting the *best*)(MEU). But italics should be used only for such necessary emphasis; never as a means of shouting at the reader. Queen Victoria was apt to lead her loyal subjects astray in using what may be called gesticulatory italics:

'We are *all* so particularly well, including Pussy, that we intend, to my great delight, to prolong our stay till next Monday. This place has a peculiar charm for us both, and to me it brings back recollections of the *happiest* days of my otherwise *dull* childhood—where I experienced such kindness from you, dearest Uncle, which has ever since continued. It is true that my *last* stay here *before* I came to the throne, from November '36 to February '37, was a peculiarly painful and disagreeable one, but somehow or other, I do *not* think of those times, but only of the former *so* happy ones.'

The use of the exclamation mark in brackets to call attention to a word or phrase is to be deplored and avoided. One example will suffice: 'Perhaps he will be successful at his third (!) try.'

Emphasis is also indicated by structural abnormalities in the sentence—i.e. by placing a word or phrase in an unusual position. Most of the sentences quoted under INVERSION are examples; one or two others follow. The emphasis falls on the words in italics.

(*a*) Object before the verb:

'*Two Men* I honour, and no third'.
'*To do good and to distribute*, forget not'.

(*b*) Introductory 'It is, was—':

It is *my* book I have lost, not yours; It was *Tom*, not Jack, who bowled at the pavilion end.

(*c*) Apposition and Repetition:

'*All, all* are gone, *the old familiar faces*'.
'*Trelawney, he*'s in keep and hold,
Trelawney, he may die'.

(*d*) 'Only':

To stop the bus, ring the bell *once* only.

end-stopped. See BLANK VERSE.

enforce. In Mod.E. idiom *enforce* is transitive with an impersonal object: *enforce* peace, laws, regulations. The old construction 'enforce a person to (or to do) a thing' is no longer permissible. In Mod.E. *force* would be substituted for *enforce*.

English. For the term as applied to the sonnet see SONNET.

enhance. *Enhance* cannot have a personal object (or subject, in the passive). A man may *enhance* his reputation; his reputation may *be enhanced*; but you cannot *enhance* a person in reputation; and a person cannot *be enhanced*.

enjambment. See BLANK VERSE.

-(e)n plurals. A few modern nouns have a plural in *-en*, representing the *-an* plural of the OE. 'weak' declension. The only simple one remaining in common use is *oxen*. Two nouns, *children* and *brethren*, have an *-en* plural added to an older plural of their own. The OE. noun *cild* belonged to the neuter declension and made its plural *cildru*, which became *childer* in ME. *Brother* had a mutation plural *brether*. The archaic and poetical word *kine* is another double plural in *-en*. OE. *cu* had a mutated plural *cy* (represented in archaic *kye*); *kine = cy + en*. Shakespeare has the plural *shoon* (shoes):

> 'How should I your true love know
>   From another one?
> By his cockle hat and staff,
>   And his sandal *shoon*.'

But we have to go back to Chaucer for *toon*, the *-(e)n* plural of *toe*:

> 'Lyk asur were his legges, and his *toon*.'

Chaucer also has *hosen* (the plural of *hose*), *foon* (foes), and *eyen* (eyes):

> 'His *eyen* twinkled in his heed aright,
> As doon the sterres in the frosty night.'

enquire, inquire. The spelling with *in-* is recommended by OED for the verb and also for the noun *inquiry*. Though SOED (1933) supports this recommendation, the modern tendency is to write *enquire, enquiry*.

ensure. See ASSURE.

envoy. The parting lines or stanza of a poem, particularly one written in a fixed artificial form, e.g. the BALLADE. The envoy is usually written as if addressed directly to a patron, or other particular person, the lines frequently beginning 'Prince!'

epic. Every nation has its earliest history—the history of its struggle for existence against nature and hostile tribes—shrouded in myths which in course of time take concrete form as heroic poetry. Fragments of this poetry are chanted or recited by bards at the feasts held by warriors after battle. Eventually the fragments are gathered together and welded into the form of a complete poem by some 'compiler', and the result is an epic—an heroic poem glorifying its hero, and, through him, the nation to which he belongs. It was the genius of the great epic poet Homer that raised the heroic sagas of Greece to the dignity of works of art— the *Iliad* and the *Odyssey*. The main theme of the *Iliad* is the wrath of Achilles, its special 'hero', at the slight put upon him by Agamemnon, and his final return to the field and slaying of Hector; that of its sequel, the *Odyssey*, is the adventures that befell Odysseus in the course of his return from the Trojan War to his kingdom of Ithaca. Virgil, glorifying Aeneas, and through him the greatness of the Emperor Augustus and of the Roman people, wrote the *Aeneid*—a prophetic vision woven into a romantic story of a legendary age. This national epic breathes a sense of the greatness of Rome, rising from its humble origin in the far-distant past, through its long struggle for supremacy, to the 'world-power' of the Augustan régime.

Investigating the rules of heroic poetry, Aristotle turns to the *Iliad* and the *Odyssey*. Here is Beeching's summary of his conclusions:

'The fable or theme of an epic must have dignity. It must represent great actions and involve great issues. Also it must be single and entire; not like a chronicle whose events have no real connexion with each other. Further, it must not be too large. The "Trojan War" would be a subject fulfilling the first two conditions of nobleness and unity, but it would be unmanageable. Homer therefore is content with but one incident in it, the wrath of Achilles; and other events not arising out of this, but necessary for its proper comprehension, are added in episodes.'

In English the only true epic, i.e. the only poem which strictly conforms to the definition of an epic given above, is *Beowulf*. It consists of 3,200 lines and is perhaps the earliest considerable poem in any modern language. The manuscript belongs to the late tenth century, though the date of its composition is uncertain. In later times we have a great poem with epic qualities, *Paradise Lost*, which Milton models on Homer, especially in the management of the plot. For instance, the poem opens with Satan in Hell. The story of his fall is reserved for an episode in later books. Like the writers of the classical epic, Milton makes frequent use of similes, in many of which he loses touch with the comparison he is attempting to make, and which become in consequence detached pictures, cameos of pictorial beauty. He introduces mythological machinery, even invoking the assistance of a Muse as Homer does. He is fond of catalogues. Just as Homer devotes the bulk of the second book of the *Iliad* to cataloguing the names and numbers of the hosts of the Greeks and of the Trojans, so Milton devotes much of the first book of his epic to an enumeration of the chiefs of the fallen angels, afterwards known as the heathen deities of the Syrians, Arabians, Egyptians, and Greeks.

Spenser's *Faerie Queene*, Byron's *Don Juan*, and Wordsworth's *Prelude* have all been labelled epics, as have Tennyson's *Idylls of the King* and Browning's *The Ring and the Book*. Arnold's *Sohrab and Rustum* is not an epic; but the poet himself calls it 'an episode' from the semi-mythical period of Persian history.

epigram (literally = writing upon, an inscription) is a brief and pointed saying, one which conveys much meaning in few words. Terseness is the natural characteristic of epigram. Verbal contradiction may be used to command attention and urge the reader to consider for himself the important truth so disguised. Bacon, Pope, and Macaulay are masters of epigrammatic expression:

'We take cunning for a sinister or crooked wisdom' (Bacon).

'Man never is but always to be blest' (Pope).

'One thing and one thing only could make Charles dangerous—a violent death' (Macaulay).

Cf. PARADOX, OXYMORON, ANTITHESIS, EPITAPH.

From its original meaning, a verse inscribed, e.g. on a tomb, epigram came to mean, in the words of Dr. Mackail, 'a very short poem summing up as though in a memorial inscription what it is desired to make permanently memorable in any action or situation. It must have the compression and conciseness of a real inscription, and in proportion with smallness of its bulk must be highly finished, evenly balanced, simple, lucid.' Let us quote an example from the prolific Martial:

> 'Nubere vis Prisco: non miror, Paula; sapisti.
> Ducere te non vult Priscus: et ille sapit.'

('You want to marry Priscus, Paula. I'm not surprised. Wise woman! Priscus doesn't want to marry you. Wise man!')

S. T. Coleridge defines the term in an epigram:

> 'What is an epigram? a dwarfish whole:
> Its body brevity, and wit its soul.'

epitaph (= on a tomb) means 'words, usually verses, inscribed on a tombstone or monument'. Here is a facetious example taken from a churchyard in the city of Newcastle-on-Tyne:

> Here lies Robert Wallis,
> Clerk of All Hallows,
> King of good fellows
> And maker of bellows.
> He bellows did make to the day of his death,
> But he that made bellows could never make breath.

Cf. EPIGRAM.

The epitaph is also a literary form, not really intended for inscription on a tombstone, though following the convention. Examples are: the epitaph at the end of Gray's *Elegy*; Mr. A. E. Housman's 'Epitaph on an Army of Mercenaries'; Ben Jonson's and Milton's epitaphs on Shakespeare. Here is Milton's epitaph:

> 'What needs my *Shakespear* for his honour'd Bones,
> The labour of an age in pilèd Stones,
> Or that his hallow'd reliques should be hid
> Under a Star-ypointing *Pyramid*?
> Dear son of memory, great heir of Fame,
> What need'st thou such weak witnes of thy name?
> Thou in our wonder and astonishment
> Hast built thy self a live-long Monument.
> For whilst to th'shame of slow-endeavouring art,
> Thy easie numbers flow, and that each heart
> Hath from the leaves of thy unvalu'd Book,
> Those Delphick lines with deep impression took,
> Then thou our fancy of it self bereaving,
> Dost make us Marble with too much conceaving;
> And so Sepulcher'd in such pomp dost lie,
> That Kings for such a Tomb would wish to die.'

epithet. In Grammar a term sometimes applied to the attributive adjective.

epode. See ODE.

equal(ly). (*a*) *Equally* is never followed by *as* in Mod.E. In such sentences as 'I am interested in detective stories equally as you', the *as* should be *with*. In such a sentence (quoted from MEU) as 'The Opposition are equally as guilty as the Government' *equally* is tautological. If *as* is omitted the correct idiom with *equally* is: 'The Opposition and the Government are equally guilty.'

(*b*) It takes at least two things to be equal. The construction illustrated in 'Even the poet who is equally a man of action or a man of the world' is incorrect, unless *equally* simply means *also* (the poet = a man of action or a man of the world). If it means that the poet is a man of action in the same degree as he is a man of the world, *or* must be replaced by *and*: 'Even the poet who is equally a man of action *and* a man of the world.'

-er, -or. The English agent suffix is *-er*. It is the common suffix with native verbs (*doer, teacher, buyer, seller, singer*, &c.). The corresponding Latin suffix is *-or*. MEU says that 'English verbs derived from the supine stem of Latin ones—i.e. especially most verbs in *-ate*, but also many others such as *oppress, protect, act, credit, possess, invent, prosecute*— usually prefer the Latin form to the English one in *-er*'.

Some forms important to remember are: *abduct*OR; *abett*OR; *adapt*ER; *collect*OR; *conjur*ER; *conquer*OR; *correct*OR; *corrupt*ER; *decant*ER; *desert*ER; *dispens*ER; *digest*ER; *distribut*OR; *eras*ER; *eject*OR; *govern*OR; *idolat*ER; *impost*OR; *promot*ER; *propell*ER; *purvey*OR; *sail*OR; *tail*OR.

especially, specially. *Especially* means 'to an exceptional degree'; *specially* means 'for one purpose and no other'. 'The weather has been *especially* cold lately', but 'I came *specially* to see you'.

esq. For use and position see LETTER-WRITING.

ethic. For ethic dative see DATIVE CASE.

euphemism, euphony, euphuism. The prefix *eu-* is the Greek adverb = well, favourably.

In wholesome fear of their natural gods, primitive nations tried to appease them by soft speech. Thus the Greeks called the Furies, the terrible avenging goddesses, the Eumenides (the well-disposed ones); the dangerous foggy sea, now more appropriately called the Black Sea, the Euxine (i.e. the sea favourable to strangers), and so on. With similar intent the Cape of Storms is now called the Cape of Good Hope, and the largest (and most stormy) ocean the Pacific. Such substitution of a less harsh or disagreeable word or phrase for a more accurate but more offensive one is called *euphemism*, i.e. pleasantness of speech. As literary examples here are two from *Macbeth*:

(*a*) 'He that's coming
  Must be *provided for*'
  (a terribly grim euphemism for the murder of King Duncan).

(*b*) 'Fleance, his son . . .
  . . . must *embrace the fate*
  Of that dark hour'
  (i.e. must be murdered at the same time as Banquo).

Euphony is pleasantness or smoothness of sound, a matter of acquired taste and the delicacy of a trained ear.

Euphuism is the name given to a high-flown or affected style of writing, from *Euphues: the Anatomy of Wit*, a prose romance by John Lyly, written in this style and published in 1579. Its principal characteristics are excessive use of antithesis, emphasized by alliteration and other devices, and of fantastic allusions to historical and mythological personages and natural history. Shakespeare satirizes *euphuism*, e.g., in *1 Henry IV*, where Falstaff's 'for though the camomile, the more it is trodden on the faster it grows, yet youth, the more it is wasted the sooner it wears' more than merely glances at Lyly's 'Though the camomile the more it is trodden and pressed downe, the more it spreadeth; yet the violet the oftener it is handled and touched, the sooner it withereth and decayeth.'

even. *Even* is one of those adverbs which easily slip out of position in the sentence. A simple example will explain the correct usage, and serve as a warning against carelessness. Given a sentence, it is possible by adding *even* to it to get three distinct meanings:

Sentence: 'I am not disturbed by your threats.'

(i) *Even* I am not disturbed by your threats (let alone anybody else).

(ii) I am not *even* disturbed by your threats (let alone *hurt, annoyed, injured, alarmed*).

(iii) I am not disturbed *even* by your threats (*even* modifies the phrase, the emphasis being on the *threats*).

It is also possible, though perhaps rather awkward, to put *even* immediately before *your*, and so give *your* the emphasis (*your* threats—let alone anybody else's).

Obviously the intended meaning must be decided upon before *even* is placed in position; and the test is that *even* must come into close association with the word or phrase that is singled out for emphasis or for contrast with another. If idiom does not permit this nearness, *even* must be flung overboard and another construction found.

-ever. (*a*) The suffix *-ever* may be added to the words *who, which, what, where,* and *how*. The archaic suffix was *-soever*. *Who(so)ever, which(so)-ever,* and *what(so)ever* are sometimes used as simple pronouns (= *who, which, what*), as in 'Whosoever will may come', and 'Whatever is, is right'. But all the compounds with *-ever* are most commonly used in a concessive sense:

'Whatever you do, don't take unnecessary risks' (= 'Though you do everything else' . . .).

'Where'er you walk' . . . (= 'Though you walk everywhere' . . .).

'Whoever goes, I shall not be affected' (= 'Though everybody or anybody go' . . .).

'However strong you are, you should be careful not to overstrain yourself' (= 'Though you are remarkably strong' . . .).

The other forms of the pronouns are, accusative: *whom(so)ever*, and genitive: *whose(so)ever*.

Note that *ever* is a separate emphasizing adverb after interrogative pronouns and particles: 'Who ever was that?' 'Why ever did you come?' (not *whoever, whyever*). But MEU regards this use as colloquial; though it has a legitimate use in emphasizing that the speaker has no idea what the answer will be. But it is certainly not allowable in writing except in reproducing colloquial speech.

(*b*) *Syntax*. A difficulty arises in connexion with the use of *whomever*. MEU explains that *whoever* is like *what* in that it contains its antecedent in itself. Its case is therefore decided not by the main but by the subordinate clause. So 'He wrote to *whoever* invited him' is correct, the *whoever* being subject of the relative clause, and the antecedent, which would be object of *to*, is contained in it; but *whomever* is necessary in 'He wrote to *whomever* he invited', since now it is itself object of the verb in the subordinate clause.

ever so. See NEVER SO.

everybody else. Genitive *everybody else's*. See ELSE.

everyday is an adjective: '*everyday* life in Rome', '*everyday* clothes'; 'every day' is an adverb phrase of time: '*Every day* I am getting better and better', 'I see him *every day*'.

exceeding(ly), excessive(ly). The former implies *very much*, the latter *too much*. The differentiation in meaning is a comparatively modern one. Jane Austen (died 1817) writes 'I have an excessive regard for Jane Bennet', as well as 'Really, Mr. Collins, you puzzle me exceedingly'.

except, excepting. The important uses are as follows:
  (*a*) *except*—as a preposition before nouns and adverb phrases: 'all *except* the Nonconformists'; 'There will be rain everywhere *except* in the southern counties'. In such constructions *excepting* is not idiomatic in Mod.E. The MEU example is: '... *excepting* in countries where special causes operate' (say, *except*). But
  (*b*) *excepting* coupled with a negative has prepositional force: 'not *excepting* the fifth form'. Cf. *not excepted*, the absolute construction with the past participle: 'the fifth form *not excepted*'. Cf. also PROVIDED.

exclamation mark. The exclamation mark (!) should always be used after 'grammatical' exclamations, which are classified by MEU thus:
  (*a*) interjections, as *oh!*, *alas!*;
  (*b*) words or phrases used as interjections: *Heavens!*, *By Jove!*;
  (*c*) sentences containing the exclamatory *what* and *how*: *What a catch!*, *How hot it is!*;
  (*d*) wishes: *Confound you!*, *God forbid!*;
  (*e*) ellipses and inversions due to emotion: *To think of it!*, *Not a word!*;
  (*f*) apostrophes: '*Milton! thou shouldst be living at this hour*'.
Outside these definite uses MEU says that the exclamation mark is suitable to the expression of 'scornful' quotation, to the unexpected, the amusing, the disgusting, or something that needs the comment of special intonation to secure that the words shall be taken as they are meant. One or two examples are given: *And you told me he could not play!*; '*For the first time in his life—in the world's life indeed—he tasted—crackling!*'; '*But, when they came from bathing, thou wert gone!*'
For the position of the exclamation mark with inverted commas, see INVERTED COMMAS.

expedient, expeditious. The former is nearly always used predicatively and means 'advantageous'; the latter means 'done (or doing) speedily', 'prompt'. 'It is *expedient* that we should use *expeditious* means of putting condemned criminals to death'.

explicit. See IMPLICIT.

explosives. See CONSONANTS.

express. See DECLARE.

extent of place. For the accusative of extent of place see ACCUSATIVE CASE.

extenuate. The word does not mean 'excuse' and cannot have a personal

object. You *extenuate* (i.e. 'thin down') the evil in a person, not the person
for that evil. So *Othello*: 'Nothing extenuate, nor set down aught in
malice', and *Julius Caesar*: 'his glory not extenuated'.

-ey. The temptation is not to drop the mute *e* before the adjectival
suffix -*y*, and write *shakey, nosey, wavey*; but the rule is: mute *e* is never
written before the adjectival -*y* except (*a*) when the root word itself ends
in -*y* ('thy skyey speed' in Shelley's *To a Skylark*, not *skyy* or *skiey*);
(*b*) when the root word ends in -*ue*: *bluey* and *gluey*.

eye rhyme. See RHYME.

facilitate = 'to make easy'; we therefore do not facilitate a person but
a deed or operation: 'The fine weather *facilitated* the picking of the straw-
berries'; not, 'The pickers were *facilitated* in their work'.

factitious, fictitious. *Factitious* (<Lat. *facere, factum*, to make) means
'designedly got up', 'not natural', 'artificial' (COD). Sir Thomas Browne
speaks of '*factitious* gems', in which sense Mod.E. would use *artificial*.
A factitious meeting, argument, value is one that has been designed or
made for a particular purpose.
  Fictitious (<Lat. *fingere, fictum*, to feign) means 'feigned', 'counterfeit',
'not genuine'. A fictitious account or report is one that is a lie; a fictitious
name or character is one that is assumed; a fictitious document is one
that is sham or counterfeit.

factitive. In grammar, the term applied to verbs of *making, considering,
calling*, which have with their normal object an objective complement,
noun or adjective: 'They will never make a wicket-keeper *captain*';
'We called him *Archibald*'; 'They made him *go*' (where the objective
complement is an adjective).

faerie, faery, fairy. *Fairy* is the workaday word, used of any subject of
Titania (or Queen Mab) and Oberon who happens to visit the earth on
Midsummer Night or at any other time. The land of the fairies is Fairy-
land. *Faerie* is the dim mysterious region of the imagination, the magic
of dreams: it might be used, for instance, of the setting of poems like
Kubla Khan, Christabel, and *La Belle Dame sans Merci*. As an adjective
faerie or *faery* has two chief literary associations: (*a*) in Spenser's title
The Faerie Queene, and (*b*) in Keats's phrase (in the *Ode to a Nightingale*)
'*faery* lands forlorn'.

failing. In the familiar type of phrase 'failing him', 'failing his agreement'
failing is a preposition. When it follows the noun it is a present participle
in the absolute construction:
  Failing a heavy rainfall soon, the drought will become serious (preposition).
  The rainfall *failing*, the drought became serious (absolute construction).

Notice that as a preposition *failing* is conditional: 'if the rainfall is not
heavy soon'; in the absolute use it usually states a reason: 'as the rainfall
failed'. Cf. EXCEPT, EXCEPTING.

fair. *Fair* is an adverb in such phrases as: 'bid *fair*'; 'fight *fair*'; 'play
fair'; 'speak one *fair*'. The temptation to use *fairly* in these expressions
should be avoided.

f and v. The question whether an original f > v in inflected or derivative forms arises in connexion with

(a) Plurals of nouns in -*f* and -*fe*. No rule concerning the retention of *f* or the change to *v* in the plural can be given. The following is an alphabetical list of some of the more important words concerned. In the second column the dual plural forms printed in small capitals have a note to themselves. Where no note is indicated it is to be inferred that the first of the two forms given is preferable.

beef	BEEVES; BEEFS
calf	calves
elf	elves
grief	griefs
half	halves
handkerchief	handkerchiefs; -ves
hoof	hoofs; hooves
knife	knives
leaf	leaves
life	lives
loaf	loaves
mischief	mischiefs
oaf	oafs
proof	proofs
relief	reliefs
roof	roofs
scarf	scarves; scarfs
safe	safes
self	selves
sheaf	sheaves
shelf	shelves
staff	STAFFS; STAVES
strife	strifes
thief	thieves
turf	turfs; turves
wharf	WHARFS; WHARVES
wife	wives

(b) Other derivative words:

Word	Notable derivatives
calf	calve (verb); calves-foot or calfs-foot
knife	knife, knive (verbs)
leaf	leafy (adj.)
lief	LIVELONG; liefer
life	LIFELONG
mischief	mischievous
oaf	oafish
proof	prove (verb). Note spelling.
safe	save (verb); safety; saviour
scarf	scarfed; scarved
scurf	SCURFY; SCURVY
self	selfish; SELVEDGE; SELVAGE
thief	thieve (verb); thievish
turf	turf (verb)
wharf	wharfage; wharfinger
wife	HOUSEWIFE; -wifery

farther, further. (a) For forms and etymology see DOUBLE COMPARA-TIVES.

(*b*) MEU says that no useful distinction can be made between the two forms in use, but that the preference of the majority is for *further* in all meanings; '*farther* is not common except where distance is in question'. It hazards the opinion that it is less likely that a differentiation between the two will be established than that *further* will become universal. So also the verb *to further* is far more common than *to farther*, which might possibly be confused in speech with *to father*.

fault. 'I am *at* fault' means I am puzzled; 'I am *in* fault' means I am to blame.

fear. There are two constructions after the noun ('There is no fear'; 'for fear'):

(*a*) *of* +noun, pronoun, or gerund—'There is no fear of his escaping'; 'for fear of robbers';

(*b*) a clause in apposition introduced by *that* or *lest*—'There is no fear that he will escape'; 'for fear he will be robbed'. After 'for fear' the conjunction is very frequently omitted. Avoid *as to* before the clause ('There is no fear as to whether . . .'). Cf. DOUBT and QUESTION AS TO.

feasible. MEU gives a warning against the use of the word in the sense of *possible* or *probable*: 'It is *feasible* that . . .' (correct to *possible* or *probable*). *Feasible* means 'do-able', 'able to be done'; it is therefore used correctly in: 'A meeting would be *feasible*'; 'A protest is *feasible* but scarcely expedient.' In such sentences *possible* in its secondary sense ('able to be made, done') could be used; but *feasible* cannot be substituted for *possible* in the sentence: 'It is *possible* that there will be snow during the next twelve hours.'

feature. When the article in MEU was written the use of *feature* as a verb ('featuring Charlie Chaplin', &c.) was still rarely seen except on cinematograph advertisements. A note added in 1924, however, records its appearance in the advertisement of an outfitter. In 1934 it had become almost what Fowler would have labelled a 'vogue word'. At any rate, it has established itself in the reviewer's vocabulary. Novels and even poems *feature* characters nowadays. But it is still too early to say whether or not what has seemed for twenty years an ugly Americanism will become established in English.

female. For the difference between *female* and *feminine* see FEMININE.

feminine. **1.** For feminine gender see GENDER; for feminine rhyme see RHYME; and for feminine ending see BLANK VERSE.

2. The difference between *feminine* and *female* may be roughly summed up thus: *female* is originally a noun and afterwards a noun used attributively as an adjective, and is used of sex; *feminine* is an adjective meaning 'not merely of or for women, but of the kind that characterizes or may be expected from or is associated with women' (MEU). MEU says: 'When the question is *Of or for which sex?*, use *female*; when the question is *Of what sort?*, use *feminine*.' A few typical examples follow:

female	feminine
companion	friendship
attendant	attention
servant	curiosity
ward	pursuits

'Female education' means 'education for females'; 'feminine education' means 'that which tends to cultivate the qualities characteristic of women'.

few. 1. *Few* as a noun is plural in Mod.E. As an adjective it cannot qualify a singular noun (cf. its antonym, *many*).

2. *Fewer* is used of numerical quantity, *less* of quantity in bulk or size. The application of this simple rule will solve all difficulties with *fewer* and *less*. 'The fewer men the greater share of honour' is a good and familiar example of the correct use. Note, however, that *fewer*, like the positive *few*, qualifies a plural noun only. 'A *fewer* number of people' is wrong, '*fewer* people' right. See also LESS.

3. '*Few* is opposed to *many*; *a few* to *none* . . . A *few* forms with the noun a collective, which, however, is followed by a plural verb'—COD. The sentences 'Few and short were the prayers we said' and 'A few prayers were said' illustrate the difference between *few* and *a few*, as well as the syntactical point quoted above.

fictitious. See FACTITIOUS.

finite and infinite. The *finite* parts of the verb are the parts which are 'limited to' a subject, i.e. are 'bounded by' number and person: I *saw*; We *are going*; He *has been injured*. The infinite parts are those which have no relation to a subject, but which

(a) may be with the AUXILIARY verb an element in a compound tense, like *going* in the present continuous tense '(we) *are going*', quoted above;

(b) may act as adjective or noun. See GERUND, INFINITIVE MOOD, PARTICIPLES.

flats. See CONSONANTS.

flee, flow, fly. 1. The forms are:

	Pres. Simp.	*Present Part.*	*Past Simp.*	*Past Part.*
to flee	I flee	fleeing	I fled	fled
to flow	It flows	flowing	It flowed	flowed
to fly	I fly	flying	I flew	flown

2. The most likely confusions are:

(a) of *flowed* with *flown*. 'The river has *overflown* its banks' ('overflowed') will serve as an example of the common error, and as a warning. But the confusion is as old as Shakespeare. 'I would be loth to have you *overflown* with a honey-bag' exclaims Bottom (*M.N.D.*). Mr. Pepys, too, falls into the mistake; he is vexed, he writes, to find his house *overflown* with a thaw.

(b) of *to flee* with *to fly*. The distinction is not difficult if *to flee* is used only with the underlying sense of *to escape*. There are three possible constructions:

(i) absolute—'I fled down the street' (*sc.* from somebody or something);

(ii) with *from*—'I fled from the angry tiger';

(iii) transitive—'I fled him down the nights and down the days'; 'I fled the country.'

To fly is used

(i) literally—'Birds fly'; 'The Prime Minister flew to Geneva'; 'Boys were flying kites'; 'Alcock and Brown were the first two Englishmen to fly the Atlantic' (for the last two sentences see TRANSITIVE);

(ii) as a vivid exaggeration for *run, hurry*—'I flew upstairs'; 'I flew from my house to the station' (rarely used in any other than the Past Simple Tense);

(iii) as equivalent of *flee* (in present tense only): 'You must fly the country for a while' (Thackeray); 'He is compelled to fly from the company of the good' (Jowett);

(iv) metaphorically—'I flew into a temper'.

OED, s.v. *flee*, says: 'The confusion between the verbs *flee* and *fly* occurs already in OE. . . . In modern English the association of the two verbs has the curious result that the ordinary prose equivalent of L. *fugere* is *fly* with past tense and past participle *fled* . . . while *flee* has become archaic, being confined to more or less rhetorical or poetic diction.' The points to memorize are: *fleeing, fled*, not *flying, flew*, are the present participle and the past participle respectively of *to flee*; and *to flow* is a weak verb; therefore its past form is *flowed* not *flown*.

fly. *Flies* is the plural = insects; *flys* the plural = carriages. See Y > I.

follows. See AS FOLLOWS.

foot. The unit of metre in verse (see METRE and RHYTHM). In English verse the main feet may be classified thus:

RISING RHYTHM

(a) Foot of two syllables, unstressed + stressed (× ´), called the *iamb* (adjective, *iambic*):

The cur|few tolls | the knell | of part|ing day

(b) Foot of three syllables, two unstressed + stressed (× × ´), called the *anapaest* (adjective, *anapaestic*):

And the sheen | of their spears | was like stars | on the sea

FALLING RHYTHM

(a) Foot of two syllables, stressed + unstressed (´ ×), called the *trochee* (adjective, *trochaic*):

Through the | shadows | and the | sunshine

(b) Foot of three syllables, stressed + two unstressed (´ × ×), called the *dactyl* (adjective, *dactylic*):

Take her up | tenderly

Rarely occurring feet are the *spondee*, consisting of two equally stressed syllables (´ ´):

Rocks, caves | lakes, fens | bogs, dens | and shades | of death

and the *amphibrach* (× ´ ×):

Most friendship | is feigning

for. In Mod.E. *for* is a co-ordinating conjunction; it does not (like *because* and *since*) join a subordinate clause to a main clause; i.e. it does not introduce an adverb clause of reason. In any but a very short sentence a semicolon (not a comma) is the stop before *for*. The example is from MEU: 'This is no party question; for it touches us not as Liberals or Conservatives, but as citizens.' In the following sentence the archaic use as a subordinating conjunction (= *because*, *since*) is illustrated: 'They are . . . jealous *for* they are jealous' (Shakespeare).

for-, fore-. *Fore-* has the same significance as the *fore* in *before*; *for-* is an OE. intensive prefix meaning 'out and out', 'completely', or (half negative) 'against', 'without'. A few common words in which the prefixes occur are given: *fore-*: forearm, foreboding, forebears, fore-fathers, FOREGO, foreman, forewarn; *for-*: forbid, forgather, forget, for-give, FORGO, forlorn, forsake, forspent, forswear. In *foreclose* and *forfeit* the prefix is <Lat. *foris*, 'outside', and the natural English spelling would be *for-*; the *fore-* in *foreclose* is on analogy with the ordinary English *fore-* illustrated above. See also FOREGO, FORGO.

forceps. For number see SINGULAR-PLURAL NOUNS.

forecast. The past forms are *forecast* (not *-casted*). Cf. BROADCAST.

forego, forgo. The difference between the words is fairly obvious from the prefixes, though it is not always observed even by educated writers. *For-* is the OE. prefix seen in *forsaken* and *forlorn*, *forgive* and *forget*, and has a kind of negative intensive effect; thus *forgo* means 'go alto-gether without'. *Fore-* is the adverbial prefix of time; *forego* means simply 'go before'. The following examples will illustrate the distinc-tion: 'He has voluntarily forgone his privileges'; 'the foregoing article'; 'a foregone conclusion' ('decision or opinion come to in advance of the evidence or necessary facts'—COD).

foreign plurals. The following are the chief foreign nouns 'borrowed' in English that have kept their native plural form:

Singular	Plural
(a) *French*	
adieu	adieux
beau	beaux
bureau	bureaux
tableau	tableaux
(b) *Latin* (only everyday words are given. Scientific *ad hoc* words nearly always have the Latin plural.)	
appendix	appendices
axis	axes
bacillus	bacilli
basis	bases
FORMULA	FORMULAE
genus	genera
INDEX	INDICES
radius	radii
species	species
terminus	termini
tumulus	tumuli

Addenda, data, desiderata, errata, memoranda, strata are all Latin neuter plurals, having singulars in *-um*; and they should all be treated as plurals in English. *Stamina* (pl. of Lat. *stamen*) is now used in English as a singular.

Singular	Plural
(c) *Greek*	
crisis	crises
criterion	criteria
ellipsis	ellipses
hypothesis	hypotheses
parenthesis	parentheses
phenomenon	phenomena
thesis	theses
(d) *Italian*	
BANDIT	BANDITTI
dilettante	dilettanti
(e) *Hebrew*	
CHERUB	CHERUBIM
SERAPH	SERAPHIM

for ever, not *forever*. See IRREGULAR UNIONS.

formal words. Below is given a short haphazard list of what MEU calls 'formal words'—those we use when 'we tell our thoughts, like our children, to put on their hats and coats before they go out'. It is interesting to remind ourselves how one or two of them occur in everyday life. In the well-dressed language of the army the troops *commence* operations and *proceed* from one barracks to another; in the theatrical advertisement the play *commences*; in the genteel language of business *pay* becomes *emoluments*, and *buy* becomes *purchase* (though we say 'Buy British'). Actual trade-names are particularly interesting: *inflator* (for *pump*), *half-hose* (for *socks*), *vest* (for *waistcoat*). A few formalities belong to the majestic kingdom of the law: 'You are hereby *summoned* (called upon) to appear at 10 o'clock in the *forenoon* (morning).' We are startled to find an ordinary London bus called a 'Metropolitan Stage Carriage'. The safest rule in writing and speech is to use formal words only when the occasion is formal. In the ordinary ways of life language, like ourselves, is more comfortable in its workaday clothes. Here is the list; the corresponding informal words are given in brackets:

accommodation (room)
announce (give out)
bear (carry)
cast (throw)
cease (stop)
close (shut)
collation (meal)
comestibles (food)
commence (begin)
complete (finish)
conceal (hide)
conveyance (carriage)
dispatch (send off)
don (put on)

donation (gift)
draw (pull)
emoluments (pay)
endeavour (try)
evince (show)
expedite (hasten)
extend (give)
felicitate (wish joy)
forenoon (morning)
imbibe (drink)
inquire (ask)
luncheon (lunch)
mucilage (gum)
obtain (get)

peruse (read)
physic (medicine)
preserve (jam)
proceed (go)
purchase (buy)
remark (say)
remove (take away)
seek (try, look for)
suborn (bribe)
summon (send for)
sustain (suffer)
valiant (brave)
veritable (real or positive)
vessel (ship)

former, latter. The words should not appear in any but technical or commercial English, where they may sometimes be useful. But in literary English as a means of avoiding repetition of a noun they are to be avoided. In a sentence like 'Mr. Jones and Mr. Smith are next-door

neighbours; the former is a Civil servant and the latter a Bank manager'
there seems to be some justification for them; but even here the way out
of the threatened repetition is so simple and obvious (use relative clauses
qualifying Mr. Jones and Mr. Smith) that *former* and *latter* need not
have been called into service. Even as the sentence stands there is much
to be said for repeating the actual nouns. See also LATE.

formula. The plural *formulae* has been anglicized into *formulas* in
colloquial language and often in ordinary narrative and descriptive
writing. *Formulae* is therefore in Mod.E. restricted to mathematical
and scientific English; in wider uses (e.g. a political formula) the plural
is *formulas.* Cf. INDEX.

forward, forwards. The OED makes a distinction between the two
words that is scarcely tenable to-day. It is best to choose by instinct,
or according to the euphonic needs of the sentence. *Forward* seems to be
prevailing over *forwards* and will probably in the end altogether dis-
place it.

fuchsia. So spelt (< Fuchs, a German botanist); pronounced fū′sha.

-ful. Nouns ending in *-ful* (*handful, spoonful,* &c.) make their plural by
adding *s* to the *-ful*—*handfuls, spoonfuls,* not *handsful, spoonsful.*

full stop (or 'full point' or 'period'). (*a*) The full stop ends a sentence, and
is followed by a capital as the first letter in the next sentence (if any):
'Rejoice evermore. Pray without ceasing. Quench not the spirit. Despise
not prophesyings. Prove all things; hold fast that which is good. Abstain
from all appearance of evil.'

(*b*) The full stop (or 'full point') is used to mark an abbreviation or contraction. MEU advocates the omission of the stop when the first and
last letters of the word are used in the abbreviation. Thus: *Geo.* for
George, Jan. for *January, Ezek.* for *Ezekiel,* but *Mr* for *Mister, yd* for
yard, and *Bart* for *baronet.* This usage, however, is by no means established, witness RCR, from which the following notes are quoted:

When necessary, the names of the months to be abbreviated, as below:

Jan. Feb. Mar. Apr. May June
July Aug. Sept. Oct. Nov. Dec.

Where the name of a county is abbreviated, as Yorks., Cambs., Berks., Oxon.,
use a full point; but print Hants (no full point) because it is not a modern
abbreviation.

4to, 8vo, 12mo, &c. (sizes of books), are symbols, and should have no full point.
A parallel case is that of 1st, 2nd, 3rd, and so on, which also need no full points.

Print lb. for both sing. and pl.; not lbs. Also omit the plural -*s* in the following:
cm., cwt., dwt., gr., gm., in., min., mm., oz. Insert the plural -*s* in tons,
yds., qrs.

MS. = manuscript, MSS. = manuscripts.

Print PS. (not P.S.) for postscript or postscriptum; MM. (messieurs); S.S.
(steamship), but s.s. (screw steamer); H.M.S. (His Majesty's Ship); H.R.H.;
I.W. (Isle of Wight); N.B., Q.E.D., and R.S.V.P.

It is interesting to note that RCR recommends *1st, 2nd, 3rd* without
the full point (= full stop) on the ground that they are symbols, not
contractions. The custom in printing contracted words may be studied
from many examples in the text of this book. See also APOSTROPHE.

further. See FARTHER.

fused participle. See GERUND (5).

future in the past. This tense marks an action as future from a past point of view. It is used

(a) in simple sentences and main clauses, e.g. 'These measures *would act* as a deterrent in two ways' (i.e. were sure to act). 'When summer came, they *would begin* to make preparations to mobilize the army' (i.e. they were going to begin . . .).

(b) in subordinate clauses, e.g.

I knew that { you *would come*.
we *should find* you here.
he *would be hurt* by your words.

Note: When *should* (in 1st person) and *would* (in 2nd and 3rd persons) are used with conditional force, we have the future (and future perfect) in the past as equivalent to tenses in the subjunctive, e.g.

I *should like* (*should have liked*) to tell you.
You *would be* certain to tell me.
If I had known I *should have* told you.
If he had known he *would have* told me.

g. For *g* hard or soft see C AND G.

gallicism. A gallicism is an idiom, mode of expression, significance or form of word borrowed from French, but translated into or adapted in English. Thus the word *banality* is a gallicism, being an English form of the French *banalité*; INTRIGUE is a gallicism when it is given its French significance in English; the phrases 'leap to the eyes', 'a thousand thanks', 'give furiously to think' are gallicisms, being literal translations of the French 'sauter aux yeux', 'mille remerciements' and 'donner furieusement à penser'.

MEU's advice is to avoid gallicisms when they 'presuppose the reader's acquaintance with the French original'; to use them, indeed, only when they are so thoroughly naturalized as to be no longer recognizable as gallicisms.

gallows. For number see SINGULAR-PLURAL NOUNS.

gaol, jail. The two spellings exist side by side, and there is nothing to choose between them in ordinary use. *Gaol* is derived from Norman French, and *jail* from the Southern or standard French. COD says that *gaol* is always used in official and legal English.

gender. There is no gender in English nouns, since English is no longer an inflected language. Old English had declensions (masculine, feminine, and neuter) of both nouns and adjectives (in the same way, though not as completely, as Latin). With the loss of inflexion, distinctions for gender in nouns vanished. In Mod.E., too, adjectives (including the articles and demonstratives) have no inflexion except for comparison and, in the case of the demonstratives *this* and *that*, for number. So there can be no indication, as there is in French, of the gender of a noun through the adjective or article that qualifies it. In Mod.E., therefore, *son* and *daughter*, *husband* and *wife*, *brother* and *sister* are simply nouns that happen to represent persons of different sex. Even those nouns which have related forms for male and female (*poet, poetess*; *governor, governess,* &c.) cannot be said to have gender.

True gender does survive, however, in certain pronouns: (*a*) the third person demonstrative, in the singular forms only—*he, she, it*; and (*b*) the relative, where there is a distinction between personal and neuter—*who, which*.

genitive case. The genitive case of a noun or pronoun is that case which expresses that the person or thing represented by the noun either (*a*) possesses or (*b*) appertains to the thing or person represented by another noun in the sentence.

1. *Form.* The genitive case is represented (*a*) in nouns by the inflexion 's or s' (see APOSTROPHE) and in pronouns by a special inflected form, or (*b*) by the case-phrase, *of*+relative pronoun.

2. *Syntax.* The inflected genitive of nouns is generally used as an adjective as in '*Caesar's* spirit', 'the *raven's* feathers', where the genitive expresses possession, and in 'a *boys'* school', 'a *week's* holiday', 'a *dog's* life', where the genitive expresses the idea of appurtenance or association. For the adjectival use of the pronoun see POSSESSIVE. The inflected genitive of both nouns and pronouns is, however, sometimes a true noun or pronoun used predicatively as complement of the verb: 'That book is *Tom's*'; ' 'Tis *mine*, and I will have it.'

Note that the adjective phrase, *of*+noun, as genitive is always adjectival: the leg *of the table* (= the *table's* leg), the books *of the year* (= the *year's* books). But the combination *of*+noun has many idiomatic uses outside the purely genitival. Thus: the city *of Rome*; He died *of fever*; It was kind *of them*; made *of wood*.

3. *Partitive Genitive.* The genitive phrase following a word that indicates in its meaning a part of a whole, e.g. *part, any, each*, the superlative of an adjective:

> 'The second part *of the question* must be attempted.'
> 'Any *of the above-mentioned articles* may be chosen.'
> 'The last *of all the Romans*, fare thee well.'

4.   'Any dear friend *of Caesar's*'.
                                      That dog *of yours*.

Of this usage Jespersen says that it sometimes, but not always, has a partitive sense, as in the sentences quoted (= any dear friend of Caesar's [friends]; that dog of your [dogs]); but that 'the construction was employed chiefly to avoid the juxtaposition of two pronouns, "this hat of mine", "that ring of yours" being preferred to "this my hat", "that your ring", or of a pronoun and a genitive, as in "any ring of Jane's", where "any Jane's ring" or "Jane's any ring" would be impossible'. The construction was so convenient that it was extended to uses in which no partitive sense is logically possible: 'this face, these eyes, of mine'.

5. *Objective Genitive.* In such genitive phrases as 'the fear *of Death*', 'the murder *of Caesar*', the genitive is said to be *objective*—*Death* and *Caesar* acting as a kind of object of the action implied in the noun. Contrast with the second phrase 'Caesar's death', which is a normal or subjective genitive. 'Caesar's murder' means, if it is an objective genitive, 'the murder of Caesar by somebody else'; 'Caesar's murder' means as an ordinary subjective genitive 'Caesar's murder of somebody else'.

6. *Idiomatic use of 'your'.* See YOUR.

genius. *Genii* is the plural when the word has its original meaning of 'spirit', 'presiding deity':

> 'Still had she gazed, when midst the tide
> Two angel forms were seen to glide,
> The *genii* of the stream.'

Geniuses is the plural of the noun in its secondary meaning, 'a man possessed with a spirit', i.e. with inspiration in some department of art or science:

> 'Einstein and Marconi are two of the greatest *geniuses* of all time.'

gerund. **1.** The gerund is an infinite part of a verb with the same form as the present participle, i.e. it ends in *-ing*: *doing, singing, writing*.

2. The gerund acts as a noun. It may be used precisely as the ordinary noun in the sentence—i.e. as subject, object, complement—and especially after a preposition, where it takes the place of the infinitive:

(*a*) *Seeing* is *believing*.
  (First gerund, subject; second gerund, complement)
(*b*) I hate *writing letters*. (Object of verb)
  'Graham began *pacing the room*.'
  (Object of verb, completing its sense; gerund corresponding with the prolative infinitive. See INFINITIVE MOOD (*d*).)
(*c*) 'In *returning* and rest shall ye be saved.'
  After *seeing* the play, we went home. (Object of preposition)

The gerund retains its verbal force; for the verb part in *-ing* which does not retain verbal force see 4 below.

3. The gerund, like most nouns and like the infinitive, may be used as an adjective. In the phrase 'the laughing Cavalier', the word *laughing* is an ordinary present participle qualifying *Cavalier*; the phrase means 'a Cavalier who is laughing'. But in the phrase 'a writing desk' the word *writing* is not a present participle. The phrase means, not 'a desk that writes', 'but a desk *for writing*'—i.e. the adjective *writing* stands for preposition+gerund. It is called the *Gerundial Adjective*.

4. Note the verb part in *-ing* that has (unlike the present participle and the gerund—both also parts in *-ing*) divested itself completely of verbal force and become a pure noun. It is guarded from all possible verbal activity by the definite article before and the preposition *of* after it: 'The *churning* of milk bringeth forth butter; and the *wringing* of the nose bringeth forth blood.' Contrast 'The act of *churning*' or '*Churning* milk bringeth forth butter', where *churning* is first an intransitive gerund governed by *of*, and second a transitive gerund, subject of the sentence.

5. MEU has six columns of entertaining denunciation of the misconstruction called 'fused participle'. Briefly, the error arises from a reluctance to recognize the gerund as a noun and a willingness to fob it off as a participle. Two simple examples will make the matter clear:

(*a*) The children wanting to go does not influence us.
(*b*) I did not know of him leaving the town.

In sentence (*a*) the subject is evidently supposed to be *wanting*, since *does* is singular; but that would leave *children* high and dry in the sentence, with no grammatical connexion whatever. Evidently, then, *children* and the participle *wanting* are intended to make together a singular notion as subject (hence 'fused participle'). But grammatically *wanting* must be subject, i.e. it must be a gerund, not a participle, and the accompanying noun or pronoun must become possessive, qualifying it:

'The children's wanting to go does not influence us.'

So in (b) *leaving* is the true object of the preposition *of*, i.e. it is a gerund, and must be qualified by the possessive *his*: 'I did not know of his leaving the town'. The following sentence from a daily newspaper shows the error as it occurs in common use:

'The fact of a *train taking* two hours to crawl from Waterloo to Clapham Junction sufficiently indicates the nature of its (the fog's) sudden regional descents' (correct to 'train's taking').

The distinction to make is that between a participle qualifying a noun and a gerund qualified by a possessive noun or pronoun. It may be added that the error of the 'fused participle' often occurs because the true gerund construction with the possessive noun or pronoun seems awkward. The remedy is to reconstruct the sentence.

6. Some nouns, adjectives, and verbs are idiomatically followed by the infinitive, and some by the gerund. MEU gives certain representative examples, a few of which are set out in the table below:

Word	*followed by*		*not to be confused with*	
objection	to		refusal	
habit	of		tendency	
plan	of		determination	
idea	of		inspiration	
resistance	to	+ gerund	refusal, reluctance	+ infinitive
equal	to		sufficient	
unequal	to		incompetent	
commit (self)	to		threaten	
confess	to		profess	
object	to		refuse	
succeed	in		avail	

Note that in the sentences 'It is my duty to reprove you', 'It is my habit to walk three miles before breakfast', 'It was a good idea to wait until tomorrow' the infinitives (*to reprove, to walk, to wait*) have no real syntactical relation with *duty, habit, idea*. Each of them is the real subject of its sentence ('*To reprove* is my duty', &c.) and is independent of the noun immediately before it. But it is unidiomatic to say or write 'The duty to reprove him fell upon me', 'His habit to walk three miles before breakfast kept him healthy', 'Your idea to wait till tomorrow was a good one'.

gerundial infinitive. See INFINITIVE MOOD (*d*).

get. MEU admits the somewhat ugly expression 'have got' ('I have got a new bicycle') to colloquial but not to literary English.

gibe. The *g* is soft, a variant spelling being *jibe*.

glance, glimpse. When you *take* or *give* a glance at something you *get* or *catch* a glimpse of it.

gradation. Gradation, sometimes called *ablaut*, is 'a series of relations between primary vowels by which alone the stems of a strong verb are differentiated' (Wyatt). In OE. there were seven 'gradation rows', i.e. groups of vowel relations distinguishing the seven different types of strong verb. Thus the principal parts of the verb *crēopan* (creep) in OE. were:

Infinitive	*Past Sing.*	*Past Plural*	*Past Participle*
crēopan	crēap	crupon	cropen

the 'gradation row' being ēo ēa u o.

That particular verb, like many others, has become weak in Mod.E., but gradation survives in a modified form in the strong verbs that remain, e.g.: take—took—taken; sing—sang—sung. See also STRONG AND WEAK VERBS.

grand. When *grand* is added to the names of relatives (father, mother, &c.) the hyphen is used only if without it there would be (*a*) some doubt as to the syllabication or pronunciation of the words, (*b*) some awkwardness in the spelling, (*c*) a false accentuation. Hence:

With hyphen—
    (*a*) grand-aunt, grand-uncle;
    (*b*) grand-dad, grand-daughter;
    (*c*) grand-nephew, grand-niece (in *grandnephew, grandniece*, the stress would normally fall on the first syllable, *grand*).

Without hyphen—
    grandchild, grandfather, grandmamma, grandmother, grandpapa, grandparent, grandsire, grandson.

Where *grand* occurs in titles OED gives no hyphen: Grand Duchess, Grand Duke, Grand Master.

gray, grey. Either spelling is correct.

greenness. So spelt. When *-ness* is affixed to an adjective ending with *n* the *n* of the adjective is not dropped; *thinness* is another example. Cf. *withhold*.

groin, groyne. *Groin*, part of the body, of a building; *groyne*, a breakwater.

gutturals. See CONSONANTS.

half. Half of them *is* or *are*? The rule is that when the noun or pronoun following *of* is singular, *half* is considered singular: 'Half of our heavy task *was* done'; but when the noun or pronoun following *of* is plural, *half* is considered plural: 'Half of the apples *were* bad'. The same remarks apply to *lots of* and *heaps of*.

hang. In modern idiom, pictures and bacon are *hung*, murderers are *hanged*.

hardly, scarcely. The idiom is, Hardly, scarcely had/was he . . . *when* (not *than*); '*Hardly* had it begun to rain *when* we arrived'; '*Scarcely* was he out of sight *when* you came'. See THAN.

heaps of. For number see HALF.

heir apparent, presumptive. An *heir apparent* is one whose title cannot be overthrown by any possible birth; an heir *presumptive* loses his title if an heir apparent is born. The old meaning of *apparent* was 'unquestionable'—that which actually appears.

help. The sentence 'Don't cough more than you can help', which was given for correction and explanation in a recent examination paper, is classed by MEU as a 'sturdy indefensible', and by OED as 'erroneous'. The logical form, which has never become idiomatic, would be 'Don't cough more than you *cannot* help'; but the simplest way to avoid what is certainly an ugly and illogical idiom is to substitute *must* for *can help*: 'Don't cough more than you must'.

hendiadys (Greek = 'one thing by means of two'). Two words co-ordinated may be used instead of an expression in which one qualifies the other grammatically. Good examples can be found in Virgil, e.g.:

dirae ferro et compagibus artis
Claudentur Belli portae,

i.e. 'the gates of war grim with closely-welded plates of iron'.

It is chiefly a poetic ornament in Greek and Latin, and is little used in English. 'Nice and cosy', 'try and do' are true examples.

heroic couplet. Iambic pentameters rhyming *aa*, *bb*, *cc*, &c.—the chief measure of eighteenth-century verse, perfected by Pope. The following three extracts, all from Pope himself, illustrate the suitability of the couplet, with its rhythmical precision, to (*a*) semi-humorous or mock heroic verse, (*b*) moralizing, (*c*) satire. The essence of the heroic couplet was its perfect and almost mechanical synchronizing of sense with rhythm, each couplet being (in the finest examples of the measure) itself a unit of the thought.

(*a*)
> Meanwhile, declining from the noon of day,
> The sun obliquely shoots his burning ray:
> The hungry judges soon the sentence sign,
> And wretches hang that jurymen may dine;
> The merchant from th' Exchange returns in peace,
> And the long labours of the toilet cease.
> Belinda now, whom thirst of fame invites,
> Burns to encounter two advent'rous knights,
> At ombre singly to decide their doom;
> And swells her breast with conquests yet to come.
> Straight the three bands prepare in arms to join,
> Each band the number of the sacred Nine.
> Soon as she spreads her hand, th' aërial guard
> Descend, and sit on each important card:
> First Ariel perch'd upon a Matadore,
> Then each according to the rank they bore;
> For sylphs, yet mindful of their ancient race,
> Are, as when women, wondrous fond of place.
>   Behold, four kings, in majesty rever'd,
> With hoary whiskers and a forky beard;
> And four fair queens whose hands sustain a flow'r,
> The expressive emblem of their softer pow'r;
> Four knaves in garbs succinct, a trusty band,
> Caps on their heads, and halberds in their hand;
> And party-colour'd troops, a shining train,
> Draw forth to combat on the velvet plain.
> (From *The Rape of the Lock*)

(*b*)
> Know then this truth (enough for man to know)
> 'Virtue alone is happiness below'.
> The only point where human bliss stands still,
> And tastes the good without the fall to ill;

Where only merit constant pay receives,
Is blest in what it takes, and what it gives;
The joy unequall'd if its end it gain,
And if it lose, attended with no pain;
Without satiety, though e'er so bless'd,
And but more relish'd as the more distress'd:
The broadest mirth unfeeling folly wears,
Less pleasing far than virtue's very tears:
Good, from each object, from each place acquir'd,
For ever exercis'd, yet never tir'd;
Never elated, while one man's oppress'd;
Never dejected, while another's bless'd:
And where no wants, no wishes can remain,
Since but to wish more virtue, is to gain.

(From *Essay on Man*)

(c)

Peace to all such! but were there one whose fires
True genius kindles and fair fame inspires;
Blest with each talent and each art to please,
And born to write, converse, and live with ease:
Should such a man, too fond to rule alone,
Bear, like the Turk, no brother near the throne,
View him with scornful yet with jealous eyes,
And hate for arts that caus'd himself to rise;
Damn with faint praise, assent with civil leer,
And, without sneering, teach the rest to sneer;
Willing to wound, and yet afraid to strike;
Just hint a fault, and hesitate dislike;
Alike reserv'd to blame or to commend,
A timorous foe and a suspicious friend;
Dreading e'en fools, by flatterers besieg'd,
And so obliging that he ne'er oblig'd;
Like Cato, give his little senate laws,
And sit attentive to his own applause;
While wits and Templars every sentence raise,
And wonder with a foolish face of praise—
Who but must laugh, if such a man there be?
Who would not weep, if Atticus were he?

(From the *Epistle to Doctor Arbuthnot*. This is Pope's satirical description of Addison.)

heroic quatrain. See QUATRAIN.

hight. Hight is 3rd singular present and past tense and past participle of an obsolete verb (OE. *hatan*, cf. Germ. *heissen*) = is (was) called. It is the only verb found in English with a passive sense. So in German: Er heisst Wilhelm = He is called William.

She Queene of Faeries *hight*
(Spenser)
This grisly beast, which Lion *hight* by name
(Shakespeare)

The word is obsolete in Mod.E.

historic, historical. *Historic* means famous or likely to become famous in history; *historical* means based on, vouched for by, history. Thus a character, an occasion, a building can be *historic*; evidence, method, a novel can be *historical*.

As a grammatical term *historic* is applied to tense and (in Greek) to mood used of past events. So in graphic narration the *historic present* tense is used to bring past events more vividly before the reader's mind.

In Latin the *historic infinitive* is sometimes used, instead of historic tenses of the indicative, of sudden events or of events following in rapid succession.

homonyms. MEU says: 'Homonyms are separate words that happen to be identical in form', and gives as example *pole* (OE. = 'stake') and *pole* (<Greek, 'the terminal point of an axis'). The nouns *host* meaning a large number (of people, things), derived from Latin *hostis* = enemy, and *host* meaning landlord of an inn, entertainer of guests, derived from Latin *hospes* = guest, are homonyms.

homophones. Words of the same sound but of different spelling and meaning: e.g. *piece, peace; rain, rein, reign.*

Horatian ode. See ODE.

housewife. There are two pronunciations: (i) 'housewife' (as spelt) in the ordinary domestic meaning of a mistress or manager of the house; (ii) 'huzif' (in which there is the common elimination of *w*, as in *sword* and *Woolwich*) meaning a case containing materials for sewing. MEU notes that 'huzif' was the pronunciation in the first meaning up to the 16th century, when the associations of the contraction *hussy* called for another pronunciation of the word in its dignified matronly meaning. The plural of (i) is *housewives* and of (ii) is *housewifes* ('huzifs').

how.
'I told him about how you were chosen to play for the school.'
'I am very glad you have drawn attention to how suitable the site is for an observatory.'
Both sentences offend the eye and the ear. The first one illustrates the common tendency to introduce an unnecessary preposition before the noun clause, object of *told*. In the second sentence the writer has forgotten that a preposition should, if possible, govern an actual noun or pronoun. It is possible here; so the sentence should run: 'I am glad you have drawn attention to the suitability of the site for an observatory.'

however. When *however* is an adverb (= nevertheless, &c.) it modifies the whole sentence or clause in which it stands, and is separated by a comma or commas from the rest of that sentence or clause:
> However, we will look into the matter later.
> The weather, however, was too bad for us to carry out our plans.

When it is an adverbial conjunction of concession (see -EVER) it is not separated by a comma from the word it modifies:
> However strong you are, you need a little rest.
> He is always willing to help, however tired he is.

human, humane. Up to the eighteenth century the two spellings were used indiscriminately for either meaning. In that century, however, *humane* was fixed as the spelling of the adjective representing the meaning 'merciful' as distinct from the ordinary sense of *human*. Shakespeare has 'Ere human statute purged the gentle weal', where the modern spelling would be *humane*.

humans, for 'human beings', is simply a vulgarism. 'Dozens of cases of sunstroke are reported daily, and altogether humans and animals are suffering severely'—from a well-known newspaper.

hybrids. Hybrids are words that are made up of parts derived from two or more different languages. Thus *grandfather* has a French prefix and an English root; *bicycles* has a Latin prefix (*bi*-), a Greek root (cycle < *kuklos*, a wheel), and an English inflexion for the plural; all weak verbs derived from other languages have the English dental suffix as the sign of their past.

hypallage (Greek = 'interchange') is the transference of an adjective or adverb from the word with which it naturally goes to another with which it is associated. Such an epithet is said to be 'transferred'. Examples:

> 'Let us speak
> Our *free* hearts each to each'

(i.e. Let us speak our hearts freely);

> 'Melissa shook her *doubtful* curls'

(i.e. In doubt Melissa shook her curls).

hyperbole (Greek = 'over-shooting'), a figure in which the bounds of strict veracity are over-shot, not for the sake of deceit but on account of emotion and for the sake of emphasis or humour. Thus we talk of 'tons of money', 'a thousand thanks', a person of 'no brains'. In literature we have Shakespeare's

> 'If thou prate of mountains, let them throw
> Millions of acres on us, till our ground,
> Singeing his pate against the burning zone,
> Make Ossa like a wart.'

and Pope's

> 'Belinda smiled, and all the world was gay.'

hysteron proteron (Greek = 'later earlier'), placing first what normally comes last, 'putting the cart before the horse', as in Virgil's 'moriamur et in arma ruamus'. Thus Dogberry, in *Much Ado*, 'Masters, it is proved already that you are little better than false knaves, and it will go near to be thought so shortly.'

iamb. See FOOT.

-ible. See -ABLE, -IBLE.

-ics. For number of scientific words in *-ics* see MATHEMATICS.

identical. The constructions are: (*a*) A is identical *with* B; (*b*) A and B are identical; (*c*) two (or more) persons, things are identical. 'Each of the books was identical in binding' is logically and grammatically impossible; but, as usual, the distributive *each* has put into the mind a plural which does not exist in reality. Write: 'The bindings of the books were identical' or 'The books were identical in binding'. Here is a less obvious example from a newspaper: 'It is difficult to explain on what grounds the discrimination between them and other students was made, for in each case the offence and apology were identical.' This does not, and could not, mean that the offence was identical with the apology; it means, and should say, that the offences and the apologies of the students were identical. The truth is the word *identical* has embarrassed the construction of the sentence almost beyond hope. 'All the students committed the same offence and offered the same apology' is a safe, if drastic, amendment.

idiom. MEU says that the closest possible translation of the Greek word is a 'manifestation of the peculiar'. The article goes on:

'English idiom is the same as natural or racy or unaffected English; that is idiomatic which it is natural for a normal Englishman to say or write; to suppose that grammatical English is either all idiomatic or all unidiomatic would be as far from the truth as that idiomatic English is either all grammatical or all ungrammatical; grammar and idiom are independent categories; being applicable to the same material, they sometimes agree and sometimes disagree about particular specimens of it; the most that can be said is that what is idiomatic is far more often grammatical than ungrammatical.'

It will be convenient and helpful to classify idioms in four sections: (*a*) grammatical; (*b*) 'ungrammatical'—i.e. those in which idiom and grammar disagree; (*c*) prepositional; (*d*) metaphorical. A brief note with one or two examples will explain each type:

(*a*) *Grammatical*. Here we have peculiarities in the laws of grammar and syntax: e.g. the use of both *shall* and *will* as auxiliaries in the future tenses; the use of continuous tenses in the Present and Future; the use of the impersonal *it* as an anticipatory subject, and of the adverb *there* as an introductory word in a sentence, with which we may compare the French idiom *il y a*; and, perhaps the most helpful of all English idioms, the use of the noun as adjective ('a spring day'; 'a newspaper scare').

(*b*) *Ungrammatical*. A paragraph from Mr. Logan Pearsall Smith's invaluable and delightful *Words and Idioms* will serve as both explanation and example:

'Idiomatic transgressions are of two kinds, the rules of grammar may be broken, or the rules of logic. Of these, the first kind, the ungrammatical phrases made acceptable by usage, are the most obvious, and in any old-fashioned book on good English will be found lists of these wild creatures of talk, nailed up, like noxious birds and vermin, by the purists and preservers of our speech. The phrase "It's me" is a familiar instance; other instances are "who did you see?" "than whom", "very pleased", "try and go" (for "try to go"), "different" or "averse" *to*, the split infinitive, the use of the superlative when only two objects are compared ("the best" instead of "the better of the two"), and phrases like "less than no time", "more than pleased", "as tall or taller than you".'

Mr. Pearsall Smith instances, as examples of the breaking of the rules of logic, the double comparative and the double negative. All this must, however, be modified by the statement that what is permissible in speech is not always permissible in writing. Argument along these lines has an element of fallacy in it; it makes shifting sand of the King's English. So most of the phrases and constructions dealt with in the paragraph quoted, and many more, are treated separately on their merits under their alphabetical headings.

(*c*) *Prepositional*. The idiom controlling the use of definite prepositions after certain verbs and other parts of speech ('compare *with*', 'different *from*') is treated separately, under the special heading PREPOSITIONAL IDIOM. The use of the preposition in idiomatic phrases is illustrated in the following ten: 'by chance', 'at last', 'after all', 'in time', 'by day', 'on trust', 'of course', 'for instance', 'to hand', 'in fact'. Another important prepositional idiom is the addition of a preposition (or, to be grammatically precise, an adverb particle) to a simple verb, thereby giving the verb a twist of meaning. Thus with the simple verb *to look*, we have 'to look *up*', 'to look *into*', 'to look *over*', 'to look *on*'; with *to give*, we have 'to give *in*, *up*, *out*'; with *to take* we have 'to take *in*, *up*, *on*, *upon*'.

(*d*) *Metaphorical*. Under the heading METAPHOR is given a short list of metaphorical phrases that have become common idioms in speech and writing. In *Words and Idioms* idiomatic phrases are classified according to their origin—e.g. from games, from hunting, from animals, from religion and the Bible, from commerce, from music, from the theatre, from food and eating, from the weather. Here are a few out of the hundreds Mr. Logan Pearsall Smith has collected:

'To have all one's eggs in one basket'; 'to leave out in the cold'; 'to have other fish to fry'; 'to sell like hot cakes'; 'to turn up trumps'; 'to blow one's own trumpet'; 'to be in the limelight'; 'to shut up shop'; 'to rob Peter to pay Paul'; 'a broken reed'; 'to leave no stone unturned'.

ie and ei. The only working rule is: When *ie* or *ei* is pronounced as *ee*, the *i* comes before the *e* except after *c*. There are five important exceptions: *weird, seize, counterfeit, weir,* and *plebeian. Leisure, neither, heir, neighbour, friend, height,* and *freight* are some words to be remembered.

if. *If* is
    (*a*) a conjunction introducing an adverb clause of condition:
> '*If* music be the food of love, play on.'
> '*If* I should die, think only this of me.'

There is a special use of the conditional *if* without APODOSIS in exclamatory sentences:
> *If* only I had known !
> *If* he hasn't won after all !

    (*b*) a conjunction (= *whether*) introducing a noun clause (indirect question):
> I don't know *if* you are right.
> I will see *if* there will be time to catch the train.

    See also ADVERB CLAUSE and AS.

illegible. See ELIGIBLE.

illicit. See ELICIT.

illiteracies. The following is the (intentionally illiterate) last sentence of a leader in *The Times* bewailing the misuse of words and constructions in English:—'If these sort of things go on, whom will say if in time the England language shall not be nothing but a string of nouns, like some savage dialects are.' The leader pokes fun at certain colloquialisms (and worse) that are dealt with in this book under the following headings: SORT, WHOM, SHALL AND WILL, DOUBLE NEGATIVE, IF, WHETHER, LIKE. Other similar 'illiteracies' will be found in their alphabetical position: SPLIT INFINITIVE, BETWEEN, AGGRAVATING, UNIQUE, &c.

illusion. See ALLUSION.

imbue, infuse. The confusion of the constructions with the two words is illustrated in the following formulas:
> To *imbue* a person *with* courage. ⎱ RIGHT.
> To *infuse* courage *into* a person. ⎰
> To *infuse* a person *with* courage. WRONG.

imperative mood. The imperative is the mood of command of the verb: 'Go!'; 'Greet the unseen with a cheer!' In Mod.E. the subject (second person singular or plural) is usually understood, except when it is emphasized (as in: 'I can't manage this; *you* try'), but in older English it was more often expressed—'Go and do *thou* likewise' (AV). The imperative is not to be confused with the subjunctive of wish in a main sentence: 'God *save* the King!' 'So *be* it!' (See SUBJUNCTIVE MOOD.) In indirect speech the imperative becomes an infinitive after a verb of commanding (*command, tell, instruct,* &c.): 'He told them *to go* and (to) *do* likewise'. The use of the infinitive (omitting *to*) after *please* ('Please *come*') is a polite softening of the actual command 'Come!'. 'Please *to come*' is archaic.

imperial, imperious. Both words are derived from Latin *imperium*. *Imperial* means 'belonging to an empire or to an emperor', and hence 'august', 'magnificent'. The Imperial City was Rome, The Imperial Institute is a building in London commemorating Queen Victoria's Jubilee of 1887 and devoted to the promotion of trade between parts of the British Empire. *Imperious* means 'haughty', 'overbearing', 'tyrannical'. Shakespeare uses 'imperious Caesar', 'most imperious Agamemnon', showing that in his day the word could also be used in the sense of 'imperial'.

impersonal verbs. A true impersonal verb is one that has no grammatical subject. Only two such verbs survive in Mod.E., me*seems* and me*thinks* (= it seems to me), where *seems* and *thinks* are impersonal and *me* is dative case. The logical subject of the impersonal verb consists of a noun clause, e.g.:

Methinks *I am a prophet new inspir'd.*

In ME. *liketh* was used impersonally as in Mod.E. *if you please* (= if it may *please* you). A survival of this use, but with a grammatical subject, is found in AV: 'For this *liketh* you, O ye children of Israel.'

implicit, explicit. *Implicit* = lit. 'folded up in', 'implied': 'His attitude was *implicit* in the answer he gave you' (i.e. 'it was folded up, hidden in—'). So the secondary meaning of this word is implicit (i.e. is implied) in its primary meaning; as an adjective qualifying nouns like *faith, obedience, confidence*, it means 'complete', 'absolute'. 'The starting-point of this usage' (says MEU) 'is the ecclesiastical phrase *implicit faith*, i.e. a person's acceptance of any article of belief, not on its own merits, but as part of, as "wrapped up in", his general acceptance of the Church's authority; the steps from this sense to *unquestioning*, and thence to *complete* or *absolute* or *exact* are easy.'

Explicit = 'unfolded', stated in detail, expressly stated and not merely implied—hence definite, outspoken: 'He was glad to have had this opportunity of speaking out; what had before been *implicit* in this strange relationship was now *explicit*'.

imply. There is a tendency for *imply* to usurp the meaning and use of *infer*. You may *infer* from a letter the acceptance of your offer; but the letter *implies* (not *infers*) that acceptance. The use of *infer* for *imply*, however, though it offends against Mod.E. idiom, is at least as old as Milton. SOED quotes 'Consider first, that Great or Bright infers not Excellence' (*Paradise Lost*, viii. 91).

i-mutation. I-mutation means the change of a back vowel sound (e.g. *a, o, u*) into a front vowel (e.g. *e, y* [*i*]) by assimilation to the front sound *i* or *j* which originally followed in the next syllable: thus *a, o>e; u>y*, later *i*. This change took place before there was any written record of

English, perhaps in the fifth and sixth centuries A.D. It occurs in many OE. forms and leaves its mark in Mod.E. Thus the primitive plural of the noun *man* was *manniz*; in the OE. form the *a* of the stem was mutated (changed) to *e* by the influence of the front vowel *i* in the suffix: hence OE. sg. *man(n)*, pl. *men(n)*, with loss of the primitive ending which caused the mutation. The clearest Mod.E. survivals are similar noun plurals, e.g.: *woman, women; foot, feet; tooth, teeth; goose, geese; brother, brethr(en); mouse, mice; cow, ki(ne)*. A few odd forms are interesting. A *book* was originally writing inscribed on a tablet of *beech*-wood; the vowel of *feed* is mutated from the vowel of *food*. In *old, elder, eldest* we have a Mod.E. example of mutated comparative and super-lative forms. The adjectives *strong, long, broad* have corresponding abstract nouns with mutated vowels: *strength, length, breadth*. A few verbs have mutated vowels in the present forms but not in the past: *sought, seek; thought, think*.

in-, un-. Shakespeare's 'uncapable of pity' reminds us, through the fact that Mod.E. prefers *incapable*, that there is a changing fashion in the use of *in-* and *un-*. Moreover, words that are closely associated in etymology or meaning are liable to have different prefixes. OED says: 'The modern tendency is to restrict *in-* to words obviously answering to the Latin types, and to prefer *un-* in other cases.' The following examples are taken from the MEU article:

unable	inability
unanimated	inanimate
unapproachable	inaccessible
unapt	inept }
	ineptitude }
unceasing	incessant
uncivil	incivility
undigested	indigestible
undiscriminating	indiscriminate
undistinguished	indistinguishable
unexpressive	inexpressible
unjust	injustice
unlettered	illiterate
unlimited	illimitable
unpractical	impracticable
unquiet	inquietude
unreconciled	irreconcilable
unredeemed	irredeemable
unresponsive	irresponsible

It is worth while remembering that (1) words in *-ed* have *un-*, not *in-*, as a rule (*inexperienced* being the only exception); (2) words in *-ing* always have *un-*; (3) words in *-ible* and in *-ent* usually take *in-*.

incomplete predication (verb of). The transitive verb completes the predicate with its object; the intransitive verb itself completes the predicate. But there are a few intransitive verbs that, not themselves completing the predicate, demand a noun or adjective as COMPLEMENT—i.e. 'completer'. The chief of them is the verb *to be*; *to appear, to seem, to look, to become*, are other examples. Thus normally the words 'Caesar is' do not make a sentence, although *is* is intransitive and might therefore be expected to form a complete predicate. But once a noun is supplied as 'complement' the sentence becomes complete: 'Caesar is king.' So in the preceding statement the word *complete* is the complement of *becomes*. Such verbs are called *verbs of incomplete predication*. It is noteworthy that most of them may be also normally intransitive (i.e. completing the predicate). Thus *to be* is sometimes used in the sense of 'to exist': 'Whatever *is* is right' (where the first *is* is normally intransitive = 'exists', and the second is a verb of incomplete predication, with complement *right*); 'That that *is is*' (where both verbs are normally intransitive). So in 'A ghost *appears*' the verb itself forms a complete predicate.

inculcate. The idiom is 'inculcate a thing *in* or *upon* a person', not 'inculcate a person *with* a thing': "They inculcated in him fine ideas and expensive tastes' (not: 'inculcated him with fine ideas . . .'). Cf. AFFLICT.

index. The scientific plural is usually *indices*; the plural in more general senses is usually *indexes*. There is a law of *indices* in algebra; a book may have two *indexes*.

indicative mood. The indicative mood is the mood relating to a matter of fact, e.g.:

> 'This is true' (a statement of fact),
> 'Is this true?' (a question as to a matter of fact),
> 'How true this is!' (an exclamation as a matter of fact).

indict, indite. *Indict* (which is pronounced as if spelt *indite*) is the legal term. The constructions are: to indict a person (*a*) for a crime, (*b*) as a criminal, (*c*) on a charge. *Indite* is now hardly more than a fancy term for 'write', often used jocularly in Mod.E.

indirect speech ('Reported Speech'; 'Oratio Obliqua').

(*a*) 'I want', said the Prime Minister, 'to make England a land fit for heroes to live in.'

The Prime Minister's actual words are quoted, and the sentence is punctuated accordingly. Here, however, are his words 'reported' by a third person:

(*b*) The Prime Minister said that he wanted to make England a land fit for heroes to live in.

No longer are the actual words of the speaker quoted. The quotation marks therefore disappear; the Prime Minister is referred to in the third person, since he is not now the person speaking; and, as the speech is reported *after* it took place, the tense of the verb has gone backward into the past. Sentence (*a*) is written in *direct* and sentence (*b*) in *indirect* speech.

In indirect speech (i.e. actual speech reported by a third person or by the speaker or by the hearer):

(i) the pronouns are all altered, if necessary, so that their relations with the 'reporter' and his hearer or reader, rather than with the original speaker, are expressed; this means that they will frequently all be changed into the third person.

(ii) the verb tenses usually recede into the past (e.g. Present Simple > Past Simple; Future Simple > Future in the Past).

(iii) adverbs often change for time and place (*now* > *then*; *here* > *there*); and the demonstrative *this* > *that*.

(iv) commands as well as statements become indirect. Questions often become indirect, but may remain direct (see passage below).

(v) exclamations are either omitted or recast in statement form.

Special care has to be taken with pronouns; it is easy to fall into ambiguity. Thus the indirect form of the following sentence 'I told him *I could not see him to-day*' would be 'He told him he could not see him that day', and the pronouns (i.e. the second *he* and the second *him*) are ambiguous. The only way out of the difficulty in this particular example is the cumbersome and objectionable one of explaining the doubtful pronoun or pronouns with its appropriate noun in brackets. But in simpler cases the substitution of a noun for a pronoun will generally eliminate the ambiguity. Most of the points referred to are illustrated in the following examples:

(a) Direct Speech.

'Oh, that's all right,' Miller replied cheerfully. 'Give us a start. I shan't complain if it comes to nothing.'

'Well,' Thorndyke said reluctantly, 'I was thinking of getting a few particulars as to the various tenants of No. 51 Clifford's Inn. Perhaps you could do it more easily and it might be worth your while.'

'Good!' Miller exclaimed gleefully. 'He "gives to airy nothing a local habitation and a name"!'

'It is probably the wrong name,' Thorndyke reminded him.

'I don't care,' said Miller. 'But why shouldn't we go together? It's too late to-night, and I can't manage to-morrow morning. But say to-morrow afternoon. Two heads are better than one, you know, especially when the second one is yours. Or perhaps,' he added, with a glance at me, 'three would be better still.'

Indirect Speech.

Miller replied cheerfully that it was all right. He asked Thorndyke to give them a start. He wouldn't complain if it came to nothing. Thorndyke replied reluctantly that he was thinking of getting a few particulars as to the various tenants of No. 51 Clifford's Inn. Perhaps Miller could do it more easily and it might be worth his while. Miller gleefully expressed his delight, exclaiming that Thorndyke gave 'to airy nothing a local habitation and a name'. Thorndyke reminded him that it was probably the wrong name. Miller said he didn't care, and asked[1] why they shouldn't go together. It was too late that night and he couldn't manage the next morning. But he suggested[2] they should say the next afternoon. Two heads were better than one,[3] especially when the second one was Thorndyke's. He added, with a glance at the third man,[4] that three might be better still.

Notes.

1. Or, omitting 'asked', make the question indirect as it stands: Why shouldn't they go together? Note that this question, though indirect in style, is still syntactically a direct question.
2. Or, omitting 'suggested': 'Let them say the next afternoon.'
3. The parenthetic 'you know' does not appear in the indirect speech.
4. If the narrator is an outside person a noun must stand here; and as the actual name ('Jervis') is not known from the context, the person can be indicated only by some such phrase as this. If the narrator in indirect speech were the original speaker, the *me* would stand.

(b) Direct Speech.

The fact that opinion grounded on experience has moved one way does not in law preclude the possibility of its moving on fresh experience in the other; nor does it bind succeeding generations, when conditions have again changed. After all, the question whether a given opinion is a danger to society is a question of the times and is a question of fact. I desire to say nothing that would limit the right of society to protect itself by process of law from the dangers of the moment, whatever that right may be, but only to say that, experience having proved dangers once thought real to be now negligible, and dangers once very possibly imminent to have now passed away, there is nothing in the general rules as to blasphemy and irreligion, as known to the law, which prevents us from varying their application to the particular circumstances of our time in accordance with that experience.

Indirect Speech.

He said that the fact that opinion grounded on experience had moved one way did not in law preclude the possibility of its moving on fresh experience in the other; nor did it bind succeeding generations, when conditions had again changed. After all, the question whether a given opinion was a danger to society was a question of the times and was a question of fact. He desired to say nothing that would limit the right of society to protect itself by process of law from the dangers of the moment, whatever that right might be, but only to say that, experience having proved dangers once thought real to be now negligible, and dangers once very possibly imminent to have now passed away, there was nothing in the general rules as to blasphemy and irreligion, as known to the law, which prevented men from varying their application to the particular circumstances of their time in accordance with that experience.

individual.

'The ship was crowded with passengers; most of them were poor consumptive *individuals*.'

'We led our horses along dark, silent, and deserted streets, till we found an *individual* who directed us to a large, gloomy, and comfortless inn.'

These sentences, both from Borrow's *The Bible in Spain*, illustrate a familiar use of *individual* as a noun for 'person', 'man'. The use is to be condemned as an unnecessary spoiling of a good word. *Individual* is originally an adjective, meaning 'distinctive', 'peculiar', 'particular'— the opposite of 'general'; and when used as a noun should keep the fundamental idea of particularization; that is, it should be used in contrast to such ideas as 'the crowd', 'the public', 'society in general': 'He was, after all, but one individual in the clamouring crowd.' Since, however, there are comparatively few sentences in which the word may be used as a noun, in the necessary distinctive sense, it is wiser and safer to think of it first and foremost as an adjective, and to use it as a noun only when the contrast with *general* is deliberate and obvious.

indulge. The constructions are:
(*a*) indulge an emotion, a thought, an idea (i.e. give it full rein);
(*b*) indulge yourself in emotion, day-dreaming, ambitions, &c.;
(*c*) indulge in emotions, hopes, ice-cream.

infer. See IMPLY.

infinitive mood.
1. *Form.* In OE. the infinitive had an inflexional termination (-*an*, -*ian*): *helpan* (to help), *drincan* (to drink), *lufian* (to love). This form was used as a noun in OE. and was often preceded by *to* as a kind of prefix: *to helpanne, to drincanne, to lufianne.* With the loss of the inflexion, this became the form of the modern infinitive, the *to* 'being reduced to a mere sign without any meaning of its own'—SOED.

2. *Main Uses.* The infinitive is used:
(*a*) (without the *to*) to make up compound tenses with the auxiliaries *shall* and *will, do, may*: 'I shall, do, may *go*'.

(b) as a noun precisely like an ordinary noun (except after a preposition, where a gerund replaces the infinitive, since the *to* will not admit of another preposition before it):

> '*To err* is human, *to forgive* divine.' (subject)
> '*To do* good and *to distribute* forget not.' (object)
> '*To see* him is *to love* him.' (complement)

(c) as an adverb mainly to indicate purpose after an intransitive verb (usually of motion): 'I come *to bury* Caesar, not *to praise* him' (Infinitive of Purpose).

(d) as an adjective sometimes 'the equivalent of a future participle' (SOED), sometimes acting for a gerund phrase and hence called gerundial infinitive.

> 'The best is yet *to be*' (= future participle).
> 'A house *to let*'; 'There is work *to be done*' (gerundial infinitive).

Thus the infinitive may occur in all three types of phrase—noun, adverb, and adjective. One or two special or idiomatic uses may be noticed:

(i) Sometimes an infinitive completes the sense expressed in a verb (other than an auxiliary) or an adjective: 'I can *do* all things'; 'I am anxious *to go*'. This is frequently called the prolative infinitive (Lat. *pro+latus*, 'carried over').

(ii) The infinitive is used with a noun in the accusative to make the equivalent of a noun clause after verbs of *thinking* and *knowing*. See ACCUSATIVE CASE (*a*).

(iii) In the sentence 'To think he should have deceived me!' the infinitive is exclamatory, and is so full of meaning that it is used idiomatically for a whole clause.

See also SPLIT INFINITIVE and GERUND.

inflict. See AFFLICT.

infringe. By long-established usage and by origin *infringe* is transitive (infringe *a rule, regulation, right, privilege*, &c.) but modern usage has tended to make it intransitive, followed by *on* or *upon*, especially when it occurs in connexion with words like *domain, territory, boundary* ('infringe *upon* your domain', &c.). The advice given in MEU is to stick to the transitive use and when 'the temptation to insert *on* or *upon* becomes overpowering', to resort to *trespass* or *encroach*.

infuse. See IMBUE.

ingenious, ingenuous. *Ingenious* means 'clever', and may be used both of man himself and of his many inventions; *ingenuous* means 'frank', 'artless'. 'To quench the blushes of ingenuous shame', a familiar line in Gray's *Elegy*, should help to fix the word in the memory.

ingratiate. In Mod.E. *ingratiate* is always reflexive: 'ingratiate oneself' = 'make oneself agreeable'. It cannot be used in the sense of 'please (another person)', as in the example pilloried by MEU: 'Even if it does ingratiate the men, it will only be by alienating the women.'

in law. Relatives 'in law' originally included 'step-' relatives. When Sam Weller spoke bitterly of 'mother-in-law', he was referring to the second Mrs. Tony Weller, the 'vidder' who had beguiled his father into a second 'wenture'. To-day he would call her his step-mother; and his own wife's mother would be his mother-in-law.

'In Memoriam' stanza. See QUATRAIN.

innate, instinct (adj.). The constructions are: 'innate in (a person)'; '(a person, &c.) instinct with'. Examples: 'Skill in batting is *innate* in some men'; 'His batting was *instinct* with confidence and courage.'

in order that. *In order that* is followed by *may* or *might*, sometimes (but not often) by *shall* or *should*, never by *can* or *could*, *will* or *would*.

inquire. See ENQUIRE.

instance. Writers are apt to fly to *instance* as a refuge from *case*, 'not realizing that most instances in which *case* would have damned them are also cases in which *instance* will damn them' (MEU). See CASE.

insure. See ASSURE.

intelligence is quickness of understanding, sagacity—a quality possessed in varying degrees by other animals besides man, e.g. monkeys, performing horses in a circus.

    Intellect is the faculty of knowing and reasoning—a quality not by any means always found even in man.

    Hence an *intelligent* person is merely one who is not stupid or slow-witted. The epithet is more or less patronizing. But an *intellectual* person is one distinguished from the average man by qualities of mind. The epithet is respectful, even if generally tinged by suspicion or dislike.

interjections (Lat. *inter* = among, *iactus* = thrown) are words used to call the attention of the person addressed (e.g. 'Hallo!'), or to express a feeling such as joy, grief, surprise (e.g. 'Hurrah!' 'Alas!' 'Ha!'). These words, as the etymology of *interjection* implies, may be 'thrown into' a sentence without interfering with its grammatical structure. On the other hand, we cannot always remove interjections from a sentence and leave that sentence with complete sense. Thus in

        'O for a Muse of fire that would ascend
          The brightest Heaven of invention!'

the interjection 'O [for a Muse]' is elliptical for 'O I long [for a Muse]'. Sometimes an interjection may be equivalent to a whole sentence. Thus 'Alas!' = *ha las*, i.e. *ah+las* (= weary) means 'Ah [I am] weary'.

    Note that interjections are single words. Groups of words such as 'How awful!' are not interjections but elliptical exclamatory sentences, the subject and part of the predicate not being expressed. Nor are commands like 'Come!' 'Hark!' interjections; they are complete sentences with their subjects not expressed.

internal rhyme. See RHYME.

into. *Into* (one word) is a simple preposition; you walk *into* a room, you get *into* your clothes, but you go *in to* dinner (where *in* is an adverb modifying *go* and *to* is the preposition).

intrigue. The COD definition is: 'carry on underhand plot; employ secret influence (*with*); have a liaison (*with*)'. The SOED admits 'as a recent gallicism' the sense 'to excite the curiosity or interest of', and gives the quotation, dated 1905: 'The story itself does not greatly *intrigue* us.' MEU roundly condemns this use, with the observation that *intrigue* in this sense is 'one of the gallicisms, and literary critics' words, that have no merit whatever except that of unfamiliarity to the English reader, and at the same time the great demerit of being identical with and therefore confusing the sense of a good English word'. But the condemnation is too strong, and somewhat unreasonable. Words have always had the privilege in English of taking upon themselves allied meanings; so why not *intrigue*? The worst that can be said of it in the sense of 'interest' or 'perplex' is that it has become what MEU calls a vogue-word, and is therefore usually a symptom of mental laziness.

invaluable, valueless. *invaluable*: 'not able to be valued', i.e. beyond value—the prefix *in-* is negative; *valueless*: 'without value'—the suffix *-less* is negative.

inversion. Inversion is the 'turning round' of the sentence, i.e. putting the subject after the verb. It is usual (*a*) in questions, except those introduced by interrogative pronouns or adjectives; (*b*) in exclamations; (*c*) in commands in poetical or archaic language (where the subject is actually expressed); (*d*) in conditional clauses without *if*; (*e*) when the predicate is insignificant (in length, &c.) compared with the subject, or when it is desired to emphasize one part of the predicate, especially a negative; (*f*) in verse, for metrical reasons; (*g*) with *said* used parenthetically. Examples are:

(*a*) '*Is Brutus* sick?' '*Shall not the judge* of all the earth do right?' '*Shall Caesar send* a lie?'
(*b*) 'How beautiful upon the mountains *are the feet* of him that bringeth good tidings!'
(*c*) 'Upon the right hand I; *take thou* the left.'
(*d*) *Should the weather* be wet, the fête will not be held.
(*e*) There *is no doubt* that rain is on the way (instead of 'No doubt is that rain . . .'). Among those invited were *A, B, C, and D.* 'Silver and gold *have I* none.' Never *did I dream* that it would come to this. Only once *did I succeed* in seeing him.
(*f*) 'Thus *spake he*, clouded in his own conceit.'
(*g*) 'I have thought over the matter', *said the fellow*, 'and my master will be angry if I loiter here.'

Outside such normal use inversion becomes a mere trick for effect, and a trick that has very little to recommend it. The three following examples are taken from MEU:

'By diligent search in sunny and sheltered places *could some short-stalked primroses* be gathered.'
'He laid down four principles on which alone *could America go* further.'
'He looked forward, as *do we all*, with hope and confidence.'

inverted commas (quotation marks). It is remarkable in an age peculiarly contemptuous of punctuation marks that we have not yet had the courage to abolish inverted commas. Some time ago a reviewer in the *Times Literary Supplement* solemnly argued that Emily Brontë's famous lyric 'No coward soul is mine' derives a wonderful inner meaning from the fact that, in the manuscript, there is not a single full stop—nothing indeed but three somewhat haphazard commas—throughout the poem. Yet inverted commas live on and thrive, an unnecessary puzzle to the writer and an eyesore to the reader. After all, they are a modern invention. The Bible is plain enough without them; and so is the literature of the eighteenth century. Bernard Shaw scorns them. However, since they are with us, we must do our best with them, trying always to reduce them to a minimum. A few hints are given:

(*a*) Use inverted commas only for actual quotations (from literature) and for direct speech. Titles of books, names of ships, &c. are better italicized, i.e. underlined in writing (see TITLES).

(*b*) In direct speech only the actual words of the speaker are enclosed in inverted commas; at such explanatory clauses as *he said, he answered*, the inverted commas are 'broken'—i.e. an inverted comma is placed after the last word before the clause and before the first word after the clause. The other punctuation follows the meaning and context. Thus, the following passages of direct speech:

(i) 'I intend to go to London to-morrow.'
(ii) 'It is raining hard; so we shall have to postpone our visit.'
(iii) 'My house stands at the top of the hill. If you let me know when you are coming, I will meet you at the station.'

are broken like this:

(i) 'I intend', he said, 'to go to London to-morrow.' (Note that in this sentence the commas marking off the clause *he said* act as brackets—i.e. *he said* is parenthetical.)
(ii) 'It is raining hard,' he said; 'so we shall have to postpone our visit.' (Here the comma after *hard* is to mark the pause between the direct speech and the 'breaking' clause, and the original semicolon is placed after the 'breaking' clause.)
(iii) 'My house stands at the top of the hill,' he said. 'If you let me know when you are coming, I will meet you at the station.' (The full stop follows *said*, and the direct speech begins again with a capital letter.)

(*c*) In ordinary straightforward quotation and direct speech other stops (e.g. question marks, semicolons, &c.) stand inside the second inverted comma: 'Are you coming?'; 'Alas!'; 'I am ready.' Problems arise when one quotation or one piece of direct speech occurs inside another. The best practice is for the main quotation or direct speech to be enclosed in single inverted commas, and the subsidiary quotation or indirect speech in double inverted commas. Other stops have to be inserted in their places appropriate to the sense. The following sentences illustrate the rule, and also show how serious a plague inverted commas can become:

'I heard him say, "I shall be returning to-morrow".' (Even this punctuation is not entirely logical; there should be a full stop before the double inverted commas after *to-morrow*.)
'Who said "When shall we three meet again?"?' (The only sensible thing to do is to avoid writing sentences of this type. Logically the conglomeration of question marks and inverted commas at the end must stand, though in practice we should probably make one question mark do for two. At any rate the abolition of inverted commas would simplify matters.)

Here, finally, is a passage printed as it stands in the AV—a convincing argument against inverted commas. It is an instructive and melancholy exercise to insert the inverted commas modern practice would demand:

And Obadiah said, Art thou that my lord Elijah? And he answered him, I am: go tell thy lord, Behold, Elijah is here. And he said, What have I sinned, that thou wouldest deliver thy servant into the hand of Ahab, to slay me? And now thou sayest, Go, tell thy lord, Behold, Elijah is here. And it shall come to pass, as soon as I am gone from thee, that the spirit of the Lord shall carry thee whither I know not. And Elijah said, As the Lord God of Hosts liveth, before whom I stand, I will surely show myself unto him to-day.

See under INDIRECT SPEECH.

inverted foot. See METRE.

iridescent. So spelt; not *irridescent*. (From Latin *iris, iridis*.)

irony (Greek = 'dissimulation'). A statement is sometimes made more emphatic by the use of words connoting the opposite of what is really meant. This constitutes *irony*. Thus Cordelia speaks ironically of her unnatural sisters as 'the *jewels* of our father', and Macbeth asks his hired murderers:

> 'Are you so gospell'd
> To pray for this *good* man and for his issue?'

i.e. for Banquo and his son Fleance. Similarly Antony in his speech to the Roman crowd makes repeated reference to Brutus and the other conspirators against Caesar as *honourable* men.

Two special forms of irony may be noted:

(*a*) Socratic irony, the peculiarly exasperating pretence of ignorance on the part of Socrates, used to confute his opponents in debate. Socrates would innocently ask his opponent for a definition of, for example, one of the most familiar notions of ethics. He would then cite cases in which this definition is clearly at fault, and would end by making his victim contradict himself out of his own mouth. 'It would seem so'; 'apparently'; 'it looks like it'—such are the admissions wrung out of his opponents by a display of verbal ingenuity. However, 'Socratic irony' usually implies a pose of ignorance assumed in order to entice others into a display of supposed knowledge.

(*b*) Dramatic or Tragic Irony. The incidents of most Greek plays were thoroughly familiar to the spectators from their childhood days. The spectators were in the secret beforehand (although the characters were in the dark), for the range of legends on which the plays were based, e.g. Troy and its sequel, the fortunes of the royal house of Thebes, the Argonauts, the adventures of Herakles, was limited. Hence words uttered by the actors often had a dramatic value to the Athenian audience while they were of trifling import to those on the stage. In this difference between the surface meaning for the actors and the underlying meaning for the spectators lay what was called *dramatic irony*.

The fact that the women in Shakespeare's comedies frequently disguise themselves as boys leads to a sort of irony. In *Twelfth Night*, for example, on the first occasion on which Viola meets the Lady Olivia, the latter asks, 'Are you a comedian?' to which Viola replies, 'No . . . and yet I swear I am not that I play'—an allusion which the audience would understand, though Olivia would not, a remark addressed by the speaker to the audience as a secret shared by the speaker and the audience.

In Shakespearian tragedy, too, irony finds a place. King Duncan has been murdered by Macbeth. The porter of Macbeth's castle has had his full share in the general feasting and drinking in honour of the King's visit, and in his drunken humour imagines that he is porter at the gate of hell. Irony thus helps to intensify the tragic intensity of the scenes preceding and following. Similarly, Macbeth 'requests the presence' of Banquo at his solemn supper, and ironically bids him 'fail not our feast', though he has made full arrangements to have him murdered that very evening.

irregular unions. While we have compounds like *altogether*, *whatsoever*, *notwithstanding*, *nevertheless*, in English, there are a few groups of words which look as if they should have joined themselves together, but actually have not. *All* and *right* remain single; they have never joined forces as *alright*. There is no such adjective in English as *nearby* (= neighbouring: 'a nearby stream') though a well-known modern novelist writes 'The nearby station was a gateway to one of the playgrounds of Europe.' *Common* has never compounded itself with *sense* except as an attributive adjective, when it has a hyphen, though we have *commonplace* and *commonwealth*. *For* and *ever* do not yet make one word on this side of the Atlantic. Calverley wrote:

> 'Forever! 'Tis a single word!
> And yet our fathers deem'd it two;
> Nor am I confident they err'd;
> Are you?'

The answer, as yet, is No.

irregular verbs. See ANOMALOUS.

-ise, -ize. Since it is impossible to tell which English verbs end in *-ise* and which in *-ize* without some fairly intimate knowledge of English, Greek, Latin, and French etymology; and since there are some English verbs which must end in *-ise*, not in *-ize* (e.g. *advertise*, *comprise*, *exercise*), the advice here given is to end them all in *-ise*. The reader will nevertheless notice that in this book the *-ize* ending is used for many verbs; and the reason is that the Oxford University Press, together with many other printers, prefers the *-ize* in those verbs whose etymology demands it. In ordinary writing the point is of little or no importance; in writing for print one is justified in leaving the decision to the printer, who settles the matter according to the rules of his House.

Italian. For the term as applied to the sonnet see SONNET.

italics. For the legitimate use of italics see under EMPHASIS and TITLES.

i and y. The following spellings are taken from a number recommended in MEU:

(a) in i	*(b) in y*
cipher	gypsy
lichgate	pygmy
silvan	wych-elm
siphon	
siren	
stile (over which you help lame dogs)	
tire	

Most of these preferences are for etymological reasons, and only three of them (*tire*, *gypsy*, and *pygmy*) run counter to popular usage. We probably avoid the *y* in *gypsy* and *pygmy* because of a rooted, if unconscious, objection to having more than two comparatively uncommon letters (like *y*) in a word. Thus we will cheerfully write *gypsies* and *pygmies* but hesitate at *gypsy* and *pygmy*. The spelling *tyre* has probably become too familiar to be ousted by dictionary influence, though *tire* has the advantage of revealing its etymological connexion with *attire*. A tyre or tire is the 'dress' of a wheel.

jail. See GAOL.

jargon. MEU defines jargon thus: 'talk that is considered both ugly-sounding and hard to understand: applied especially to
  (i) the sectional vocabulary of a science, art, class, sect, trade, or profession, full of technical terms;
  (ii) hybrid speech of different languages;
  (iii) the use of long words, circumlocution, and other clumsiness.'

Of these
  (i) is legitimate and necessary. A man must talk in the terms of his trade if he is talking about his trade. It is when he introduces his own technical vocabulary into ordinary conversation or writing that his jargon becomes reprehensible. The truth is we all have, according to our interests, a vocabulary of our own; and terms that are familiar and natural to us become jargon to another. Indeed, it may be said that the language owes some of its richest metaphors to 'class' jargon. Through language we are able to overstep, in some measure, the barriers that separate us in actual life. It is only in the excessive use of technical or particular language that we offend;
  (ii) is seen at its best, or worst, in (a) scholars who know so much of other languages that they have forgotten the possibilities of their own, and (b) people who know so little of other languages that they want to show off that little to the best advantage, by sprinkling their speech or writing with foreign tags and phrases;
  (iii), though by no means the monopoly of journalists, is roughly, if somewhat unjustly, defined in the term *journalese*. Writing in newspapers, which is intended to be human nature's daily food, must of necessity be both hurried and toothsome. Unfortunately the journalist in striving after effect nearly always achieves a pinchbeck smartness which outside the pages of a newspaper (and sometimes even inside them) becomes irritating and ridiculous. He is, indeed, the supreme example of the professional 'jargonist' noted under (i). Worst of all, the food he offers us has long ago become stale. His figures and idioms have, by constant use, developed into *clichés* or hackneyed phrases—'the happy pair' for 'the bride and bridegroom'; 'to be made the recipient of' for 'to be given'; 'to share two goals' for 'to draw' (in football). Any effort he may make to avoid such tarnished language results not in a return to directness and simplicity but too often in more absurd striving after the picturesque. One example will suffice. The Australians made a big score—that is the simple fact. A morning newspaper had it: 'The Australians brought the pitcher too often to the well of runs.' Other examples may be found in any newspaper, any morning or evening.

journalese. See JARGON.

judgement, judgment. The first is preferable. See under MUTE E.

jussive subjunctive. The subjunctive of command—i.e. the subjunctive used idiomatically as an imperative: '*Wind* we up the height.'

But the normal prose construction is *let*+accusative and infinitive. See LET.

just. *Just exactly* is tautological, since *just = exactly*.

kerb. See CURB.

kind. See SORT.

kindly requested. This is a foolish phrase, in which the writer attributes to himself the kindness he intends to attribute to the reader. 'You are kindly requested to close the door' can mean only that the request is kindly made by the person who made it; but he probably meant 'Will you be kind enough to close the door?'

knit. The past form *knit* is often (though not always) used of brows, and *knitted* is used of jumpers and socks.

l. (i) Final *l* preceded by a single vowel is usually doubled before a suffix beginning with a vowel: a notable exception is *(un)paralleled*. See DOUBLE CONSONANTS.

(ii) Words ending in *-ll* usually drop one *l* when they become part of a compound. Thus *fulfil, welcome, wilful, almost, altogether, skilful, until*. The principal exceptions are *farewell, freewill, wallflower, tallboy, landfall, fullness*, all true compounds. It is noteworthy that the dropping of *l* takes place only in true (not hyphenated) compounds. Thus in *fullblooded* and *well-documented*, *full* and *well* are definite adverbs modifying past participles, not actual parts of compound words. Note also *all right*.

Full as a suffix is always spelt *-ful* (*beautiful, handful*, &c.).

When *-ll* occurs before a suffix beginning with a vowel both *l*'s remain: *installed, spelling* (but *spelt*).

labials. See CONSONANTS.

last. See LATE.

late. *Late* has two comparatives and two superlatives, whose meaning and use are set out in the table below:

later	the normal comparative, meaning 'more late' in time; it is both adjective and adverb: 'a *later* performance'; 'I will see you *later*.'
latter	used in the phrase 'the latter' (of two things) = the second in the order of their original mentioning; it is, therefore, a pronominal substitute for the sake of avoiding repetition: 'Mr. Jones and Mr. Smith were the finalists; the latter won by one hole.' Where more than two persons or things are originally mentioned use *last*, not *latter*. *Latter* is also still used (though archaically) in the stereotyped locutions 'latter-day' and 'his latter end'. See FORMER.
latest	means 'last up to now only', whereas *last* means 'last of all', 'final'. Mr. X's *latest* poems are those hot from the press; if he dies before he can write any more they will be his *last*. Mr. A. E. Housman's title *Last Poems* was meant to express his intention of publishing no more.
last	See above under *latest*. It is noteworthy that *last* cannot be replaced by *latest* in idiomatic phrases like 'last Tuesday', 'last year', 'at the last minute'.

Latin abbreviations. A few of the most important Latin abbreviations used in English are given below:

Abbreviation	in full	English
e.g.	exempli gratia	for instance
i.e.	id est	that is (to say)
viz.	videlicet	namely
cf.	confer	compare
cp.	compara	compare
q.v.	quod vide	which see
ab in(it).	ab initio	from the beginning
ad fin.	ad finem	toward the end
ad lib.	ad libitum	at pleasure
A.D.	Anno Domini	in the year of our Lord
c(ap).	caput	head, chapter
cc.	capita	heads, chapters
D.V.	Deo volente	God willing
verb. sap.	verbum sapienti	a word to the wise man (is sufficient)
et seqq.	et sequent-es, -ia	and those persons (things) that follow
etc.	et cetera	and the rest
ob.	obiit	he (she) died
ib(id).	ibidem	in the same place
loc. cit.	loco citato	in the passage cited
nem. con.	nemine contradicente	no one opposing
o(p). c(it).	opere citato	in the work quoted
Q.E.D./F.	quod erat demonstran-dum/faciendum	which was to be proved/done
s.v.	sub voce	under the heading
v.l.	varia(e) lectio(nes)	variant reading(s)

latter. See LATE and FORMER.

laudable, laudatory. *Laudable,* passive, 'worthy to be praised'; *laudatory,* active, 'praising, giving praise': a *laudable* ambition, desire to get on; a *laudatory* speech, article.

lay, lie. (i) *Forms:*

Infin.	Pres. Simp. T.	Past Simp. T.	Present Part.	Past Part.
to lie	I lie	I lay	lying	lain
to lay	I lay	I laid	laying	laid

(ii) *Syntax.* It is very easy to confuse the two verbs, especially if their forms are not properly memorized. Briefly, *to lie* is a strong verb, having the characteristic vowel change in the past forms, and the *-n* participle; *to lay* is a weak verb, with the characteristic dental endings. *To lie* is intransitive, and *to lay* is a transitive 'causative' verb formed from it (OE. *licgan* = to lie; *lecgan* = to lay). See under CAUSATIVE VERBS.

lend, loan.

'Sir,—Among the misused words which need your protection surely *loan* should find a place. It used to be a substantive. Now even reputable persons are changing its nature and using it as a verb, deserting its lawful rival *to lend*. Yours faithfully, RELENT.'—From a letter to *The Times*.

'*loan*. The verb has been expelled from idiomatic southern English by *lend*, but was formerly current, and survives in U.S. and locally in U.K.' (MEU).

Moral:
(i) Verify your facts before you write to *The Times*.
(ii) In idiomatic Mod.E. say and write 'I *lent* him (not I *loaned* him) a book.'

lens. See SINGULAR-PLURAL NOUNS.

less. (i) *Less* as a comparative adjective is the opposite of *greater* and *more*, and is used of quantity and size, not of numbers (see FEW): 'There were *fewer* boys absent this week' but 'The percentage of absentees was *less*'; 'There was *less* reason to be afraid' but 'There were *fewer* causes for fear'.

As *fewer* is always used with a plural noun, so *less* is nearly always used with a singular. 'There were less boys in the form' would mean, if it could mean anything, 'There were smaller boys in the form.'

(ii) *Lesser* is a double comparative form, used as an attributive adjective: 'the lesser light' (i.e. the moon); 'the lesser (evil) of two evils'.

(iii) *More or less* is an adverbial phrase which by constant and careless use has lost nearly all its meaning. It is used literally and correctly in 'The crops will feel the effect of the drought more or less according to the quality of the soil'; it is used loosely and colloquially in 'He is more or less drunk'. The colloquial use is better kept out of writing. Note that *more or less* cannot be adjectival where *more* and *less* severally are not adjectival. Thus it is possible to say and to write, 'There will be more or less jam available according to the number present', but not 'The wood was in a more or less state of decay'.

lest. *Lest* is idiomatically followed by *should* or the subjunctive ('Lest we should forget' or 'Lest we forget'); never by *will* and *would*. Cf. IN ORDER THAT.

let (= permit) is followed by an object in the accusative and infinitive construction, e.g. I shall let *you remain* here. But the imperative is often used with the accusative and infinitive as a periphrasis for a jussive subjunctive in 1st and 3rd persons, e.g. 'Let us/him go at once', and this construction frequently causes an error in case on the part of the thoughtless or would-be genteel, as in

Let you and *I* share in this task.
Let *they* who raise the spell beware the Fiend.

See CASE.

letter-writing. The following points are worth noting in the writing of a letter:

(i) The letter should be headed with the address of the writer, and the date written immediately below the address.

(ii) The salutation comes first, on a line by itself. If the letter is a private one, the salutation consists of the conventional 'Dear' or 'My Dear' followed by the Christian name or surname of the person to whom the letter is addressed. The normal business letter, written, e.g., to the Secretary or Manager of a Company, the Editor of a newspaper, the chief of a Government Department, begins 'Dear Sir', or more formally 'Sir'. If the letter is not addressed to an individual, but to a number of persons forming a committee or company, the correct formal salutation is 'Gentlemen'. A lady, whether married or unmarried, is always formally addressed as 'Madam'. For the mode of addressing persons of title and rank refer to any good Year-Book or Diary.

(iii) The conventional ending is 'Yours . . .' followed by an adverb that varies according to the degree of familiarity between writer and addressee, from the 'affectionately' of relationship or intimate friendship to the 'faithfully' of business. If a present participle like 'Hoping' or 'Trusting' is used before the ending, care must be taken to insert the personal pronoun (*I*, *we*), for the participle phrase to qualify. 'Trusting you will be able to deal with the matter quickly, Yours faithfully' is incorrect in syntax; write 'I am (We are) yours faithfully'.

(iv) In a business letter, where the name of the person or persons addressed is not mentioned in the salutation, the name or title, with the address, should be written either at the top or at the bottom left-hand corner of the letter.

(v) In addressing the envelope, the courtesy title *Esquire* (normally contracted to *Esq.*) is written after the name when the initials are known. When *Esq.* is used, no other title can stand before the name. *Esq.* should never be used unless the Christian name or initials precede the surname. Letters denoting degrees, &c. follow the *Esq.*—'J. Smith, Esq., M.A.', not 'J. Smith, M.A., Esq.'.

The title *Reverend*, usually contracted to *Rev.*, should never be used with the surname only; use the initials if they are known (the Rev. J. Smith), but if they are not known, use *Mr.* with *the Rev.* (the Rev. Mr. Smith). See also REVEREND, REVERENT.

licence, license. The noun always ends in -*ce*; the verb may have *s* or *c*, but the modern tendency is to prefer *s* on the analogy of *practise* and *prophesy*. See PRACTICE, -SE.

lie. See LAY.

lifelong, livelong. *Lifelong* means 'during the whole length of life': 'a lifelong friendship'; 'a lifelong interest in politics'. *Livelong* was originally *lieflong* (< OE. *leof*, 'dear', 'precious', from the same root as *love*: we keep it in the phrase 'lief and dear'), and was a mere intensive form of *long*. The confusion in spelling with *live* did not occasion any change in meaning. We have the word mainly in the phrases 'the live-long day', 'the livelong night'. The confusion with *live* had already taken place in Milton's time:

> 'And young and old come forth to play
> On a Sunshine Holyday,
> Till the live-long daylight fail.'

lighted, lit. The two forms are not completely differentiated in Mod.E. *Lit* is the more usual for the past tense, and *lighted* for the past participle and participial adjective: 'I *lit* the candle'; 'I have *lighted* (or *lit*) the candle'; 'a *lighted* candle'.

lightning. The noun is *lightning*, without an *e*; *lightening* is the participle, gerund, &c. of the verb *to lighten*.

like. 1. *Like* is (*a*) an adjective—not a preposition (though it may be regarded as governing an accusative) and certainly not a conjunction. In the sentence 'He is like his father' *like* qualifies *he* (i.e. it is the predicate adjective). In OE. both *like* and *near* take the dative (just as in Latin *similis* takes either the genitive or the dative, and *proximus* takes the dative), and it is therefore best to regard 'father' as dative. But there is no objection to our regarding it as accusative governed by the adjective. Sentences such as 'I cannot work like you do', where *like* is acting as a conjunction, are grammatical solecisms. The conjunction corresponding to *like* is *as*. In archaic and poetical English 'like as' is used as a compound conjunction:

> 'Like as the waves make towards the pebbled shore,
> So do our minutes hasten to their end.'

(*b*) an adverb in such sentences as: 'She sang *like* a nightingale'; 'He drank *like* a fish'.

2. When *like* introduces an adjective phrase, special care must be taken to see that the phrase qualifies precisely the noun intended. Thus in the sentence 'Like Henry VIII, the reign of Elizabeth was a period of naval expansion', there is intended to be a comparison of one reign with another. As the sentence stands, *like* qualifies 'reign'; so that the 'reign' is actually likened to the King, Henry VIII—which is absurd. Amend therefore—'Like Henry VIII's (reign)', or, better, 'Like that of Henry VIII'. So in the following sentence 'Like the Efficient Baxter a few minutes before, sudden emotion had caused him to upset his cup', *like* qualifies 'emotion'—which again is absurd. Recast: 'Like the Efficient Baxter, he was overcome . . .'

See also SIMILAR.

liquids. See CONSONANTS.

loan. See LEND.

loose, loosen. The antonym of *loose* is *bind*; that of *loosen* is *tighten*.

Lord's (the cricket ground). So spelt, not *Lords'* or *Lords*. It was originally the meadow of one John Lord.

lots of. For number see HALF.

luxuriant, luxurious. Both adjectives are derived from the same source as the noun *luxury*; *luxuriant* is restricted to the expression of abundance or prodigality, and is an epithet applied particularly to leaves, flowers, foliage, hair. *Luxurious* is the adjective expressing human luxury or indulgence: *luxurious* tastes, food, ways of living—the opposite of *simple* or *economical*.

lyric. Literally a poem to be sung to the music of a lyre. The following quotations (*a*) from OED, (*b*) from Palgrave's Preface to the *Golden Treasury*, indicate the meaning and scope of the term in modern usage:

(*a*) Short poems (whether or not intended to be sung), usually divided into stanzas or strophes, and directly expressing the poet's own thoughts and sentiments.

(*b*) The Editor is acquainted with no strict and exhaustive definition of lyrical poetry. . . . Lyrical has here been held essentially to imply that each poem shall turn on some single thought, feeling, or situation.

madam. So spelt as a mode of addressing an English lady. As a prefix to a foreign lady's name *madame* is the spelling. *Madame* is sometimes used by English ladies professionally—especially in music. The plural of *madam* is *ladies*; of *madame* is *mesdames*.

majority. The word follows the ordinary rules for number given under COLLECTIVE NOUNS; but in the sense 'most', 'more than half', it usually has a plural verb: 'The majority *are* in favour...'; 'The majority of my friends *agree*.'

malapropism. In one of the most humorous of the articles in MEU Fowler speaks of Mrs. Malaprop (a character in Sheridan's *The Rivals*) as 'the matron saint of all those who go wordfowling with a blunder-buss'. She provides amusement in the play by confusing words that have an accidental likeness, as in the famous phrase 'a nice derangement of epitaphs', a malapropism for 'a nice arrangement of epithets'. Such word confusion was a familiar stage-trick in the days of Shakespeare and is so still. Dogberry with his 'most *senseless* and fit man for the constable of the watch', and 'to talk is most *tolerable* and not to be endured'; Bottom with his 'and there we may rehearse more *obscenely* and courageously'; and old Gobbo with 'that is the very *defect* of the matter, sir' are some of the exponents of the art. But the essence of malapropisms, whether those of the lady herself or (by an anachronism) those of Dogberry, Bottom, and Gobbo, is an exaggeration of ignorance that leads to the ridiculous. A list of words that may easily be confused in all seriousness and present real difficulties in speech and writing is given under the article WORD-CONFUSION.

manuscript. The contraction is: singular MS., plural MSS. Write 'a MS.', not 'an MS.'

many a. *Many a* is distributive in effect, and requires a singular verb: 'Many a man *is*' (not *are*). The temptation to give it a plural verb is likely to arise only in inversion with *there*, as in the sentence quoted in MEU: 'While there *have* been many a good-humoured smile...' (correct to '*has* been').

mathematics. Singular or plural in function? It depends on use: singular if used (*a*) as the ordinary scientific term, or (*b*) with a singular complement following: 'Mathematics includes the theory of mechanics'; 'Mathematics is his strong point'; plural if used with the transferred meaning of 'the ability to work with figures', when it is often qualified by a possessive adjective or by *the*, *such*, &c.: 'His mathematics are not good.' The same general ruling applies to other words in *-ics*: *acoustics*, *classics*, *dynamics*, *ethics*, *hysterics*, *physics*, *politics*, *tactics*.

matter. See NO MATTER WHO.

may. See CAN.

means. *Means* = 'income' takes a plural verb: 'My means are not equal to the demand upon them'.

Means (to an end) is singular when it is qualified by *a*; plural or singular when it is (*a*) unqualified, (*b*) qualified by *the*, (*c*) qualified by an ordinary adjective (without *a*):

> A means of overcoming the difficulty *is* likely to be found.
> Such a means *was*...; A secret means *was*...
> 'The means *do* (or *does*) not justify the end.'
> Such secret, effective means *are*...

measure. The idiom is *in great measure*, not *to a great measure*. The second is due to confusion with *to a great extent*.

measures. See NUMBERS.

mendacity, mendicity. *mendacity* (Lat. *mendax*, *-acis*, lying), the practice of, a tendency to, lying; *mendicity* and *mendicancy* (Lat. *mendicare*, to beg), the condition of being a beggar.

metaphor. 1. *Description.* 'Application of name or descriptive term to an object to which it is not literally applicable' (COD). The word comes to us through French from the Greek *meta-* in the sense of 'change', and *phero* 'I bear'. It means, therefore, a transfer of significance. Thus, to take a couple of familiar examples: A ship, in the literal sense, is a vessel that travels over the sea; a desert is a waste or 'sea' of sand; the camel crosses the desert as the ship crosses the sea; so the camel, by *metaphor* or transference of meaning, is called 'the ship of the desert'. When Shylock says to Portia

> 'I charge you by the law
> Whereof you are a well-deserving pillar',

he expresses in metaphor his idea of an upholder of the law; that is, he speaks of a person (Portia) as if she were blocks of stone or marble, and of the law as if it were a building. It will be noted from these two examples that the metaphor is, in effect, a vivid development of the simile. The simile says merely that one thing is *like* another; the metaphor that one thing *is* another.

Metaphor is so common a figure of speech that often we scarcely realize when we are using it. It may occur not only in nouns but also in verbs, adjectives, and adverbs. Many words have both a literal and a metaphorical meaning. Thus the word *light* is used in its literal sense in such phrases as 'by the light of the moon', 'the speed of light', and in its metaphorical sense in 'The manuscript throws new light upon the spelling of the medieval scribes'. In this sentence, too, the verb *throws* is used metaphorically. When we talk about 'a *biting* wind' the adjective is metaphorical; by metaphor, that is, the wind is endowed with teeth and the ability to use them. There are many metaphors in English that have become fixed or stereotyped. The following list, which is adapted from one contributed by entrants in an *Observer* competition, will both illustrate these common metaphorical usages and indicate the variety and scope of the metaphor generally. Every metaphorical phrase given is so familiar as to need no explanation:

> Burning the candle at both ends.
> Leaving no stone unturned.
> Taking the bull by the horns.
> Sowing wild oats.
> Hitting the nail on the head.
> Letting the cat out of the bag.
> Making hay while the sun shines.
> The last straw.
> Blowing your own trumpet.
> Bury the hatchet.
> Making both ends meet.
> Playing second fiddle.
> Get into hot water.
> Thin ice.

Food for thought.
Forging a link.
Sinews of war.
By leaps and bounds.
Split hairs.
Ghost of a chance.
Bee in one's bonnet.
Taking courage in both hands.
Long arm of coincidence.
Swallow an insult.

All these phrases are based on *metaphor* or 'transfer of significance'; and most of them have become *idioms* or peculiarities of language. For further treatment see IDIOM.

MEU makes an interesting distinction between 'live' and 'dead' metaphors. The words *sift* and *examine* are given as examples. *Sift* keeps some suggestion of its literal sense ('to pass through a sieve') in such a phrase as 'to sift the evidence'; but there is for English ears no suggestion of metaphor in 'to examine the evidence', although the word *examine* is originally from the Latin *examen*, the tongue of a balance, and means literally 'to weigh'. So in Mod.E. the word *talent* has lost all hint of metaphor; it was originally a weight of metal (gold, silver), and gets its modern metaphorical meaning from the Parable of the Talents (Matt. xxv. 14–30).

The use of metaphor as a figure for picturesque effect is sufficiently illustrated in the following examples:

(1) From the Preface to the AV:

'For whereas it was the expectation of many, who wished not well unto our *Sion*, that, upon the setting of that bright *Occidental Star*, Queen *Elizabeth*, of most happy memory, some thick and palpable clouds of darkness would so have overshadowed this land, that men should have been in doubt which way they were to walk and that it should hardly be known who was to direct the unsettled State; the appearance of Your Majesty, as of the *Sun* in his strength, instantly dispelled those supposed and surmised mists, and gave unto all that were well affected exceeding cause of comfort.'

(2) *Macbeth*, v. v. 19–28:

'To-morrow, and to-morrow, and to-morrow,
Creeps in this petty pace from day to day,
To the last syllable of recorded time;
And all our yesterdays have lighted fools
The way to dusty death. Out, out, brief candle!
Life's but a walking shadow, a poor player
That struts and frets his hour upon the stage,
And then is heard no more: it is a tale
Told by an idiot, full of sound and fury,
Signifying nothing.'

(3) A specimen of Burke's use of metaphor, from his *Letter to a Noble Lord*:

'The Duke of Bedford is the leviathan among all the creatures of the crown. He tumbles about his unwieldy bulk; he plays and frolicks in the ocean of the royal bounty. Huge as he is, and whilst "he lies floating many a rood", he is still a creature. His ribs, his fins, his whalebone, his blubber, the very spiracles through which he spouts a torrent of brine against his origin, and covers one all over with the spray,—everything of him and about him is from the throne. Is it for *him* to question the dispensation of the royal favour?'

2. *Faulty use of Metaphor.* Errors in the deliberate use of metaphor may be briefly classified as (*a*) not sustaining the metaphor—i.e. mingling the metaphorical and the literal; (*b*) overdoing metaphor—i.e. working it to death; (*c*) mixing metaphors—i.e. introducing two distinct and often incongruous images into the working out of one figure.

Examples:

(*a*) (i) 'The means of education at the disposal of the Protestants and Presbyterians of the North were stunted and sterilized' (MEU). (The subject *means* is literal, the verbs *stunted* and *sterilized* are metaphorical.)

(ii) 'It is like a house that has not been built of brick laid on well laid brick, but put together of large slabs of material, and one can see that while Miss Evans was writing one of these slabs, nothing else counted for her.' (The writer manfully tried to sustain the brick-and-slab metaphor, but was betrayed into the ludicrous mixture of literal and metaphorical 'write a slab'.)

(iii) 'The torrent of marching feet' (a phrase once used by Mr. Ramsay MacDonald).

(*b*) 'Then the long arm of coincidence rolled up its sleeves and set to work with a rapidity and vigour which defy description' (MEU). (An extreme example of what in these days is a rare fault, since our use of metaphor is far more often unconscious than deliberate. As MEU hints, metaphor is generally overdone nowadays only for humorous effect.)

(*c*) (i) 'I will now embark upon the feature on which this question hinges'.

(ii) 'The scourge of tyranny had breathed his last'.

(iii)   'Was the hope drunk
Wherein you dress'd yourself? Hath it slept since?
And wakes it now?'

See also PERSONIFICATION.

metathesis. *Metathesis* is the changing of places by two sounds in a word. Thus in *ask* the *k* sound and the *s* sound have changed places, the OE. form being *acsian*—which survives in the provincial *ax*, *aks* for *ask*. But *r* is the letter most given to the trick. Chaucer wrote 'with lokkes *crulle*', where we say '*curled*' or '*curly*'. '*Burn*' and '*brand*' are of the same derivation (OE. '*brinnan*'); '*three*', '*third*' and '*thrice*'; '*work*' and '*wrought*'.

The fact that the OE. for *third* was *thridda* is reflected in the word *Riding* (of Yorkshire). *Thriding* (= the third [part]) lost its *th* 'owing to preceding -t(h) of *east*, &c.' (COD).

-meter (Greek = measure), another form of 'metre'. It is the unit of metrical measure that is repeated a number of times (expressed by the Greek numerals) in a line of verse. Thus *monometer*, *dimeter*, *trimeter*, *tetrameter*, *pentameter*, *hexameter* are one-, two-, three-, four-, five-, six-measure lines respectively. This measure is called a *foot*—a group of long and short syllables (in the classical languages), or of accented and unaccented syllables (in English). Thus Greek and Latin verse is a matter of vowel quantity, English verse of accent or stress. See also METRE.

methinks. See IMPERSONAL VERBS.

meticulous. *Meticulous* is a vogue-word of the journalist against which MEU thunders with precept and example for nearly three columns. The present use of the word (= *careful, scrupulous, punctilious*) is copied from

French usage, which has little relation to the Latin origin, *metus* = 'fear'. It is true that the synonyms already quoted should be enough for our purpose, and that if *meticulous* is used at all it should, out of respect to its etymology, be restricted to the meaning 'admitting no error' out of fear of the consequences. But the word, after all, has its uses and may be allowed a little rope. The careful man, the scrupulous man, and the punctilious man go so far and no farther; but the meticulous man adds (out of fear) the red ink, places the dot exactly over the *i*, crosses the last *t*—all little things which the others may ignore or forget. It is worth while noticing that in the OED definition, 'over-careful about minute details, over-scrupulous', *over* is plainly the most important element.

metonymy (Greek = change of name), the figure in which the name of an attribute is used for that of the thing meant, e.g. 'crown' (for king), 'Shakespeare' (for his plays), 'city' (for its inhabitants), 'kettle' (for the water in it). Cf. SYNECDOCHE.

metre. Metre is the 'measure' of the lines of verse, and in English is associated with, and dependent on, RHYTHM. Thus, in the following stanza:

> Fár from the mádding crówd's ignóble strífe
> Their sóber wíshes néver leaŕn'd to stráy;
> Alóng the cóol, sequéster'd vále of lífe
> They képt the noíseless ténor óf their wáy,

the full stress falls regularly on every other syllable, with an exception in the first line, where the stress is thrown back from the syllable *from* to *far*. In each line there are ten syllables: that is the simplest way of measuring—without reference, that is, to rhythm. As far as the rhythm is concerned, the lines may be divided into pairs of syllables, of which one is unstressed and the other is stressed. Each of these pairs is called a *foot*, and the lines may be divided thus:

> Fár from | the mád|ding crówd's | ignó|ble strífe
> Their só|ber wísh|es név|er leaŕn'd | to stráy;
> Alóng | the cóol | sequés|ter'd vále | of lífe
> They képt | the noíse|less tén|or óf | their wáy.

So, measured according to rhythm, the line has five feet, each foot consisting of two syllables of which the second is accented. The first foot of the first line is 'inverted'; i.e. the first syllable is stressed instead of the second. In technical terms, therefore, the metre of the stanza quoted may be stated thus:

(*a*) decasyllabic, i.e. 'having ten syllables' (without reference to rhythm);
(*b*) iambic pentameter (a 'five measure' of iambs).
See also FOOT and -METER.

middle. See CENTRE.

mileage. So spelt. See MUTE E.

minimize. See DIMINISH.

mixed metaphor. See METAPHOR.

mock-heroic. When a trivial incident is treated with mock gravity and invested with all the conventional machinery of the epic, we have a mock-heroic poem, a mock epic. Such is Pope's *Rape of the Lock*. The subject of the poem (which is in four cantos) is the cutting off a lock of a lady's hair. Her anger is appeased when the lock is finally wafted, as a new star, to adorn the skies. Pope republished the poem in an expanded form in which he introduced the machinery of sylphs and gnomes, and the result was renewed offence to the lady. Such too is Gray's *Ode on the Death of a Favourite Cat* (in forty-two lines), in which he proposes 'to immortalize Madame Selima for a week or fortnight'.

mood. 'Any one of the groups of forms in the conjugation of a verb which serve to indicate the function in which the verb is used; i.e. whether it expresses a predication, a command, a wish, or the like' (SOED). See under IMPERATIVE, INDICATIVE, INFINITIVE, SUBJUNCTIVE (MOOD).

moral, morale. The first (móral) is the adjective, meaning 'connected with manners, conduct, &c.', 'of (good) conduct'; the second (pronounced moráhl) is the noun, popularized during the Great War, standing for *condition, tone, general conduct*, usually in the phrase '*morale* of the troops'. The distinction in spelling between the two words is artificial, but useful, and should be retained. The recent practice of spelling the noun without *e* (after the French original) is pedantic and may be misleading, since in some contexts it may make it uncertain which word is meant.

more. (*a*) 'More than one' is considered singular: 'More than one of us *is*'; 'More than one man *was* killed'.
  (*b*) *More or less*: see LESS (iii).

motive. The construction is with *for* (+gerund, noun, or pronoun), not *in*.

mow. The participial adjective is *mown* ('new-*mown* grass', &c.), the past participle is either *mown* or *mowed*: 'The field has been newly *mown* (or *mowed*).'

multiple. For multiple sentence see SENTENCE, and for multiple subject see AGREEMENT.

mutation. See I-MUTATION.

mute e. Mute *e* at the end of words is
  (i) kept before a suffix beginning with a consonant,
  (ii) dropped before a suffix beginning with a vowel, except where it is deliberately retained to keep preceding *c* or *g* soft.
  The chief exceptions under (i) are *truly, duly, wholly*, and *ninth*; and a few words, notably *judgement, acknowledgement, fledgeling, abridgement*, are often spelt without the *e*, but the OED prefers the spelling with *e*. Examples of words in which *e* is retained under (ii) are *peaceable, advantageous, changeable, noticeable*, in which *c* and *g* would have become hard before the following *a, o*; and *singeing* where the *e* is specially retained to distinguish *singeing* (soft *g*) from *singing* (hard nasal *-ng*). *Hieing* is so spelt to avoid the double *i* in *hiing*, and *mileage* to prevent the possible pronunciation 'millage'.

mutes. See CONSONANTS.

mutual, common, reciprocal. The difference between the three words may best and most briefly be represented in diagrams:

(a) *mutual*

A⇄B

A does or is to B as B does or is to A.

Mutual is a 'give-and-take' word. The SOED gives as example: 'Mutual fear [i.e. A's fear of B and B's fear of A] is the only basis for alliance.'

(b) *common*

Common introduces a third element:

C is *common* to A and B; *common* does not necessarily suggest *mutual* relationship of A and B. In Dickens's book *Our Mutual Friend*, the friend is common to two other characters. The title has (as MEU suggests) done much to encourage the misuse of *mutual*. Here are two sentences both from broadcast talks that will clearly illustrate the error:

And they would have found further common ground in their *mutual* dislike of war and slavery, which both of them actively combated.

What the two men had in common besides their *mutual* lack of looks was a great personal courage.

Their dislike was common to them both; it was not a *mutual* dislike, i.e. a dislike of each other.

Similarly, their lack of looks was, on the showing of the sentence itself, *common*; it could not be *mutual*.

(c) *reciprocal*

A⇠⇢B

Reciprocal may be used exactly as *mutual*; it is, indeed, given as a synonym for it in COD. But it may be used as *mutual* may not be used— to indicate the state or action of only one of the parties concerned in its relation to the other. Thus A having rendered B some service B may render reciprocal (but not *mutual*) service. In other words, *mutual* must always be associated with two nouns or a plural pronoun; *reciprocal* may be used with a singular. The following examples are from SOED:

(i) 'Kindness is generally *reciprocal*.'
(ii) 'He had a right to expect from them a *reciprocal* demonstration of firmness.'

naive. This word, useful for expressing the shades of meaning that lie between such words as *artless* and *spontaneous*, *simple* and *innocent*, has not yet put off its French dress, in either spelling or pronunciation. The borrowings from French are *naïve*, *naïveté*; the desirable anglicized forms are *naive* (one syllable) and *naivety* (two syllables); the French masculine form *naïf* is undesirable in any English context.

nasals. See CONSONANTS.

nature. Such expressions as 'in the nature of', 'through the (adjective) nature of', 'of a (adjective) nature' are examples of woolly and unnecessary PERIPHRASIS, and are better avoided. If soil is 'of a chalky nature', it is, in brief, chalky soil; an accident is better attributed to the greasiness

of the road, than to the greasy nature of the road. The direct and concrete expression is always preferable to the indirect.

naught, nought. *Nought* for the cipher (o); *naught* in all other uses—
e.g. 'set at, come to, bring to *naught*'.

near. For construction with accusative (or dative) see LIKE.

near by, not *nearby*. See IRREGULAR UNIONS.

need. *Need* is an abnormal form of the verb used for all persons and both
numbers in the present and past tenses in interrogative and negative
sentences: 'Need I go?', 'He need not go.' The two examples illustrate
the fact that *need* is followed by the infinitive without *to*. *Needs, needed,
did need*, the normal forms, are, however, always followed by the full
infinitive: 'He needs to work harder'; 'They needed to be helped over
every little difficulty.'

neither ... nor. For general principles governing their use see CORRELA-
TIVES and EITHER ... OR.

neuter plurals. A few nouns that belonged to the OE. neuter declension
and had no inflexion in their nominative or accusative plural forms have
retained an uninflected plural in Mod.E. The commonest examples are:
deer, sheep, swine.

never. (i) *Never* for *not*, except where there is occasion for definite
adverbial modification for time, is a SOLECISM. 'I never did it' = 'I did
not do it' cannot stand; but 'I never saw him during my stay in London'
is correct and idiomatic if *never* is intended to have its true significance,
'not ever', 'not once'.
  (ii) *Never so* ... MEU says that the conditional idiom in 'Charm he
never so wisely' has bowed in Mod.E. from 'a notion of logical propriety' to the positive *ever so*. The logical propriety is a fallacy, but there
is no going back now to *never so*, except perhaps in verse, be it ever so
great a temptation to revert to the old for sentimental and even logical
reasons.

news. Singular in Mod.E.

nice. *Nice* has a peculiarly varied and troublous history. SOED gives its
meanings under fourteen different headings, which may be briefly
summarized thus:
  (*a*) The etymological meaning ('foolish', 'soft' < Latin *nescius*) is
     archaic, and is not found in Mod.E. even as an archaism.
  (*b*) The general sense of 'precise', 'delicate', 'minute', dates in its
     various applications and usages from the sixteenth century. This is
     the sense that survives in such Mod.E. phrases as 'a nice point', 'a
     nice distinction', 'a nice problem', and (slightly archaic) 'a nice
     (= careful) observer'.
  (*c*) The popular Mod.E. use of *nice* as a kind of maid-of-all-work
     among adjectives for 'pleasant' or 'affable' is marked colloquial in
     SOED. 'To look nice' dates from 1793; *nice* = 'agreeable' from 1830;
     and 'not nice' = 'not refined' from 1869. SOED gives a quotation
     from Jane Austen: 'The nice long letter which I have received
     from you.' The worst that can be said for *nice* in this usage is that

it is nearly always vapid and therefore to be avoided in serious writing; and the best that it is a convenient stand-by, though a great encourager of laziness, in conversation. It is difficult to imagine what we should do without *nice* in, for example, our comments on the weather; but when we go back a little and find, for example, Gilbert White speaking not tamely of a *nice* but lyrically of a *sweet* day, or Shakespeare and Milton with their vast range of adjectives for wind and weather, we begin to realize what we have lost in sacrificing our birthright in epithets for the paltry gift of so insignificant a word.

no matter who. The case of the pronoun needs care. It is easy, however, to make a test by opening out the ellipsis: *Who* did it does not matter— It does not matter *who* did it—No matter *who* did it; *Whom* it was written by does not matter—It does not matter *whom* it was written by—No matter *whom* it was written by.

nominative case. The nominative case is (*a*) the case of the subject; (*b*) in general the case of the complement in a simple sentence—see COMPLEMENT and GENITIVE CASE.

The chief idiomatic use of the nominative is in the absolute phrase (*nominative absolute*), a construction imitated from the Latin ablative absolute. In Latin a noun and a participle qualifying it, both in the ablative, make an adverb phrase of e.g. time, reason. Thus: 'Urbe capta Caesar Romam profectus est'; which literally translated is

> *The city taken,* Caesar set out for Rome.

The phrase italicized in the English sentence is a nominative absolute phrase, the noun *city* and the participle qualifying it, *taken,* being considered as nominative. The phrase is called 'absolute' (< Lat. *absolvere* 'to untie', 'to unloose') because grammatically it is free or 'unloosed' from the rest of the sentence—i.e. the participle does not qualify a noun outside its own phrase. Here are two examples, a simple one from one of R. L. Stevenson's essays, and a more difficult one from Shakespeare:

(i) '*Cities given,* the problem was to light them.'
(ii) 'For once upon a raw and gusty day,
   The troubled Tiber chafing with her shores,
   Caesar said to me . . .'

For Nominative in Apposition see APPOSITION.

none. Since *none* = 'not one' logical grammar would fix it as a singular, but idiom and OED often treat it as a plural. Where there is hesitation between singular and plural, it is wise to bring into operation the law of euphony, as explained under COLLECTIVE NOUNS.

nor.

1.   (*a*) 'He slumbers not, *nor* sleeps.'
            (*b*) He does not slumber *or* sleep.
            (*c*) He neither slumbers *nor* sleeps.
            (*d*) He does not slumber *nor* does he sleep.
            (*e*) He has no slumber, *nor* has he sleep.

Why *or* in (*b*) and *nor* in (*a*) and (*d*)? The point is that in (*b*) the *not* stands with the auxiliary outside the brackets—to speak in algebraic terms—and makes negative both the verbs inside the brackets: 'He does not (slumber or sleep)'. But in (*a*) and (*d*) the negatives go separately with the verbs. In (*a*) the verbs are simple: *slumber, sleep*; in (*d*) they are compound: *does slumber, does sleep*. Sentence (*b*) is simply sentence (*d*) with the auxiliary *does* used once instead of twice, and taking with it the negative, which itself then needs to be used only once. In sentence (*e*) the first negative is not with the verb at all but in the adjective *no* qualifying *slumber*; the negative (*nor*) is therefore necessary with the verb of the second clause. A more subtle example of this type of sentence is quoted from MEU: 'It is with no unfriendly intention to Germany *or* with any desire to question her right or her need to possess a powerful Navy.' The negative adjective *no* qualifying *intention* cannot exert its influence on *with any desire*; yet it is plain from the sense that a negative is as necessary there as it is with *intention*. Correct therefore to *nor*. But *or* could be kept if the negative is put with the verb, and both verb and negative taken (as it were) out of the brackets: 'It is not with (any unfriendly intention *or* any desire).' In sentence construction, as in algebra, a negative outside the brackets will make negative the plus sign within. A little simple bracketing is always worth while with *nor* and *neither . . . nor*.

2. *Nor* used simply without *neither* is apt to tempt the writer into a kind of double negative. The following sentences illustrate the error:

(i) A poem is not a sermon *nor* a political speech.
(ii) These feelings were not due merely to his living in Ireland *nor* to the particular mood of frustration in which this sonnet was written.

In neither sentence are the correlatives used; but in each the negative is stated, once for all, in the first clause. The following *nor*, therefore, is an additional and superfluous negative, and should be replaced by *or*. In RCR a sentence from the preface to *Lorna Doone* is quoted: 'The writer neither dares nor desires to claim for it the dignity *or* cumber it with the difficulty of an historical novel', with the interesting comment: 'The printer's reader inserted a letter *n* before the *or*; the author deleted the *n*, and thought he had got rid of it; but at the last moment the press reader inserted it again; and the word was printed as *nor*, to the exasperation of the author, who did not mince his words when he found out what had happened.'

notable, noticeable, notorious. *Notorious* means 'well known' (in a bad sense): a *notorious* criminal, district, book. The following comment, taken from a newspaper, will illustrate the difference between *notable* and *noticeable*: 'Scotland Yard should use better English. Mr. X. of Brighton was described in the official notice as having a "notable" scar on the upper lip. One difference between Mr. X. and Nelson is that Nelson's scars were *notable* without being *noticeable*, while those of Mr. X. are *noticeable* without being *notable*.'

notional verb. A notional verb is a verb of 'full' meaning, in contrast with an auxiliary; but it is important to notice that a verb which is normally an auxiliary may sometimes be used as a notional verb. Thus the verb *to be* is notional in 'Rachel weeping for her children because they *are* not'; 'That which *is*, *is*'; *to have* is notional in 'Silver and gold *have* I none'; 'I *have* a song to sing'; *shall* is notional in 'Thou *shalt* not steal' (i.e. it is

not the ordinary auxiliary of the future, but has its original meaning *must*).
See also SHALL AND WILL.

not only . . . but also. These are particularly troublesome correlatives,
chiefly because even more than others they tempt the writer into breaking the fundamental rule that each of the two correlatives must be
followed by the same kind of item in the two members of the pair
joined together (see CORRELATIVES).

Thus 'He wrote *not only* to the secretary *but also* to the president' is
correct, since each of the correlatives is followed by an adverb phrase
(preposition + noun); but 'He *not only* wrote to the secretary *but also* to
the president' is incorrect, since if the first of the correlatives is followed
by a finite verb, the second must also be followed by a finite verb. The
following two sentences illustrate the error:

I wish I could do justice to its detail and its intimacy *not only* with Dorothy's
personality *but also* the environment of hills, lakes, poetry and people in which
she spent her eighty years and wove for herself a garment of immortality.
(Correct to: 'but also with *the environment* . . .')

I have lost not only my customers, but Miss Rachel herself is gone also.

[For 'I have lost not only my customers but also Miss Rachel'. The writer has
confused the correlative construction (*not only* . . . *but also*) with the simple
construction using *and*: 'I have lost my customers, and Miss Rachel has gone
also'. It is noteworthy that the sentences do not mean exactly the same thing;
but a mixture of the two constructions makes matters worse, not better.]

noun clause. The noun clause does exactly the same work in the sentence
as the noun itself. In the following table are set out some representative
examples:

Whatever he does is a reward in itself.	Subject of sentence.
What is certain is, *that a signal change is coming over us* and *that already it has made great progress*.	Of the three noun clauses in this sentence the first is subject and the second and third complements after *is*.
Believe me, it is not necessary to a man's respectability *that he should commit a murder*.	Real subject of the sentence in apposition to the anticipatory subject *it*.
You all do know *that on the Lupercal I thrice presented him a kingly crown*.	Object of the verb *do know*: indirect statement.
I asked him *when he was leaving his present position*.	Object of the verb *asked*: indirect question.
But, remembering *that this was the man* whom Ronnie had described as being wrapped up in one of these animals, she smiled her bright smile.	Object of a participle in an adjective phrase.
Our sense, then, for *what is poetry* and *what is not*, the attractiveness of the French plays and players must not make us unlearn.	Objects of the preposition *for*.

noun equivalent. The possible equivalents of a noun in the sentence are:

(*a*) Pronouns (all types).

(*b*) Any part of speech that is for the time being used as a noun. The
adjective is by far the commonest, but other parts of speech may

become substantival—e.g. adverb or conjunction: 'the *ups* and *downs* of life'; 'If *ifs* and *ans* were pots and pans . . .', 'But me no *buts.*'

(c) Infinite parts of the verb:
   (i) the infinitive
   (ii) the gerund.

(d) Noun phrases.

(e) Noun clauses.

nouns as adjectives.

'Amongst the words that have become lost from the language some are adjectives. And when these are lost, nouns have to take their place. An example of a lost adjective is the word *hostile*. I don't believe that in the dispatches of any English leader in the field, up to and including the time of Lord Roberts, the word *enemy* has ever been used as an adjective. But now it always is, simply because of the loss of the proper adjective. Very recently I read in an important daily paper "the centre line of the eclipse". One would hardly think that the word *central* was one of our lost adjectives. Yet, if it is not lost, why use the noun to do its work? The adjective *Roman* is long since lost, for you always read of "our Rome Correspondent"; and the words *Kentish* and *Turkish*; but now the very word *English* is just beginning to go the same way, for one reads of "the England XI". The Australians were always allowed their adjective up to last year, when a few papers began to speak of "the Australia XI", as though the adjective were dead, or rather moribund, so that the noun could do its work better. For further instances one need only look at the papers to see nouns every day driving adjectives on to the dole.'

The quotation is from an essay by Lord Dunsany called 'England Language Conditions!' But, after all, what is all the fuss about? The right to use a noun as an adjective is one of the most useful and jealously guarded rights in the language. Most of Lord Dunsany's argument is fallacious. The adjective *hostile* has not disappeared from the language: it is still alive. But by a process of differentiation in meanings (always a good sign in language) the noun takes its place in certain contexts—notably, as Lord Dunsany hints, in military dispatches—instead of the adjective. Thus in Mod.E. 'the hostile objective', 'the hostile lines' would be unidiomatic. The word *enemy* has simply taken over part of the work of *hostile*; and, on the whole, does it clearly and well. The sentence about *Roman, Kentish,* and *English* is so manifestly absurd as to need little comment. But obviously our Rome correspondent need not and probably will not be *Roman*; the Kent County Council and the Kent cricket team are not necessarily *Kentish*, although a lane in Kent is a Kentish lane; and the *England* eleven (which often includes Jams and Nawabs) is not always an *English* eleven. A *Times* leader repeats the same muddled and vain objection to what is a legitimate and indeed desirable usage: 'We read again and again of the "England team" instead of the "English team".' It may be that sometimes there is a wanton and unnecessary use of the noun for an adjective. But in one at any rate of the sentences and phrases quoted the use is good, as pointing a necessary distinction, not bad, as abolishing without reason an established idiom. Whenever a noun may be conveniently used as an adjective, without ambiguity or distortion of meaning, the use is expedient. This book, for example, often uses the phrase 'dictionary definition' for 'definition (as) in/of a dictionary'; this very article mentions 'a *Times* leader' for 'a leader in/from *The Times*'; and the nouns *adjective, adverb, noun* are used to qualify *clause* and *phrase* (chiefly because there is no satisfactory adjective form corresponding with *noun*). If the usage complained of by Lord Dunsany and *The Times* makes (as it does) for clearness and preciseness, why condemn it and obstruct its progress? To reduce the whole matter to absurdity are we, because there happens to be an adjective *Oxonian*, to talk and write about the *Oxonian Dictionary*?

noun plurals. The various ways of forming the plural of English nouns are set out in the following table. Further treatment may be found under the headings indicated in the last column.

Rule	Note	See under
A. General Rule: add *s* to the singular form.	This is the rule for the vast majority of English nouns. There are certain spelling adjustments in nouns ending in (*a*) consonant + *y* (*b*) *f, fe* (*c*) a sibilant (*d*) *o*.	 (*a*) Y > I. (*b*) F AND V. (*c*) CONSONANTS. (*d*) -OS, -OES.
B. A few nouns keep plural forms that belonged to certain OE. declensions: (*a*) Plural formed by change of vowel. (*b*) Plural in *-n, -en*. (*c*) Plural as singular.	 *man—men; foot—feet;* &c. A survival of the OE. 'weak' plural in *-an*. A survival of the OE. neuter declension.	 I-MUTATION. -EN PLURALS. NEUTER PLURALS.
C. Some nouns borrowed from other languages retain their original plural form.	 A few keep their native plural and also have a normal English plural in *s*.	FOREIGN PLURALS. DOUBLE PLURALS.

number. See AGREEMENT.

numbers in writing. The convention is—in ordinary descriptive style write in words (*a*) numbers up to and including 100, especially when they are used adjectivally: 'the seven dwarfs'; 'twenty years old'; 'fifteen pounds'; 'page ten'; (*b*) ordinal numbers: 'the nineteenth century'; 'the second time'. Except in formal or technical language the symbols £, s. d. should be avoided; if, however, they are used, figures, not words, should stand with them: £6, not six £. The number of the year should always be written in figures: 'The Great War, 1914–1918'. Dates should have figures for the day, either cardinal or ordinal: 29 April 1933, or 29th April 1933. The names of Kings, Popes, and Emperors have Roman numerals: Henry V; George IV; Leo X; Wilhelm IV; or they may be written thus: Henry the Fifth; George the Fourth; &c. (with a capital letter for the number). References to passages in the books of the Bible may be written on the following model: ii/2 Corinthians ix. 27, where the Roman or Arabic numeral before the title stands for the number of the 'book' or epistle, the Roman numeral after the title for the chapter, and the Arabic numeral for the verse. So with references to plays: *I Henry IV/Henry the Fourth*, III. ii. 134 = the first part of *Henry IV*, Act 3, Scene 2, line 134. The number of the chapters in a book is usually indicated by a Roman numeral ('Chapter IV'); the number of the pages by an Arabic numeral ('page 10'), though a separate numbering with Roman numerals is often used for introductory matter such as a preface. Roman numerals are never used with the ordinal suffix: *iind*, *vith*.

The above are guiding rules and representative examples. As an additional hint the following extract from RCR will be found interesting and useful:

'Spell out in such instances as—"With God a thousand years are but as one day"; "I have said so a hundred times".'

'Insert commas with four or more than four figures, as 7,642; but print dates without commas, as 1934; nor should there be commas in figures denoting pagination, or numbering of verse, or in mathematical workings, even though there may be more than three figures.'

numbers, weights, and measures.

There is a number of nouns signifying number, weight, and measure which, though having a plural form, prefer the singular in certain uses where the meaning is plural.

We talk of a *five-pound note*, a *six-room house*, a *seven-course dinner*.

But we say *women spies*, because 'woman' retains its noun status with 'spy', cf. *men-servants*.

Why then *lady doctors*? probably euphony. Where the plural of the first word is formed by adding -s or -es it sounds better to keep this word in the singular in forming the plural of the compound.

The following list of phrases will illustrate the current idiom, and form a basis for some generalization:

two dozen eggs; dozens of people; three score years and ten; scores of mistakes; six ton of coal; tons of money; a two-ton lorry; a two-pound weight; pounds upon pounds of sugar; three foot long; a two-foot rule; answer in feet, not yards; the Five Mile Act; miles of water; two years old; a two-year-old.

In general the singular form is used if the noun is qualified by an actual numeral, especially if it joins with that numeral to make a compound adjective (as in 'two-ton lorry'). The modern tendency is to prefer the plural form in all uses except the compound adjective construction: 'He is twenty years old', but 'a twenty-year-old quarrel'. Other words affected are: *pair, hundredweight* and other units of weight, *yard* and other units of lineal measure, *gallon* and other units of capacity, *hour* and other units of time.

numerical prefixes.

The English numerals are never used as prefixes, although they sometimes make an element in compound words, e.g. *one-sided, one-handed*, 'the *two-eyed* stance'. In the following table are set out the main Latin and Greek numerical combining forms. It must be remembered that many of the words compounded with them came to us through French. There are, too, many hybrids—e.g. a Latin prefix with a Greek root or a Greek prefix with a Latin root.

Latin: *unus* (*uni-*)	one	un-animous; uni-form; uni-corn; uni-versity.
Greek: *monos* (*mono-*)	single, alone	mono-tonous (<tone); mon-ocle; mono-rail.
Lat. Gk.: *duo*	two	duo-logue.
Greek: *deuteros*	second	deutero-nomy. *(Deuteronomy* was the second book of the law.)
Latin: *bis, bi-* } Greek: *dis* (*di-*) }	twice	bis-cuit; bi-cycle; bi-ped. di-meter.
Latin and Greek prefix *tri-*	three	tri-angle; tri-pod; tri-meter; tre-foil.
Latin prefix *quadr-* }	four	quadr-ennial; quadru-ped.
Greek prefix *tetra-* }	four	tetra-syllable; tetra-meter.
Latin: *quinque* }	five	quinqu-ennial, quinque-reme.
Greek: *pente* (*penta-*) }	five	penta-meter; penta-gon; Penta-teuch.
Latin. *sex* (*sexi-*) }	six	sex-centenary; sexi-syllabic.
Greek: *hex* (*hexa-*) }	six	hexa-meter; hexa-gon.
Latin: *septem* }	seven	September.
Greek: *hepta* }	seven	hepta-gon; hept-archy.
Latin: *octo-* } Greek: *okto-* }	eight	octo-pus; octo-syllabic.
Latin: *novem* } Greek: *ennea* }	nine	{ Novem-ber. { ennea-gon.
Latin: *decem* } Greek: *deka* }	ten	{ Decem-ber, dec-ennial. { deca-logue, deca-metre.
Latin: *centum* (centi-) } Greek: *hekaton* (hecto-) }	hundred	{ centi-grade, centi-pede, cent-ury, { cent-enary. { hecto-graph, hecto-gram(me), hecto- { litre.
Latin: *mille* } Greek: *khilioi* (modern prefix *kilo-*) }	thousand	{ mile, mill-ennium, milli-metre, mill- { ion (= big thousand). { kilo-cycle, kilo-watt, kilo-gram.
Greek: *murioi*	ten thousand, vast number	myria-pod, myri-arch, myri-acanthous, myria-gramme.

O, Oh. *O* is the spelling when no mark of punctuation follows; i.e., principally, when it is used with a noun in the vocative or with a word, phrase, or clause that with it makes a unit of exclamation:

> 'O wind,
> If winter comes, can spring be far behind?'
> 'O dear! what can the matter be?'
> 'O that we were there!'

Oh is used independently; i.e. it is always followed by a stop (comma or exclamation mark):

> Oh! what would come of it?
> Oh, so you have come after all.

object. See ACCUSATIVE CASE.

objective genitive. See GENITIVE CASE.

oblivious. Oblivious *of*, not *to*.

obstacle. Obstacle *to* (progress, agreement, &c.), not *of*.

octet. See SONNET.

ode. The word *ode* is simply the Greek for 'song'. Any kind of poem written to be sung to the accompaniment of music was called by the Greeks an ode. To-day the term is used of a rhymed (rarely unrhymed) lyric, often in the form of an address, e.g. to a Nightingale, to Liberty. It is usually of exalted style and enthusiastic tone, often in varied or irregular metre, and generally 50–200 lines in length.

In Greek poetry there were two forms of the ode:

(i) The *personal*, which consisted of a number of uniform stanzas with an elaborate metrical system. Such were the odes of Sappho and Anacreon. This was the form imitated by the Roman poet Horace (cf. Marvell's *Horatian Ode*).

(ii) The *choric* ode, divided into strophe, antistrophe, and epode. This form is called Pindaric, because of its use by Pindar, the greatest of the lyric poets of Greece (died 443 B.C.). Pindar's normal ode was divided into a number of sets of three stanzas, called strophe (= 'turn', i.e. the song sung by the choir while dancing towards one side of the orchestra), antistrophe (i.e. 'counter-turn', the song sung while the choir danced to the other side of the orchestra), and epode (= 'after-song', the song sung by the united choir in the centre of the stage). These sets were identical in metrical structure, but not limited in number. Thomas Gray (1716–71) wrote two Pindaric Odes—*The Progress of Poesy* and *The Bard*. After Gray's time, the form fell into disuse, and the ode has become a succession of regular stanzas (e.g. Keats's *Ode on a Grecian Urn*, Shelley's *Ode to the West Wind*); or of irregular stanzas (e.g. Wordsworth's ode *Intimations of Immortality*, Tennyson's *Ode on the Death of the Duke of Wellington*).

of. (*a*) See GENITIVE CASE.

(*b*) Difficulties with *of*. The examples below are taken from the article on *of* in MEU; and the errors illustrated in them are explained:

(i) 'The Ministry aims not merely *at* an equitable division *of* existing stocks, but *of* building up reserves against the lean months.'
[The Ministry aims *at* what?—(*a*) an equitable division of existing stocks, (*b*) building up reserves. The second *of* should, therefore, clearly be *at*; it owes its presence here to the writer's carelessly carrying over the *of* from the previous noun, without any inquiry into its appropriateness.]

(ii) 'It could be done without unduly raising the price *of* coal, or *of* jeopardizing new trade.'
[Faulty bracketing again. The sentence, reduced to its lowest terms, says '*without* (raising or jeopardizing)'. Why, therefore, the second *of*?]

(iii) 'Lord Parmoor referred to the progress which had been made in the acceptance of the principle of a League of Nations, mentioning especially its inclusion in the Coalition programme, and *of* the appointment of Lord Robert Cecil to take charge of the question at the Peace Conference.'
[This odd mistake may have arisen in one of two ways: (*a*) the writer thought there were so many *of*'s in the sentence that one more would not do any harm, or (*b*) he forgot that his participle (*mentioning*) was transitive, with two objects—*inclusion* and *appointment*—and side-slipped (the MEU term) into the belief that he began with 'making mention of'. At any rate, the *of* is certainly an intruder.]

(iv) 'The prohibition of meetings and the printing of and distribution of fly-sheets stopped the Radicals' agitation.'
[Faulty bracketing again: {('The prohibition of meetings) and (the printing of and distribution of flysheets)} stopped the Radicals' agitation.' The passage in the main bracket is the (double) subject of the sentence. But that does not

give the meaning: *prohibition* is actually the subject of the sentence. Rebracket therefore: 'The prohibition (of meetings and *of* the printing and distribution of flysheets) stopped the Radicals' agitation.' The extra *of* is necessary to avoid ambiguity, and the *of* after 'printing' is better omitted.]

older, elder. (i) *Form.* For forms see DOUBLE COMPARATIVES.

(ii) *Syntax.* *Older* is the normal modern comparative; *elder* cannot be followed by *than*, and is used exclusively now in connexion with human family relationships: 'the elder son', 'the elder brother', 'He was the elder of the two sons'. So restricted is the use to actual family comparisons that we should usually say of one of two friends 'he was the older of the two', 'the older man of the two', not *elder*. The superlative *eldest* is similarly restricted in use. It is noteworthy that *elder*, but not *older*, may be used as a noun even in the plural number: 'the elder of a church'; 'Respect your elders.'

omnibus. See BUS.

one. Four things are to be remembered:

(*a*) *One* is not an indefinite pronoun-of-all-work, like the French *on*. In English we prefer the passive construction where French uses *on* with the active. The French notice says 'Ici on parle anglais', but the English 'French is spoken here'. Attempts at imitating the French use are apt to be comic, as in 'One must not cut one's friends, must one?' Nevertheless, *one* is a true indefinite pronoun in English and has been so used since the fifteenth century. Shakespeare has (*Romeo and Juliet*): 'Why, may one ask?' Sparingly used, it has a legitimate place in the language.

(*b*) If *one* is used as the indefinite pronoun, the use must be consistent. In the sentence (from a literary review) 'One has to live somewhere, even if you are an Englishman and a Londoner' the writer suddenly threw *one* overboard in favour of *you*. A commoner mistake is to treat *one* as the third person (demonstrative) pronoun *he, she*: 'One must not forget *his* umbrella, must *he*?' The genitive of *one* is not *his* but *one's*, but this form is a comparatively recent invention and will not be found in the older writers.

(*c*) In phrases where *one* is a numeral followed by a partitive genitive ('one of his friends', 'one of the men') it is not an indefinite pronoun with forms of its own, but is properly represented afterwards by forms of the third person (demonstrative) pronoun: e.g. 'One of the men has lost *his* ticket'; 'One of the girls has not brought *her* book.'

(*d*) *One of the*— (i) 'One of the best, if not the best, feats of bowling in recent years'. The formula is common, makes a kind of rough sense, but cannot stand in written and is better avoided in spoken English. Bracketing immediately reveals the fault: '(One of the best)+(if not the best) feats'. It is obvious that the plural *feats* cannot be associated with the second bracketed expression. The way out is to abolish the attempt at bracketing and take advantage of an idiomatic ellipsis: 'One of the best feats of bowling in recent years, if not the best (feat).'

(ii) 'One of the best men who has ever lived.' The verb has been attracted into the singular by *one*: it should agree with its subject *who*, which is plural agreeing with the antecedent *men*.

(*e*) For *one another* see EACH.

only. 'This rack is only to be used for light articles.' Is *only* out of place? Logically, yes. As the sentence stands the rack is *to be used*, not e.g. to be broken or lost or mended; the Railway Company meant that it was to be used, but only for light articles. Grammatically, yes; *only* should modify the adverb phrase 'for light articles', not the verb 'to be used'. Only custom and carelessness plead on the other side. But they are strong; and grammar under the ugly name of pedantry has to give way. It is worth while, nevertheless, keeping *only* in its place when there is no danger of falling into stilted English. And indeed sometimes the sense determines that there is only one place for *only*. 'Only a miracle can save him' cannot possibly be expressed by 'A miracle can only save him.'

onomatopoeia. Onomatopoeia is the accordance of sound with sense. It is seen in such words as *bang, cuckoo, whisper, hush, ping-pong*, which suggest their meaning by their sound. In verse it is a device used for effect, often associated with ALLITERATION. Sometimes, as in the first three examples quoted below, the onomatopoeia is a natural element in the rhythm and style of the passage in which it occurs; sometimes, as in the last three examples, it is wrought with more deliberate art:

(*a*)   The ice was here, the ice was there,
     The ice was all around;
    It cracked and growled, and roared and howled
     Like noises in a swound.
    (Here the onomatopoeia is reinforced by other devices—repetition in the first two lines and the unusual word *swound* in the last.)

(*b*)   Or ushered with a shower still,
    When the gust hath blown his fill,
    Ending on the rustling leaves,
    With minute drops from off the eaves.
    (Here it is mainly the *us* sound in 'ushered', 'gust', and 'rustling' that suggests the sense.)

(*c*)   Him the Almighty Power
    Hurled headlong flaming from the ethereal sky,
    With hideous ruin and combustion, down
    To bottomless perdition.
    (Here is the onomatopoeia of general effect brought about by subtleties of rhythm. Note, for instance, how the second line defies the normal iambic scansion, and how the word *down*, by its very position as part of a phrase that overflows into the next line, suggests 'falling' or 'tumbling over'.)

(*d*)   The moan of doves in immemorial elms,
    And murmuring of innumerable bees.
    (The famous example from Tennyson of onomatopoeia by means of liquid consonants.)

(*e*)   I heard the water lapping on the crag,
    And the long ripple washing through the reeds.
    (Another example from Tennyson—the master of artificial effect in verse. Note how it suggests two distinct sounds of water.)

(*f*)   Or by a cider-press with patient look
    Thou watchest the last oozings hours by hours.
    (Note the slow-voiced hissing of the last line.)

Onomatopoeia may even be inherent in a stanza form. Thus the short last line of the stanzas of Keats's *La Belle Dame sans Merci* gives the effect of a thing left unsaid, and therefore of mystery. The long last line of the stanzas of Shelley's *To a Skylark* following on four short ones suggests the soaring of the lark, as the overflow of the lines in the *terza rima* of the *Ode to the West Wind* suggests the wind in its turmoil.

The adjective is *onomatopoeic*.

onto. Is there such a word? MEU says (*a*) that where *on* is an adverb the two words must be separate, *on to*; (*b*) that where *on* is not adverbial one or other of the two prepositions should be used by itself as the context demands, or the two words should be joined to make a simple preposition, *onto* (like *into* and *upon*). Thus in the sentence 'We walked on to Beachy Head' *on* is definitely an adverb and the two words are therefore separated; but in the sentence 'He fell onto the pavement below' there cannot be adverbial force in *on*, and *onto* is prepositional, a variant of either *on* or *to*. The rule is therefore: (*a*) if *on* is an adverb, use *on to*; (*b*) if *on* is not adverbial, and its association with *to* is necessary to the sense, use *onto*; (*c*) do not use *onto* where simple *on* or *to* expresses the meaning intended.

opportunity. *Opportunity* is followed by *of*+gerund, not by *of*+noun, which construction belongs to *advantage*. You take the opportunity *of visiting* him, but you take advantage *of his presence* in London to visit him.

or (i) See EITHER . . . OR.

(ii) For syntax of *or* and *nor* see NOR.

(iii) 'We need something more before we can conclude that Germany is going to be democratized in any effective way, or before we can be sure that this move also is not a weapon in the war.' This is a sentence quoted in MEU to illustrate wrong repetition after *or*. As the sentence stands it means that we need something more *either* before we conclude *or* before we can be sure; but the intended meaning is that we need something more before we can conclude *or* be sure (i.e. both, not one or the other; in effect, *or* = *and*). It is another instance of faulty bracketing; the omission of 'before we can' after *or* will set the sentence right.

-or. For -*or* as agent suffix see -ER; and for -*or* and -*our* see -OUR.

oratio obliqua. See INDIRECT SPEECH.

-os, -oes. The general guiding rule for the plural of nouns ending in *o* is: Nouns in -*o* whose plural is freely used (except those in which the -*o* is immediately preceded by another vowel), and monosyllables, have -*oes*; all others have -*os*. But this rule is so far from being safe that the following list of words in -*o* whose plural is likely to be used is given for reference:

albino:	albinos	fiasco:	fiascos
archipelago:	archipelagos	folio:	folios
arpeggio:	arpeggios	go:	goes (as in 'I had several
banjo:	banjoes		*goes* at it')
calico:	calicoes	hero:	heroes
cameo:	cameos	magneto:	magnetos
cargo:	cargoes	magnifico:	magnificos
crescendo:	crescendos	manifesto:	manifestos
domino:	dominoes	no:	noes
dynamo:	dynamos	photo:	photos
embryo:	embryos	potato:	potatoes

It is to be noted that contracted words like *photo* and *dynamo*, whose plurals are in common use, are an exception to the rule.

other. (*a*) *Other* is a comparative and is followed by *than*, not by *but*: 'There was no other way open *than* to go.' (*b*) 'It could not possibly have been carried out *other* than by the mammoth vessels' (MEU). What is wrong? *Other* is an adjective or a pronoun, never an adverb; but an adverb is needed here. *Otherwise* is the adverb corresponding with *other*; correct therefore: 'carried out otherwise than'. Sometimes, however, the boot is on the other leg. 'No further threats, economic or *otherwise*, have been made' (MEU). Obviously *otherwise* should be an adjective standing for the opposite of *economic*; but it is an adverb. Read: 'no further threats, economic or *other*', or, if this form seems awkward: 'no further economic or *other* threats.'

See also EACH OTHER.

otherwise. (i) See OTHER.

(ii) *Or otherwise.* MEU states that '*or otherwise* after a noun is (*a*) nearly always superfluous, (*b*) when it is not superfluous, an inferior substitute for *or* with the negative form of the preceding noun or an equivalent'. Two of its examples (which may be corrected by the omission of *or otherwise*) are:

'The success of our efforts depends on the success *or otherwise* of the German submarine campaign.'

'It is entirely for the High Court to ascertain the truth *or otherwise* of the statements.'

ottava rima ('eight-verse'). In English the eight-lined stanza in iambic pentameters, rhyming ababbcc. Byron's *Don Juan* is written in *ottava rima*. Here is one of its stanzas:

> 'A mighty mass of brick, and smoke, and shipping,
>   Dirty and dusky, but as wide as eye
> Could reach, with here and there a sail just skipping
>   In sight, then lost amidst the forestry
> Of masts; a wilderness of steeples peeping
>   On tiptoe through their sea-coal canopy;
> A huge, dun cupola, like a foolscap crown
> On a fool's head—and there is London Town!'

ought is etymologically the past tense of *owe* (e.g. Shakespeare's 'He said you *ought* him a thousand pound'), now used as a present (cf. *must*). Like *must* it takes on a past significance by the addition of a perfect Infinitive:

> I ought to/must/go.
> I ought to/must/have gone.

Failure to recognize *ought* in its past significance is the cause of the SOLECISM 'He had/did/ought', 'Hadn't/didn't/it ought?'

Note that *ought* must be followed by the infinitive with *to*; MEU quotes the following sentence illustrating the faulty usage: 'We should be sorry to see English critics asserting that they *ought* or could *have acted* otherwise.'

-our, -or. (*a*) In English some words have the *-our* ending (*favour, honour, humour*); and some, like *terror, horror*, have shed the *u*. In America the *-or* ending is standard for all words.

(*b*) English words in -*our* usually drop the *u* before the suffixes -*ous*, -*ate*, -*ation*, -*ize*:

clamour	clamorous
clangour	clangorous
humour	humorous
odour	odorous
rigour	rigorous
valour	valorous
vigour	{ vigorous { invigorate
odour	deodorize
vapour	{ vaporize { vaporous

Before the suffixes -*ite* and -*able*, however, the *u* is generally retained: *favour, favourite*; *honour, honourable*.

MEU (1926) favours *humourist* from *humour*, but COD (1929) has the single spelling *humorist*—an interesting example of English progress in eliminating the *u*. In other words, however, the spelling -*our*- is still preserved before -*ist*: *colourist*.

ours, yours, theirs. So spelt, without the apostrophe. But the AV has 'The good of all the land of Egypt is your's' and 'For their's is the king-dom of heaven'. Tennyson's 'Their's not to reason why' is probably an ellipsis for 'Theirs is not . . .'

outcome. 'The outcome of the controversy will lead to the breaking off of friendly relations between the two countries.' This is saying a thing twice. The outcome will be the breaking off; the controversy will lead to the breaking off. It is a mistake similar to 'The REASON is because'.

overflow. For technical use of the term in prosody see BLANK VERSE.

owing to. See DUE.

oxymoron (Greek = 'sharp dull', 'pointedly foolish'). A figure of speech in which two words or phrases of opposite significance are set together for effect. Tennyson was particularly fond of the figure, and the lines

> 'His *honour* rooted in *dishonour* stood
> And *faith unfaithful* kept him *falsely true*'

serve as the stock example of its use. Shakespeare has:

> 'Do that *good mischief* which may make this island
> Thine for ever.'

In *Paradise Lost* Milton has *precious bane* (used of the gold in hell) and 'raised to that *bad eminence*' (of Satan). A modern prose example is:

'. . . with no sleeves except such as were provided by a *carefully careless* scarf.'

Someone has thus neatly combined the contrarieties of the telephone as a boon and a curse:

> 'O, precious bane,
> Tormenting joy,
> Dividing chain,
> Exacting toy.'

palatals. See CONSONANTS.

paradox (Greek = 'contrary to opinion') is a seemingly absurd though perhaps really well-founded statement. The figure has been described as 'a truth doing a somersault'. Examples:

'He who goes against the fashion is himself its slave'

(Logan Pearsall Smith).

'God paints in many colours; but He never paints so gorgeously, I had almost said so gaudily, as when He paints in white'

(G. K. Chesterton).

Paradox may legitimately be used 'for illuminating with a sudden flash a neglected aspect of a subject or for clinching an argument with a memorable phrase; but this genuine use may give place to a mere striving after effect'.

parenthesis. A parenthesis is an 'aside' or 'breaking off' from the normal construction of the sentence. The words that form the parenthesis may be enclosed by (*a*) commas, (*b*) brackets, (*c*) dashes. Of the following examples those numbered (i) show the simple grammatical parenthesis, common in direct speech; those numbered (ii) the parenthesis proper; and those numbered (iii) the parenthesis for deliberate effect.

(i) It was, *as I have told you*, a difficult problem.
There were, *he suggested*, certain other people who should be consulted.
He is a man who *I know* is honest.
(In this type of sentence, where the parenthesis follows a relative pronoun, the commas are usually omitted—often with the unfortunate result that the relative pronoun is forced into the accusative, as if it were the object of *know* instead of the subject of its own clause. See CASE.)
His fit of anger, *which was the cause of our quarrel*, was soon over.
(A non-defining clause: see also RELATIVE PRONOUN.)

(ii) (*a*) *Explanatory parenthesis.*
The fête will take place next Thursday (3 June).
We (the boys and I) are coming over to see you to-morrow (Friday).
He said that he (John) quite agreed.
(A necessary but awkward device when pronouns are apt to become confused in indirect speech. For a note on the subject see INDIRECT SPEECH.)

(*b*) *Ordinary parenthesis.*
'He girt his fisher's coat unto him (for he was naked) and did cast himself into the sea.'

'until
Thine azure sister of the spring shall blow
Her clarion o'er the dreaming earth, and fill
(Driving sweet buds like flocks to feed in air)
With living hues and odours plain and hill.'

(iii) 'The uncertainty and quick shifting of partners—a thing which the constancy of whist abhors—the dazzling supremacy and regal investiture of Spadille —absurd, as she justly observed, in the pure aristocracy of whist, where his crown and garter give him no proper power above his brother-nobility of the Aces;—the giddy vanity, so taking to the inexperienced, of playing alone:— above all the overpowering attractions of a *Sans Prendre Vole*—to the triumph of which there is certainly nothing parallel or approaching, in the contingencies of whist;—all these, she would say, make quadrille a game of captivation to the young and enthusiastic.'
(A riot of parentheses, not uncommon in the style of Elia. The punctuation, with its apparently arbitrary commas, semicolons, and colons allied to the dashes, is Lamb's own, and cannot be reduced to any law or rule.)

'Layers of dust have accumulated (a superfoetation of dirt!) upon the old layers, that seldom used to be disturbed, save by some curious finger, now and then.'

> 'And then she cast her arms along
>   The golden barriers,
> And laid her face between her hands,
>   And wept. (I heard her tears.)'

Except where parenthesis is necessary to the meaning of the sentence, as in the examples under (i), it should be sparingly used. To use it for effect is always hazardous.

MEU gives a warning against failing to recognize a parenthesis. The example quoted is: 'A remarkable change had come over the Government, *he suggested*, since the Bill had left the Committee, and expressed doubts as to whether Mr. Masterman altogether approved of the new turn of affairs.' Here 'he suggested' is plainly a parenthesis; but the writer has forgotten it, and tried to take the *he* out of the brackets (i.e. the commas) to do duty as subject of the verb *expressed*. Recast the sentence 'He suggested that a remarkable change had come over, &c.'

The MEU rule for punctuation in connexion with parenthesis is given: 'After the second bracket or dash any stop that would have been used if the brackets or dashes and their contents had not been there should still be used.' This means, e.g., that when a bracket occurs at the end of a sentence the full stop, or question mark, or exclamation mark is placed outside the second bracket. If, therefore, the parenthesis is itself a question and it occurs at the end of a sentence, there will be two question marks, one inside and one outside the brackets. The observance of the MEU rule with dashes is rare, the second dash often being left to do its own work and that of any other stop which ought to follow it. At the end of a sentence the second dash is always omitted. Since English sentences always have a tendency to over-punctuation, it seems on the whole a wise proceeding to omit the other stop. The punctuation recommended by MEU would become a nightmare to both reader and writer.

parody. A parody is a consciously exaggerated imitation of another literary work. Its purpose is frequently to produce a ridiculous effect, to make fun of the writer of the original by turning his work to ridicule. Sometimes the metre is imitated, sometimes the sentiment, sometimes the style or mannerism, sometimes all three together. What BURLESQUE is to action or acting and caricature to form and feature, parody is to verbal expression. Thus Butler's *Hudibras*, a mock-heroic poem of the seventeenth century, is a burlesque of the hypocrisy of the Presbyterians and Independents. The pictures in *Punch* to-day regularly poke gentle fun at politicians by caricature, and its editor as regularly prints humorous parodies of various poems in which the subject-matter is up to date, while the language is a clearly marked echo of the original. But the best parody is much more penetrating than this: it implies sound and valid criticism of the original. The best parodist gets into his victim's brain and humorously applies his methods to alien subjects. Hence to parody a writer is obviously to pay a compliment to his popularity. When Shelley wrote *Peter Bell the Third* he did not write a parody of Wordsworth's *Peter Bell*, but rather a perversion. Even Lewis Carroll's 'Father William' is rather a perversion than a parody of Southey's ballad. Among the most felicitous classic examples of parody are those of the brothers James and Horace Smith in *The Rejected Addresses*. They are full of clever and genial satire unblemished by vulgarity. Of the twelve poets parodied in this book, the authors say in their Preface to the eighteenth edition:

'To the credit of the *genus irritabile* be it recorded that not one of those whom we had parodied or burlesqued ever betrayed the least soreness on the occasion, or refused to join in the laugh that we had occasioned.... "I certainly must have written this myself" said [Sir Walter Scott], "although I forget upon what occasion." ... Lord Byron wrote thus to Mr. Murray from Italy—"Tell him we forgive him, were he twenty times our satirist".'

As specimens of parodies we print

(i) part of Charles Stuart Calverley's *Wanderers*, in which the tinker takes the place of Tennyson's brook:

> I loiter down by thorp and town,
>   For any job I'm willing;
> Take here and there a dusty brown,
>   And here and there a shilling.
>
> The things I've done 'neath moon and stars
>   Have got me into messes:
> I've seen the sky through prison bars,
>   I've torn up prison dresses:
>
> I've sat, I've sigh'd, I've gloom'd, I've glanced
>   With envy at the swallows
> That through the window slid, and danced
>   (Quite happy) round the gallows;
>
> But out again I come, and show
>   My face nor care a stiver,
> For trades are brisk and trades are slow,
>   But mine goes on for ever.

(ii) part of Smith's parody of Wordsworth's style in such poems as *Alice Fell* and *We are Seven:*

> My brother Jack was nine in May,
> And I was eight on New-year's day;
>   So in Kate Wilson's shop
> Papa (he 's my papa and Jack's)
> Bought me, last week, a doll of wax,
>   And brother Jack a top.
>
> Jack 's in the pouts, and this it is,—
> He thinks mine came to more than his;
>   So to my drawer he goes,
> Takes out the doll, and, O, my stars!
> He pokes her head between the bars,
>   And melts off half her nose!
>
> Quite cross, a bit of string I beg,
> And tie it to his peg-top's peg,
>   And bang, with might and main,
> Its head against the parlour-door:
> Off flies the head, and hits the floor,
>   And breaks a window pane ...

(iii) 'April' (G. F. Bradby's parody of Masefield's 'Sea Fever'):

> I must go back to a vest again, to a winter vest with sleeves,
> And all I ask is an honest shop where the shop-men are not thieves;
> And a fair price, and a free choice, and a full stretch for dining,
> And a smooth touch on the bare chest, and a smooth inner lining,

I must go back to a vest again, for that which most I dread
Is a bad cold, a head cold, and a day, or more, in bed;
And all I ask is a friend's advice, and a short time for thinking,
A soft wool, and a man's size, and a good bit for shrinking.

I must go back to a vest again, for the April winds are bleak,
And the spring's way is a cold way, and my circulation weak;
And all I ask, when the cash is paid and we leave the shop together,
Is a warm fire, and an arm-chair, or a change in the weather.

participles. 1. *Form.* The two participles of the verb in English are
(*a*) the present participle, which always ends in *-ing*;
(*b*) the past participle, which has an *-n* (*-en*, *-n*) ending in strong verbs
and a dental ending (*-ed*, *-d*, *-t*) in weak verbs. See STRONG AND
WEAK VERBS. A compound made of present+past participles (e.g.
having seen) acts as the perfect tense form of the present participle.
The 'compound participles' recognized by Fowler (*King's English*)
are: *having seen, being about to see, about to see; having been seen, being
seen, about to be seen, being about to be seen*.

2. *Syntax.* Both participles may
(*a*) occur in the compound tenses of the verb—the present participle in
the continuous and the past participle in the perfect active and all
the passive tenses. See TENSE;
(*b*) act as simple adjectives: 'a *flowing* stream'; 'a *singing* bird'; 'a *broken*
promise'; 'a *twisted* skein';
(*c*) act as adjectives in the ABSOLUTE phrase;
(*d*) act as adjectives in an ADJECTIVE PHRASE, qualifying a noun or
pronoun in the main clause. In each of the following sentences
the adjective phrase is italicized, and the word qualified is printed
in small capitals:

Leaving the highway, WE turned into the grounds of the castle.
Worn out by long watching, the SOLDIER fell asleep.
I heard the CHOIR *singing carols*.

The adjective phrase containing the present participle is far more common
and idiomatic than that containing the past participle.

The position of the participle phrase in the sentence is important, as the
following examples of incorrect uses show:

Standing on the bridge, the AEROPLANE hovered above us.
Shattered into a thousand pieces, HE picked up the valuable vase.

The simple rule is to keep the participle phrase as near as possible to
the noun or pronoun it qualifies.

Note particularly the common error where the main clause begins with
the introductory *there*:

Having given this warning against possible disappointment, there is little left
for the reviewer to praise. (Qualifying *little*? Certainly not *reviewer*,
though he apparently issued the warning. But the error here is not really
an error of *position*. No change in the position of the clause would really
mend the sentence; the only remedy is to change the construction to an
absolute: 'This warning having been given.' The 'there is' construction is
always dangerous when there are participles about; the writer himself should
have been warned by that.)
Written under the inspiration of a friendly pipe, there is mellowness in these
random jottings. (*Mellowness* is, but *jottings* should be, qualified.)

Sometimes, especially when there is an impersonal construction in the main sentence, the participle phrase is left 'hanging', with nothing at all to qualify:

> *While welcoming the start that has been made in this report*, it must not be forgotten that other important aspects remain to be investigated.
>
> Now, *having found Rolfe*, it is impossible for him to doubt that his hero was worth finding.
>
> (In both sentences the participle phrase apparently qualifies the impersonal *it*.)

For 'fused participle' see GERUND.

parts of speech. The work of the parts of speech is summarized in the following table:

Noun	Acting as: (*a*) Subject of Sentence. (*b*) Direct or Indirect Object of Verb. (*c*) Object of Preposition. (*d*) Nominative in Absolute Phrase. (*e*) Complement to a verb of incomplete predication. (*f*) In apposition to another noun.
Pronoun	As Noun, except (*f*). A pronoun may stand in apposition to a noun or pronoun.
Verb	(*a*) Finite: the 'word' whose function is predication, expressing the action done by, or the state of, the subject. (*b*) Infinite: acting as adjective, adverb, or noun in a phrase, or acting as subject, object, or complement in a sentence. See FINITE AND INFINITE.
Adjective	qualifying a Noun or Pronoun.
Adverb	modifying chiefly Verb, Adjective, and Adverb, and more rarely, Preposition and Conjunction. It may also modify a complete predicate, or a whole phrase or sentence.
Preposition	governing a Noun or Pronoun, or a Noun Equivalent (e.g. a Noun Clause).
Conjunction	(*a*) *simple*: linking together words (e.g. two nouns, two prepositions) and phrases; *and*, *but*, *or* are the chief examples. (*b*) *co-ordinating*: joining together clauses that have the same rank and function in the sentence. (*c*) *subordinating*: joining a dependent clause to the clause on which it is dependent. See also under CORRELATIVES.

See also INTERJECTION.

passed, past. *Passed* is the spelling when the past participle (of the verb *to pass*) is used in verbal senses; *past* is the spelling when the past participle has passed into an adjective.

passive voice. The simple construction with the transitive verb in a sentence is:

	Subject	Verb	Object
	The lion	beat	the unicorn.

In such a sentence the verb is said to be in the *active voice*, since the subject performs the action. When, however, the subject suffers the action the verb is in the *passive* (Lat. *pati*, *passus*, suffer) *voice*:

	Subject	Verb	Instrument or Agent
	The unicorn	was beaten	by the lion.

Note that in such a sentence as 'I cut myself', where the subject apparently suffers the action, grammatically the object *myself* is the sufferer and the verb is active. See REFLEXIVE.

The passive tenses of the verb are made up of a tense of the verb *to be* + the past participle: 'I was beaten'; 'It is written.'

pathetic fallacy. Sometimes Nature is so strongly personified by poets as to be regarded as taking a definite interest in human action. We have then what Ruskin called the *Pathetic Fallacy*: e.g. Nature's mourning when Eve plucked and ate the forbidden fruit:

> 'Earth felt the wound, and Nature from her seat,
> Sighing through all her works, gave signs of woe,
> That all was lost.'

patronymic. A patronymic is a name that indicates the relationship of son or daughter to father. Thus *Johnson* is by origin a patronymic (though now merely a surname), meaning the 'Son of John' Certain affixes have a special patronymic significance. In Greek *-ides* was the usual suffix to indicate 'the son of'—*Alcides*, the son of Alceus. We have in English the obvious and familiar *-son*; the prefix *Mac* from the Scottish; the prefix *ap* from Welsh, represented in its shortened form in the surname *Pritchard* (= ap Richard, 'the son of Richard'); the OE. suffix *-ing*, as in *Browning*; the Norman prefix *Fitz* (= French *fils*), as in *Fitzjohn, Fitzpatrick*; and the Irish affix *O'* in *O'Reilly, O'Donnell*.

Patronymics are not used in modern English, except very occasionally in dialects. Even this use has died out now, though there is a reminder of it in the name of an inn very well known in the West Riding, 'Bill's o' Jack's'—i.e. '(Bill the son of Jack)'s' (where the o' has of course nothing to do with Irish *O'*).

pay. Makes past forms *paid* (not *payed*). See Y > I.

pence, pennies. *Pence* is the collective of price, compounded with the numbers up to but not above eleven (*twopence, fourpence, elevenpence, fifteen pence*); *pennies* is used for the coins as such, without reference to their potential purchasing power. In syntax, *pence* is singular—'There is *fourpence* on the table' where the fourpence is regarded merely as a sum of money, which might be made up indifferently of varying numbers of pennies and halfpennies. But 'There are *four pennies* on the table', where the emphasis is on the coins as separate objects.

pentameter. See -METER.

people. People is a collective noun when it = (i) nation, (ii) the common folk, populace, as opposed to the aristocrats and ruling classes. As (i) it is usually considered singular ('The British people is notoriously fond of sport'); and has a plural of its own: 'the white peoples'; as (ii) it is plural: 'The people have never been so badly treated as they have been during the past two years.' In all other uses *people* is a normal plural (= men and women).

perfect. This grammatical term, applied to tense, refers to *completeness* of the action and not to time (Lat. *perfectus* = complete). Thus the *present perfect*, made up of the present auxiliary 'have' and the past participle, e.g. 'I have lived', denotes completeness of action in the present time; the *past perfect*, made up of the past auxiliary 'had' and the past participle, e.g. 'I had loved', denotes completeness of action at some time in the past; and the *future perfect* similarly refers to action as completed at some time in the future, e.g. 'I shall have lived.'

Note (*a*) The present perfect is sometimes made up of the auxiliary 'be', instead of 'have', especially with verbs implying motion (as in other modern European languages), e.g.

> Your uncle *'s come.*
> 'The noble Brutus *is ascended.*'
> 'How *are* the mighty *fallen!*'
> '*Is* our whole dissembly *appeared?*'

(*b*) To the tense-form consisting of 'should ('would') have' and the past participle, e.g. 'I should have come', the name *future perfect in the past* is given. This tense marks a completed action as future from a past point of view.

perfect infinitive. It is often difficult to know when the simple infinitive and when the perfect infinitive should be used. The latter form expresses the occurrence of events *prior to* the time of the main verb, and there is no trouble when the main verb is present, e.g. 'He seems *to have enjoyed* his holiday' (i.e. at some previous time); 'He ought *to have gone* to town yesterday' (contrast with, 'He ought *to go* to town tomorrow'). But what is to be said about 'He intended *to have gone* yesterday'? Some grammarians defend it as implying that his intention was frustrated; others affirm that his intention in the past is adequately expressed by the past indefinite 'intended', which, therefore, ought to be followed by the simple infinitive. There seems no doubt that the perfect form is often needless and often ugly, as in

'Peggy would have liked *to have shown* her turban and bird of paradise at the ball.'

The mistake is common, and wholly indefensible after *seem* and *appear*; e.g. 'They seemed *to have preferred* some more fashionable place for summering in'. Here the writer hesitates between *seem to have preferred* and *seemed to prefer*, either of which would have been correct.

period. See FULL STOP.

periphrasis is 'round-about' speech or writing—a style which, though popular, is to be avoided. It arises from an odd desire in most of us for longwindedness and effect, as in the expression 'He was the recipient of' for 'He received'. MEU gives as an example 'the year's penultimate month' for 'November'. Such words as CASE, CHARACTER, INSTANCE, NATURE, REGARD, readily lend themselves to periphrasis.

person. In grammar, pronouns are distinguished as belonging to one of three 'persons': the *first* person = the person speaking; the *second* person = the person spoken to; the *third* person = the person spoken about. The third person pronoun (*he, she, it*) is properly a demonstrative pronoun. See PRONOUNS. The tense forms of the verb inflect for person in the second singular (all tenses) and the third singular of the present simple indicative:

> First: I go
> Second: thou goest } singular
> Third: he goes

First: we go
Second: you go   } plural
Third: they go

For agreement in Person see AGREEMENT.

personate, personify. To *personate* (the commoner equivalent is *impersonate*) a man is to pretend, by disguise and gesture or simply by using his name, to be the man; to *personify* a thing, an abstract quality, is to endow it, metaphorically, with the characteristics of a human being. See PERSONIFICATION.

personification. Personification is a particular metaphor, in which the attributes of a person are transferred to inanimate or abstract things. Thus in the lines from *Hamlet*:

> 'But lo! the morn in russet mantle clad
>   Walks o'er the brow of yon high eastern hill',

the metaphor consists in the personification of *morn*. But the actual term personification is usually restricted to the figure (very common in the 18th century) in which abstract things are given personal qualities. Here are one or two examples:

> 'Disaffection reared its ugly head.'
> 'Can Honour's voice provoke the silent dust,
>   Or Flattery soothe the dull cold ear of Death?'
> 'Youth on the prow, and Pleasure at the helm.'

perspicacious, perspicuous. *Perspicacious* = 'having or showing insight', and is generally used of persons; *perspicuous* = 'clearly expressed', and is generally used of speech or writing. A *perspicacious* person (i.e. one who has clear insight into a matter) will probably be capable of making a *perspicuous* statement about it.

Petrarchan. For the term as applied to the sonnet see SONNET.

phrase. A phrase consists of a number of words which make a unit acting as a noun, adjective, or adverb in the sentence. It does not contain a finite verb but may contain an infinite part of a verb (participle, infinitive, gerund). In itself it cannot make complete sense, but can have meaning only through its relation to some part of the sentence in which it stands.

plain sailing. This is the popular and established phrase in Mod.E. But it is probably a corruption of the nautical '*plane* sailing', i.e. sailing by a *plane* chart.

pleonasm. *Pleonasm* is the use of more words than are required to give the sense intended. As in TAUTOLOGY there is redundancy, which here consists in needlessly adding what is already implied, not in repetition. Examples are: the use of double comparatives, superlatives, and negatives, and such expressions as 'equally as well', 'more preferable', 'continue to remain'. Pleonasm is not always a fault. It can be used for the sake of emphasis, as in 'Lest at any time they should see *with their eyes* and hear *with their ears*'.

plural of compound nouns. As a rule compound nouns form their plural by adding -*s* to the significant and not to the distinguishing part of the compound, especially when the significant part is a noun, e.g.

maid-servants (but maids-of-honour), hangers-on, commanders-in-chief, knights-errant, sons-in-law, passers-by, lookers-on, men-of-war, coats-of-mail.

But when the two parts of the compound are so closely united as to become practically one word, the plural is formed according to the general rule for number, i.e. by adding -s to singular. Thus spendthrifts, castaways, spoonfuls, major-generals, poet-laureates, washer-women, coverpoints, goodbyes. Sometimes both parts of the compound take the plural inflexion, e.g. men-servants, Lords-justices, knights-templars, Lords-lieutenants.

Note that the plural of Mr. Brown is 'Messrs (i.e. Messieurs) Brown', and of Miss Brown is either 'The Miss Browns' (cf. spoonfuls), or 'The Misses Brown' (cp. knights-errant).

portmanteau word. 'A word like those invented by Lewis Carroll, made up of the blended sounds and combining the meanings of two distinct words' (SOED). Most of the inventions referred to occur in the verses called 'Jabberwocky' in *Through the Looking Glass*, which Alice thinks are *rather* hard to understand. When later on she asks Humpty Dumpty the meaning of them he tells her, referring to the word '*slithy*' in the first stanza: '*Slithy* means "lithe and slimy". You see it's like a portmanteau—there are two meanings packed up in one word.' The one word in the verses that has survived in ordinary language is *chortle*:

> 'O frabjous day! Callooh! Callay!
> He *chortled* in his joy.'

The two words *chuckle* and *snort* are packed up in it.

There are a few 'facetious formations' (OED) in the manner of portmanteau words: *squarson* (= squire and parson, a term applied to the squire who was also parson of the village); *wuncle* (= the wicked uncle, in the BBC Children's Hour); *gruncle* (= granduncle); *Radiopinion* (= Radio Opinion, a magazine heading). More serious examples are: *Eurasia* (= Europe and Asia) and *Australasia* (= Australia and Asia); *Bakerloo* Railway (= Baker [Street] and Waterloo, its two original termini); *gracing* (= greyhound racing). Of the formations given, only *squarson*, *Eurasia*, *Australasia*, and *Bakerloo* have had lasting currency.

position. The importance of the position of words, phrases, and clauses in the sentence is illustrated under the following headings:

(i) *Words*
    (*a*) *Adjectives*: TRANSFERRED EPITHET.
    (*b*) *Adverbs*: EVEN, ONLY, SPLIT INFINITIVE.
    (*c*) *Prepositions*: PREPOSITION AT END.
    (*d*) *Correlatives*: CORRELATIVES, EITHER . . . OR, BOTH . . . AND, NOT
        ONLY . . . BUT ALSO.

(ii) *Phrases and clauses*: AMBIGUITY, ADJECTIVE PHRASE, ADVERB PHRASE, PARTICIPLE.

possession. *In possession of* is active, = 'holding'; *in the possession of* is passive, = 'held by': 'The thief was found *in possession of* the papers'; 'The papers were found *in the possession of* the thief.'

possessive. The term *possessive* is sometimes used for *genitive*. Since, however, the genitive case of nouns or pronouns has certain idiomatic uses only remotely connected with possession, the term *genitive* is preferable. Special care must be taken to define and distinguish 'possessive pronoun' and 'possessive adjective'. If 'possessive pronoun' means anything, it means the genitive case of the pronoun; and 'possessive adjective' means the adjective corresponding with it. In the personal pronouns and the third person demonstrative (plural and feminine singular) the distinction is one of form:

Genitive of Pronoun (Possessive Pronoun)		Possessive Adjective
First Person	mine ours	my our
Second Person	thine yours	thy your
Third Person (Demonstrative)	his hers its theirs	his her its their

In other pronouns it is one of syntax. Thus in '*Whose* is this book?' *whose* is the genitive of the pronoun; and in '*Whose* book is this?' it is a possessive adjective.

possible.

> (*a*) It would not be possible to find a better place.
> (*b*) No better place is possible to be found.

Of these two sentences (*a*) is correct, (*b*) incorrect. Why? The reason is that *possible* is an 'absolute' word, meaning in itself 'able to be done, found, &c.' It cannot, therefore, be followed by an infinitive that is intended to complete its meaning (like *to be found* in sentence (*b*)). The infinitive in (*a*) is the real subject of the sentence, not the amplifier of *possible*: 'To find a better place would not be possible.' Idiom, however, does admit of the amplification of *possible* by '*of*+noun': 'It is possible of proof.'

practice, -se. In this pair, and in the three pairs following, the *c* is the sign of the noun, and the *s* of the verb: *advice—advise*; *device—devise*; *prophecy—prophesy*. *Licence—license* is still a doubtful pair, but modern usage brings it into line with the four pairs dealt with above, *licence* for the noun and *license* for the verb.

precipitate, precipitous. *Precipitate*, adjective (pronounce -ĭt) = violently hurried, rash, unconsidered; *precipitous* = steep (like a precipice).

We can talk of the *precipitate* flight of an army after defeat, and of a *precipitous* path. Unfortunately *precipitous* is often misused as the equivalent of *precipitate*, as in the following example taken from MEU: 'Are the workers justified in taking the *precipitous* action suggested in the resolution?'

predicate, that part of the sentence which expresses the action or state of the subject, consisting of the verb (with object or complement, if any) and any modifications or qualifications. See SENTENCE.

predicative adjective. See ADJECTIVE.

preface, prefix. You *prefix* a title *to* your name; a collection of poems is *prefaced by* or *with* an essay. See PREPOSITIONAL IDIOM.

prefer. 1. Note spelling: *prefer, preferred, preferring, preference*. See under DOUBLE CONSONANTS.

2. The original meaning (<Lat. *prae*+*fero*) is to bring or carry before, used particularly of office or rank. Hence 'In honour *preferring* one another'. This use is now most common in connexion with ecclesiastical appointments; cf. *prelate* = lit. 'one who has been preferred' (<Lat. *prae*+*latum*, supine stem of *ferre*) and *preferment* = a superior office, especially in the Church.

3. With the word in its usual meaning ('choose rather', 'like better'), the idiom is

prefer [Noun or Noun Equivalent] to [Noun or Noun Equivalent]:

> I prefer rain to fog.
> I prefer this book to the one you lent me last week.

The trouble begins when *prefer* is followed by an infinitive. Then the normal idiom with *to* becomes difficult, if not impossible. 'I prefer to go to stay' obviously cannot stand; and 'I prefer to go to staying' is very little better. There are two ways out of the difficulty: (*a*) make both infinitives gerunds: 'I prefer going to staying.' This, though correct, is stilted and not idiomatic, English; (*b*) use *prefer . . . rather than*, a convenient confusion of two constructions, admitted by the OED: 'I prefer to go rather than to stay.' But it is better to throw *prefer* overboard altogether, and use the simple *rather . . . than*: 'I would rather go than stay.' *Prefer* followed by simple *than* (not *rather than*) is not allowable (see under THAN), though it is common in Mod.E. The following examples of the wrong use are taken from MEU: 'Many prefer to go bareheaded *than* to reassume the fez;' 'He prefers to suggest *than* to conclude.'

prefix. See AFFIXES; for *prefix* (verb) see PREFACE.

prejudice. The idioms are 'a prejudice *against, in favour of*', not 'a prejudice *to*'; but 'prejudicial *to*'.

preposition. The preposition governs a *noun* or *pronoun* or its equivalent, usually indicating relationship of place or time. In form it may be

(*a*) simple, e.g. *to, from, at, in*;
(*b*) compound: e.g. *out of, up to, with regard to, in respect of, as regards, on to*;
(*c*) verbal: i.e. certain present participles may be prepositional in function, the chief examples being: *considering, regarding, respecting,* and *notwithstanding*.

For the syntax of such participle-prepositions see CONSIDERING. In addition, one or two adjectives have prepositional force: LIKE and *near* are the important ones. See also PREPOSITION AT END.

prepositional idiom. Since prepositions play so large a part in English idiom, perhaps the surest sign of a foreigner whose English is not perfect is his misuse of them. Such phrases as 'in London', 'at Bath', 'by the seaside', 'in season', 'the man with the red hair', 'out of temper', 'beside himself', exemplify the idiomatic use of prepositions. And just as in common usage certain nouns in stereotyped phrases are governed, so certain verbs, adjectives, and nouns are followed, by particular prepositions. The use of prepositions before nouns in fixed or common phrases like those above is generally a matter of instinct with the Englishman. But the prepositional idiom following certain words is by no means so natural and easy a matter. Below is a table for reference of the accepted usages with some representative words. Further notes on the usages will be found under the headings of many of the words concerned.

affix	*N to* N	
agree	*to* a thing	
	with a person *on* a matter or *in* an opinion	
averse	*from* N	OED admits also *to*
compare	N *with* N	'in the sense *examine or set forth the details of a supposed similarity or estimate its degree.*' (MEU)
	N *to* N	'in the sense *suggest or state a similarity*'. (MEU)
confide	*in* N	
	N *to* N	
consist	*of* N	
	in N	
contrast (verb)	N *with* N	accent on second syllable.
contrast (noun)	*to* N	accent on first syllable.
	between+plural	
	between N and N (and 'in contrast *with*')	
converse (verb)	*with* a person *on, about* a thing	accent on second syllable.
converse (noun)	*of* N	accent on first syllable.
deduce	N *from* N	
dependent	*on* N	
differ } different }	*from* N	OED gives *to* and *than* as being regularly used in older English, but recommends *from* as modern usage. It also admits 'differ *with*': 'On this point I must differ *with* you.'
endue	N *with* N	
enforce	N *on* N	
essential	*to* N	
foist	N *on* N	
independent	*of* N	cf. *dependent* above.
induce	N *in* N	
	a person *to do* a thing	
indifferent	*to* N	cf. *different* above.
inflict	N *on* N	
infuse	*N into* N	
initiate	*into* a society	
	in a science, &c.	

instil	N *into* N	
interpolate	N *in* N	
preface	N *with* N	
prefix	N *to* N	
replace	N *with* or *by* N	
sensitive	*to* N	
substitute	N *for* N	Distinguish from usage with *replace* above.
sympathy	*with* N	MEU admits *for*, and says 'The exception sometimes taken to following *sympathy* with *for* instead of *with* is groundless'.

preposition at end. 'You must never use a preposition to end a sentence up with' is an old joke, and introduces a superstition that dies hard. True, the very word *preposition* ('placed in front of') suggests that the proper place for a preposition is in front of the noun or noun equivalent it governs. And indeed that is the place for it if its being there does not upset naturalness of diction or idiom. MEU sums up the matter thus:

'Follow no arbitrary rule, but remember that there are often two or more possible arrangements between which a choice should be consciously made; if the abnormal, or at least unorthodox, final preposition that has naturally presented itself sounds comfortable, keep it; if it does not sound comfortable, still keep it if it has compensating vigour, or when among awkward possibilities it is the least awkward.'

One or two hints will be found useful:

(*a*) The preposition must come at the end of the clause or sentence when it governs a relative pronoun that is

(i) not expressed, (ii) represented by *as* or *that*:

(i) That is the room I slept in.
(ii) The present argument is the most abstract that ever I engaged in.
'Such bitter business as the day would quake to look on.'

(*b*) It stands naturally at the end when it governs the interrogative pronoun: 'Whom did you give it to?' is less pedantic than 'To whom did you give it?'

(*c*) The so-called preposition sometimes turns out to be an adverb that is actually part of the verb. Thus in the sentence 'I will look into the matter', *into* is compounded in sense with *look*, making it in effect a transitive verb, so that the verb may be made passive with *into* standing as adverb at the end: 'The matter will be looked into.' See TRANSITIVE. In Shakespeare's English the 'preposition-adverb' *with* has the special form *withal* when it stands at the end of the sentence: 'This diamond he greets your wife *withal*.'

When the preposition does stand at the end, there arises sometimes a difficulty about case, especially with the interrogative pronoun. 'Who were you speaking to?' is so common as to be almost idiomatic. But the fact remains that *to*, though far removed, does still govern the interrogative pronoun in the accusative; and 'Whom were you speaking to?' should always be the version in writing.

presumptive, presumptuous. The former is almost exclusively a legal term meaning 'that which may be assumed to be valid or true until the contrary is proved'. Thus we speak of presumptive evidence or proof. The heir presumptive to a throne or an estate is the heir pending the birth of the heir apparent. *Presumptuous* means 'full of presumption', 'taking too much on oneself', 'unduly confident', 'arrogant'.

prevent. (*a*) The original sense was 'to come before' (Lat. *præ*+*venire* 'come'). It is so used in the Prayer Book: 'Prevent us . . . in all our doings', and in Shakespeare: 'So to prevent the time of life' (i.e. 'forestall death'). The transition to the modern sense of *hinder* or *stop* is a natural one.

(*b*) The modern constructions are (i) *prevent* (transitive) noun *from*+ gerund: 'I have prevented him from troubling you'; (ii) *prevent* with noun or gerund as object: 'His decision will prevent argument'; 'I shall try to prevent his coming'. The construction 'prevent *him* coming, doing, &c.,' is common in colloquial English, and is noted as 'Popular' in OED. But grammar demands the possessive qualifying the gerund. See GERUND.

primary, primitive. *Primary* means 'holding first place' (in time, or in importance, or in development), 'not derived'. Thus primary *meaning* (that from which others have been derived), *colour* (i.e. red, green, violet, or red, yellow, blue, which give all the others by mixture), *education* (i.e. in rudiments), *planet* (a body which revolves directly round the sun, not a satellite), *tense* (i.e. present, future, perfect, and future perfect). *Primitive* means 'early', 'undeveloped', 'rudimentary', 'uncouth'; thus primitive *customs, church, gland, tribes*.

principal, principle. *Principal* is an adjective (= chief) which may be used in certain senses as a noun. *Principle* is a noun (= 'fundamental truth as basis of reasoning; general law as guide to action; personal code of right conduct'—COD).

Principal: the four *principal* streets of the city; the *principal* character in the play; the *principal* (= the chief master) of a college; the interest on the *principal* (= the chief or capital sum of money); the *principal* clause of a sentence.

Principle: Newton formulated the *principle* of gravity; He was a man of high *principle*; He stuck to his *principles*; They refused to play cards, on *principle*.

probable. *Probable* as predicate adjective after anticipatory *it* ('It is probable') cannot be followed by an infinitive, but must be followed by a 'that—' noun clause: 'It is probable that it will happen', not 'It is probable to happen'. When it is a qualifying adjective *probable* should be followed by the present, not the future, tense: 'The probable result is (not 'will be') to antagonize the opposition.'

prolative. See INFINITIVE MOOD.

prolepsis is the anticipatory use of an adjective to express the result of the action of the verb, e.g. 'to drain the cup *dry*', 'to paint the town *red*' (i.e. until it becomes dry/red). So also:

'Heat me these irons *hot*' (Shakespeare);
'Had not spells . . . armed thee or charmed thee *strong*' (Milton).

pronouns. Pronouns are words that stand instead of nouns; they are used, that is, for the avoidance of noun-repetition. They may be conveniently classified as (*a*) *Definite*—that is, those that stand definitely for a noun expressed or inferred, and (*b*) *Indefinite*—those that have no actual relationship with a noun in their own or a neighbouring sentence, but stand *generally* for a noun. The Definite pronouns have for the most part retained their inflexions; they are classified and declined thus:

(*a*) *Personal*

		First Person (Person speaking)	Second Person (Person spoken to)
Singular	Nominative	I	[thou
	Accusative	me	thee
	Genitive	mine	thine
	Dative	me	thee]
Plural	Nominative	we	you
	Accusative	us	you
	Genitive	ours	yours
	Dative	us	you

(The plural form of the second person is in Mod.E. used also as the singular; *thou*, &c., are now used only in poetical or religious writing.)

(*b*) *Demonstrative* ('pointing out')

(i)

		Masculine	Feminine	Neuter
Singular	Nominative	he	she	it
	Accusative	him	her	it
	Genitive	his	hers	its
	Dative	him	her	it
Plural	Nominative		they	
	Accusative		them	
	Genitive		theirs	
	Dative		them	

(This pronoun is generally called the third person pronoun.)

(ii)   Singular: This   That
             Plural: These   Those

See also SUCH and SO, which are used idiomatically as demonstrative pronouns.

(*c*) *Interrogative and Relative*

		Personal	Impersonal
Singular and Plural	Nominative	who	which, what.
	Accusative	whom	which, what.
	Genitive	whose	whose
	Dative	whom	which

That and *as* are used in the nominative and accusative as relative pronouns. See RELATIVE PRONOUNS.

Most of the *indefinite* pronouns are indeclinable; but a few of them have a genitive form in 's. They may be classified thus:

(*a*) *one, someone, somebody, anyone, anybody, no-one, nobody, none, both, all.*

(b) The distributives *each, everyone, either, neither, whether*. See under DISTRIBUTIVES.

(c) *what*—an interrogative and also a 'demonstrative-relative' pronoun = *that which*. For syntax see WHAT.

proper. For the term as applied to nouns see COMMON AND PROPER.

prophecy, prophesy. See PRACTICE.

protagonist. *Protagonist* is not the opposite of *antagonist*. It means 'the actor who takes the chief part in a play—a sense readily admitting of figurative application to the most conspicuous personage in any affair' (MEU). It should not, therefore, (a) be qualified by an adjective like *chief* or *principal* or (b) be used as a synonym for *advocate*.

protasis. (Greek = 'stretching forward') is the name given to 'the first or introductory clause in a sentence, especially the clause which expresses the condition in a conditional sentence; opposed to APODOSIS' (OED).

provided. In the sentence 'Provided it is fine, we shall go', *provided* may be taken as a conjunction (= if), or the whole phrase may be regarded as absolute = '(it being) provided (that) it is fine'. The general rule for the use of *provided* in MEU will convince most hesitating users that it is simpler and safer to stick to *if*: 'A clause introduced by *provided* must express a stipulation (i.e. a demand for the prior fulfilment of a condition) made by the person who in the main sentence gives a conditional undertaking or vouches conditionally for a fact.' A single legitimate example from Shakespeare will illustrate that statement:

> 'I got a promise of this fair one here,
> To have her love, provided that your fortune
> Achieved her mistress.'

'*Providing that . . .*' should not be used in writing, though the construction is by no means uncommon in colloquial and in business English.

punctuation. All marks of punctuation except the full stop, which indicates the end of the sentence and is therefore indispensable to composition and syntax, are used for convenience in reading. Their main business is twofold: (a) to 'phrase' the sentence, showing at a glance the relationships of its various parts; (b) to indicate artificially the inflexion of the voice (e.g. in exclamation and question), and the inclusion of outside matter into the basic narrative (e.g. parenthesis, quotation, direct speech). The stops used in (a) are the comma, the semicolon, and in a less degree the colon; in (b) the exclamation mark, the question mark, brackets and the dash, quotation marks. It follows, then, that a punctuated sentence is one whose meaning and construction the reader can grasp with the minimum of effort. This does not mean that the punctuation must be lavish. Far from it. Over-stopping, especially with commas, is one of the commonest faults in writing. As far as the 'artificial' marks are concerned (i.e. those named under (b) above), the use is purely conventional, and is not uniform even among printers. It is interesting to remember that quotation marks are of comparatively modern origin, and on the whole they seem to be an unnecessary irritation in the reporting of conversation. That they are not used in the Bible does not make the Bible less easy to read.

The chief 'laws' of punctuation may be briefly summarized thus:
  (i) Remember that a great deal depends on the full stop.
  (ii) Spare the comma, and remember that there is such a mark as the semicolon.
  (iii) In artificial punctuation be consistent.
Hints and warnings are given under the names of the various stops mentioned in this general note.

purport. A difficult verb. One or two warnings are necessary as to its meaning and use. The examples are from MEU.
  (i) It cannot be used in the passive, since it is already passive in significance (= 'is supposed', 'is represented to be'). 'He had no information of a Treaty between Japan and Germany *purported* to have been made during the war.' (Correct to *supposed* or *purporting*.)
  (ii) It cannot have as subject a person as such: 'She *purports* to find a close parallel between the Aeschylean Trilogy and *The Ring*.' But it may have as subject ' a person viewed as a phenomenon of which the nature is indicated by speech, actions, &c.' (MEU): 'The Gibeonites sent men to Joshua *purporting* to be ambassadors from a far country.'

purpose. The three idioms connected with *purpose* are apt to get mixed:
  (*a*) Be to the, to little, to no *purpose*.
  (*b*) Do something to no, to little, to some, to much *purpose*.
  (*c*) Serve the, my, no *purpose*.
'It serves little purpose to go and be refused' is an example of a mixture of (*a*) or (*b*) with (*c*).
For Infinitive of Purpose see INFINITIVE MOOD, and for clauses of purpose see ADVERB CLAUSE.

quasi-adverbs. This is the term used by MEU of a few adjectives that may act idiomatically as adverbs in sentences of the type:
> 'He acted *contrary* to my wishes.'
> 'He dressed *preparatory* to going to the theatre.'
> 'He arrived *prior* to your going away.'

Other quasi-adverbs that may be used in the same way are: *according, pursuant, preliminary, previous, irrespective, regardless*.

quatrain. A four-lined stanza, or, as in the SONNET, a four-lined unit of a longer verse-form. To be noted especially are
  (*a*) *the heroic quatrain*, four iambic pentameters rhyming abab—the stanza of Gray's *Elegy*:
> 'Full many a gem of purest ray serene
> The dark unfathomed caves of ocean bear;
> Full many a flower is born to blush unseen,
> And waste its sweetness on the desert air.'

  (*b*) *the 'In Memoriam' stanza*, four iambic tetrameters rhyming abba—the stanza of Tennyson's *In Memoriam*:
> 'To-night the winds begin to rise
> And roar from yonder dropping day;
> The last red leaf is whirled away,
> The rooks are blown about the skies.'

(c) *the stanza of Fitzgerald's 'Omar Khayyám'*, four iambic pentameters rhyming aaba:

> 'The Moving Finger writes; and, having writ,
> Moves on: nor all thy Piety nor Wit
>   Shall lure it back to cancel half a Line,
> Nor all thy Tears wash out a Word of it.'

question as to. 'He will also try to supply an answer to the question as to whether Rugger or Lawn Tennis supplies the more ticklish problem for the commentator.' The 'as to', though common, is always superfluous. When the question is, as here, stated as a clause, the clause stands directly in apposition to the noun *question*: 'the question *whether Rugger ...*'. The other construction with *question* is liable to the same interference by 'as to'. 'The question as to costs was left over' is a common enough newspaper statement; but it is not English. When a simple noun (not a noun clause) is concerned in the question the idiom is 'The question of ...': 'The question of costs was left over.' Two idioms so simple and clear-cut as these do not deserve the bad treatment they so often get.

question mark. The mark (?) at the end of a direct question. For the position of the question mark in relation to inverted commas see INVERTED COMMAS.

quire. See CHOIR.

quite. *Almost quite*, *almost completely* and other phrases in which *almost* modifies an absolute word are logical absurdities. See also UNIQUE.

quotation marks. See INVERTED COMMAS.

quoth is properly the past tense of an OE. verb = to say. It is used only with direct speech, in 1st and 3rd person singular only, and always precedes its subject. Shakespeare uses it also in the 2nd singular, something like the modern abomination *says you*: 'Did they? quoth you'. The verb is combined with the third person pronoun *a* (= he) in *quotha* (= quoth he). But the word is obsolete in Mod.E.

rather. (a) 'I *had* rather' and 'I *would* rather' are equally idiomatic.
(b) *rather than*. The normal construction is illustrated in 'I would rather go than stay', where the two infinitives (*go* and *stay*) are balanced by *than*. By an extension of idiom such expressions as '*dying* rather than *surrender*', 'He *went* rather than *stay* as an unwelcome guest', where the infinitive balances another part of the verb, are justified. To substitute *surrendering* for *surrender* and *stayed* for *stay* would be unidiomatic.
See also PREFER.

re-. *Re-cover*, *re-pair*, *re-count*, *re-form*, *re-join*, *re-enforce*, and other artificial *re-* compounds are examples of ARTIFICIAL DISTINCTION.

reaction. In Chemistry we may talk of the *action* of sulphuric acid on copper and of the *reaction* of copper to sulphuric acid. When the two words are lifted out of their chemical context into the larger world of ordinary language, they retain their idiomatic constructions. If events in Germany act upon English politics, it means that English politics react, or show a reaction, to events in Germany.

reason. At least *three* warnings are necessary in connexion with the word *reason*:

(i) 'The reason is because' is a type of tautological expression that defies both grammar and logic. The correct idiom is 'The reason (why &c.) is that . . .', the *that* introducing a noun clause as complement of the verb *is*. So the sentence (from a BBC. film critic) 'The reason why I am dealing with so many pictures to-night is because I happen to have seen them all just recently' may be recast in two ways:

(a) 'The reason . . . is that I happen', (b) 'I am dealing with so many pictures to-night because I happen . . .'.

Equally bad, and almost equally common are: 'The reason . . . is due to', 'The reason . . . is on account of'.

(ii) 'because of that reason': a near relative of the error dealt with under (i). You act not *because of* but *for* a reason. *Reason* itself indicates cause.

(iii) 'The reason for the increase may be attributed to the rapid development of science during the past two centuries.' The increase may be attributed, not the reason; the reason *is* the rapid development. In all three types of sentence cited the trouble arises from a confusion of ideas that leads to a double statement of cause.

recipient. 'Sir Wilfrid Laurier, who was seventy years of age yesterday, was *the recipient of congratulations* from Mr. Asquith.' The quotation is from MEU, which asks bitterly 'Can any man say that sort of thing and retain a shred of self-respect?' The objection is to the flabby and woolly effect of the excessive use of nouns and to the circumlocutory four words instead of one: 'Sir Wilfrid was congratulated by' is briefer, clearer, and more direct. See PERIPHRASIS.

reciprocal. See MUTUAL.

recourse, resort, resource. The main idiomatic phrases are:

recourse—to have *recourse* to; without *recourse* to.

resort—in the last *resort* (and *resort* may be used in the two phrases given to *recourse* above; but *recourse* is preferable).

resource—as a last *resource*; the only *resource*; at the end of his *resources*. The commonest confusion is that between 'in the last resort' and 'as a last resource', where *resort* and *resource* are apt to change places, or one of them is made to do duty for both.

reflexive. Used in grammar of

(a) verbs whose subject and object are the same person or thing: '*He prides himself* on'; '*I sat myself* down.'

(b) pronouns which serve as objects to reflexive verbs, like *himself* and *myself* in the examples above. They are objects of the verb, but at the same time they refer to the doer of the action expressed in the verb; that is, the action performed by the subject is as it were 'thrown back' or 'reflected' on to itself. They may be summarized thus:

	First person	*Second person*	*Third person*
Sing.	myself	thyself	himself, herself, itself
Plural	ourselves	yourselves	themselves

The reflexive pronouns may also be governed by a preposition: 'I was talking to *myself*'; 'No man liveth unto *himself*'. Sometimes, especially in archaic English, the ordinary accusative form of the pronoun is used for the reflexive: 'I will bethink *me*'; 'I found the Weser rolling o'er *me*'. It is important to notice the difference between a reflexive pronoun, which is always the object of either a verb or a preposition, and an emphasizing pronoun which always stands in apposition to a noun or pronoun: 'Though the devil *himself* turn Jew'; 'I *myself* will go with you'.

regard. (i) The compound prepositional phrases 'with regard to' and 'in regard to' are generally unnecessary, since a simple preposition—e.g., *about, in*—may usually be substituted for them. Their chief legitimate position is at the beginning of a sentence, as a kind of introductory phrase: 'With regard to the other matter, we have not yet discussed it fully'; 'In regard to your proposition, there is nothing to be done.' The same rule applies to 'as regards', which has a similar use and meaning as AS TO: 'As regards the BBC., the whole principle will have to be revised.'

(ii) MEU gives a warning against the confusion of the constructions of *regard* and *consider*. *Consider* has the direct construction with the double accusative or accusative with qualifying adjective: 'I consider him a good man'; 'I consider it disgraceful'. *Regard* requires *as*: 'I regard him as a good man'; 'I regard it as disgraceful.'

(iii) *Regarding* is often used (cf. *respecting*) idiomatically as a preposition: 'There is very little to say *regarding* that other matter.' See CONSIDERING.

regretful, regrettable. The first means 'full of regret for', the second 'causing regret'. A person who does a *regrettable* action is often *regretful* afterwards.

relative pronoun. (*a*) *Forms:*

	Personal	Impersonal	Common
Nom.	who	which	that
Acc.	whom	which	that
Gen.	of whom	whose	
	whose		
Dat.	whom	whom	

As is used as a relative pronoun, especially after *such, same*. See under AS.

(*b*) *Syntax:*

1. When the relative pronoun is subject of the clause it introduces, it agrees with its antecedent in number and person. This agreement is expressed in the verb to which the relative pronoun is subject.
2. The relative pronoun is often omitted when it is not subject of the clause, as 'This is the house I mentioned to you'. Sometimes, especially in verse, the antecedent is not expressed; as in 'Who steals my purse steals trash' (= 'He who . . .').
3. *Which* is often, but *that* and *who* never, used adjectivally.
4. *Whom* and *which* may be governed by a preposition; *that* cannot be preceded by a preposition, but may be governed by a preposition standing at the end of its clause.

5. Discussing the difference between *that* and *which*, MEU arrives at the following general conclusions: (i) *that* is both personal and impersonal; (ii) *that* is often used in speech where *which* is used in writing; (iii) *that* is best reserved for defining adjective clauses, leaving *which* for non-defining clauses, except where the late position of a governing preposition with *that* would make the construction awkward.

6. The relative pronoun in all its forms does the work of a conjunction introducing a subordinate adjective clause.

See also ADJECTIVE CLAUSE, NUMBER, CASE, THAT, AS.

repel, repulse. The person who feels repulsion is *repelled*, not *repulsed*; *repulsed* means 'rejected'. The writer of the following probably did not intend to express his conviction that heaven would not reject him: 'I am awfully keen on the next life. I think it will be wonderful. Pearly gates and golden streets do not *repulse* me.'

replace. See SUBSTITUTE.

reported speech. See INDIRECT SPEECH.

resentment. The constructions are resentment *of*, *at*, *against*; never *to*.

resort, resource. See RECOURSE.

respect. (i) 'With respect to' and 'in respect of' come under the same suspicion of periphrasis, and should conform to the same rules, as 'with regard to', 'in regard to' and 'as regards'. See REGARD.

(ii) The present participle *respecting* is used idiomatically as a preposition; cf. CONSIDERING. But a simple preposition (e.g., *about*) is usually preferable.

(iii) RESPECTIVE, *respectable*, and *respectful* require a little thought and care. The first has an article to itself; *respectable* means 'able to be respected', *respectful*, 'full of respect'.

respective. *Respective* and *respectively* are words that have the effect of placing the various members of each of two groups of things or persons in their proper and intended relationship. Thus if we want to express concisely the fact that one boy, Tom, was given an apple and another boy, Jack, was given a pear, we can say, 'Tom and Jack were given an apple and a pear *respectively*.' *Respectively* implies the relationship:

> Tom————————→apple
> Jack————————→pear

It is obvious, therefore, that care must be taken with the order of the words in the two groups; if Tom is to have the apple, *Tom* and *apple* must come in the same position in their respective lists.

MEU (from which the following examples are taken) declares that *respective* and *respectively* are words seldom needed, and that they are often used merely 'for the air of thoroughness and precision they are supposed to give to a sentence'. Examples:

(i) The writing-room, silence-room, and recreation-room, have respectively blue and red arm-chairs. (Three rooms and two types of chairs. The bad syntax is the outcome of bad mathematics.)

(ii) He was a Fellow of Balliol College, Oxford, and of the University of London respectively. (There is only one person concerned; there can, therefore, be no question of the grouping [A with B and C with D] inferred by *respectively*. Say 'He was a Fellow of both . . .')

(iii) Having collected the total amount, the collector disburses to each proper authority its respective quota. (*Respective* is tautological after *each*.)

(iv) That training colleges for men and women *respectively* be provided on sites at Hammersmith and St. Pancras. (Here *respectively* is correct and necessary; to omit it would lead to the possible meaning that the colleges on both sites were for both men and women. *Respectively* makes it clear that the college on one site is for men, and that on the other site is for women. The same test may be applied to the simple example given at the beginning of this article. Without *respectively* Tom and Jack might have an apple and a pear apiece.)

retained accusative. See ACCUSATIVE CASE.

retained dative. See DATIVE CASE.

reverend, reverent. *Reverend* = deserving reverence; *reverent* = feeling reverence. As a title, *Reverend* is abbreviated *Revd.* or *Rev.* A clergyman should always have his envelope addressed thus: The Rev. J. (or John) Smith if his initial (or Christian name) is known, or The Rev. Mr. Smith, but never The Rev. Smith.

rhetorical question is the vivid expression of a statement in the form of a question. It is a device well known to orators—hence its name. For example, Carlyle's 'To us also, through every star, through every blade of grass, is not a God made visible, if we will open our minds and eyes?' is much more vivid in the form of a question than it would be as a mere statement.

rhyme. 1. So spelt: the word has the same derivation as *rhythm* (from Greek *rhuthmos*, 'flow') but comes through the French *rime*, for which reason the spelling *rime* in English is admitted by OED; but this spelling is often preferred by Saxonists on the erroneous assumption that the word is derived from OE. *riman*, 'count'.

2. A simple rhyme is the correspondence in sound of two final syllables. The rhyming syllables may be said to have normally two or three parts— a vowel, a consonant preceding, and sometimes a consonant following, the vowel. Of these the vowels and the *following* consonants (if any) must be identical in sound (not necessarily in spelling) and the *preceding* consonants must differ, in modern English rhyme. Thus, *mount—count, stuff—enough, load—rode, fox—clocks, birch—church, be—see*, are rhymes; *sight—site, write—right, soon—room, chord—cord, word—lord, go—do, two—to*, are not; though combinations such as *sight—site* (called 'identical rhymes') were once admissible and popular. *Fright* and *bright*, *blow* and *glow* are rhymes, since *fr, br, bl, gl* are considered as single consonant sounds. A rhyming syllable may be without an initial consonant; *ear—fear, ale—gale*, are rhymes.

In English rhymed verse the rhyme normally falls on the last stressed syllable of the lines. When this stressed syllable is the last in the line the rhyme is called *simple* or *masculine* or *strong*. Sometimes, however, an unstressed syllable follows the rhyming stress and the rhyme is then known as *weak* or *feminine*. Such unstressed syllables do not themselves rhyme, but are identical. Now and then, especially in jocular or humorous verse, a triple or even quadruple rhyme occurs—i.e. a rhyming stress followed by two or three identical unstressed syllables.

Simple Rhyme:

> Full well the boding tremblers learned to *trace*
> The day's disasters in his morning *face*;
> Full well the busy whisper, circling *round*,
> Conveyed the dismal tidings when he *frowned*.

Feminine Rhyme:

> Thus have I had thee as a dream doth *flatter*,
> In sleep a king, in waking no such *matter*.

Triple Rhyme:

> I've got new mythological ma*chinery*,
> And very handsome supernatural *scenery*.

Sometimes a syllable inside the line rhymes with the final syllable, to make an *Internal Rhyme*:

> The fair breeze *blew*, the white foam *flew*,
>   The furrow followed free;
> We were the *first* that ever *burst*
>   Into that silent sea.

Imperfect rhymes are such as do not conform to the above rules in every particular. Especially to be noticed are 'eye rhymes', i.e. those which exist only to the eye and not to the ear, like *quay—day*. These are sometimes admitted in English verse, perhaps because of our habit of reading verse more often than listening to it. Now and then changes of pronunciation work havoc with what was once a perfect rhyme. Thus in Pope's famous couplet:

> 'And thou, great Anna, whom three realms *obey*,
>   Dost sometimes counsel take—and sometimes *tea*',

the rhyme is imperfect in Mod.E. but was perfect in the 18th century, when *tea* was pronounced *tay*.

A special form of the imperfect rhyme is the 'cockney' rhyme. In this a syllable in *-or-* is allowed to rhyme with a syllable in *-aw-*, or a syllable in *-ar* with the long open *a*: *morn—dawn* (the most familiar one of all), *far—Africa*. Rupert Brooke, who, playfully taunting the villages about his own Grantchester, sang of the Barton men that they made cockney rhymes, was guilty at least once himself:

> 'But laughing and half-way up to heaven,
>   With wind and hill and *star*,
> I yet shall keep, before I sleep,
>   Your Ambarvalia.'

rhythm. Rhythm is 'flow' (Gk. *rhuthmos* 'flow') of sound resulting from the stress variations of the spoken language. In an ordinary sentence of conversation like 'I should be glad if you would come in and see me next Saturday' the stresses fall thus (′ = full stress; ‵ = medium stress): 'I should be glád if you would còme and sée me next Sáturday.' From that combination of stresses comes the rhythm of the sentence. In prose the falling of the stress is *irregular*; that is, the fully accented syllables do not occur at regular intervals. But in verse the fall of the stresses is fundamentally *regular*, with variations only for the avoidance of monotony. The three following passages illustrate (*a*) the normal irregular rhythm of prose, (*b*) an irregular rhythm tending to the regular in a style that hovers mid-way between prose and verse, (*c*) the regular rhythm of verse, with variations from the normal. In the prose passage the individual reader will mark his own stresses: in the verse passage the stresses are marked (´ = full stress; ` = medium stress).

(a) He was my friend and my father's friend all the life I can remember. I seem to have made foolish friendships ever since. Those are friendships which outlive a second generation. Old as I am waxing, in his eyes I was still the child he first knew me. To the last he called me Charley. I have none to call me Charley now. He was the last link that bound me to the Temple. You are but of yesterday. In him seem to have died the old plainness of manners and singleness of heart. Letters he knew nothing of, nor did his reading extend beyond the pages of the *Gentleman's Magazine*. Yet there was a pride of literature about him from being amongst books (he was librarian), and from some scraps of doubtful Latin which he had picked up in his office of entering students, that gave him very diverting airs of pedantry.

(b) Along the bed of the slanting ground, all between the stools of wood, there were heaps of dead brown leaves and sheltered mats of lichen, and drifts of spotted stick gone rotten, and tufts of rushes here and there full of fray and feathering. . . . Along and down the tiny banks, and nodding in to one another, even across main-channel, hung the brown arcade of ferns; some with gold tongues languishing; some with countless ear-drops jerking; some with great quilled ribs uprising and long jaws aflapping.

(c)

If Í should líve your épitáph to wríte
    As óne the týrant Déath doth hóld in fée,
And àt your énd in márble shóuld indíte
    The éstimáte of áll the wórld and mé;—
Thús, for your kíndness, shóuld the séntence stánd,
    Pássed by the stríctest júry òf my lóve:

'Sweet Béauty, stoĺen from eýe and fáce and hánd,
    Clúng to warm líps that dìd in músic móve'
Só, when the súbstance òf your flésh is thóught,
    Your vóice the écho òf a foólish pláy,
Thís shall be sáid: 'He gáve not áll for nóught,
    Who ìn old rímes did flíng his lífe awáy.'
      And Í am glád that àt your lást asséssing,
      Béauty shall stáy, unhármed by Déath's posséssing.

See also METRE and FOOT.

right. *Right* should hold its own against *rightly* in such sentences as:
'He did *right* to reject the offer.'
'He answered *right*.'
'If I remember *right*, he lives in Glasgow.'

But notice:
'He *rightly* rejected the offer.'
'He *rightly* refused to be bullied into submission.'

rise. See ARISE.

romantic. See CLASSICAL.

rouse. See AROUSE.

sake. In the formula 'for —'s sake' there are a few phrases in which the *s* is not inserted, and the apostrophe either stands alone or is itself omitted: *for conscience' sake*; *for goodness' sake*; *for peace' sake*. It will be noticed that the retention of the *'s* would, in each of these phrases, lead to cacophony. The MEU ruling is: 'When the enclosed word is both a common noun and one whose possessive (genitive) is a syllable longer than its subjective (nominative) the *s* of the possessive (genitive) is not used; an apostrophe is often, but not always, written'. 'For *goodness* sake' and 'for *mercy's* sake' illustrate the rule. Milton has 'for *intermission* sake'.

same. The use of *the same* for a pronoun (*it, them, they*, &c.), representing a noun already mentioned is roundly condemned by MEU as an illiteracy. But it was once a legitimate idiom: 'The same also hath sworn' (AV); '. . . grace and power faithfully to fulfil the same' (Prayer Book). It is common in commercial language: 'The specimens have been sent for your inspection; will you kindly return *the same* at your convenience?' Outside the business letter, however, it is rare; and since even there it is unnecessary, it might well be banished from the language altogether. The omission of the *the* ('will you kindly return *same*?') cannot be justified on any grounds whatever.

same . . . as.

(*a*) Miss Dwyer performed much the *same* service *that* another kindly spinster, Mary Greene, performed for another girl. ('same service *as*')

(*b*) The effort of finding words and phrases to express what they wished to say seemed to prevent many candidates from giving the *same* attention to grammatical forms *that* they had given to the translation into French. ('*as* they had given')

(*c*) The team spirit is the *same* spirit *that* creates tradition in a school or college or university. ('*as* creates', or omit *same*)

(*d*) That is the *same* street *in which* I lived for five years. ('*as* I lived in')

(*e*) That is the *same* spot *where* the accident occurred last week. (Omit *same*)

Sentences (*a*), (*b*), (*c*)—the first from a modern novel, the second from a London University examiner's report, and the third from *The Times Educational Supplement*—illustrate the error, common even among people who should know better, of using a relative pronoun instead of *as* after *same*. The construction is 'The same . . . as', where *as* represents a relative pronoun, either nominative or accusative. Sentence (*d*), however, raises a problem. *As* cannot be preceded but may be followed by a preposition (cf. THAT). The sentence must therefore be reconstructed thus: 'That is the same street as I lived in for five years.' It is better, however, when *as* would have to be governed by a preposition, to get rid of *same*. Thus sentence (*d*) is more simply and more idiomatically written: 'That is the street I lived in for five years.'

In sentence (*e*) *same* is followed incorrectly by a relative adverb or conjunction (see WHERE). If *same* is to be retained the sentence must read 'That is the *same* spot *as* that where . . .' But this awkward construction is better avoided by the omission of *same* as superfluous: 'That is the spot where . . .'

To sum up: (i) neither a relative pronoun nor a relative adverb should be used in correlation with *same*; (ii) in nominative and accusative uses *as* stands for the relative pronoun after *same*; (iii) it is wiser to avoid *same* followed by *as* governed by a preposition. See also ELLIPSIS.

scarcely. See HARDLY, SCARCELY.

scissors. For number see SINGULAR-PLURAL NOUNS.

Scotch, Scots, Scottish. As adjectives *Scotch* is preferred in England, *Scots* in Scotland, and *Scottish* (the uncontracted form of the other two) belongs to both countries. Note: Flying Scotsman, the famous express train; Scots Greys; Scots Guards.

Scotsman. 'The prevalent form used now by Scotch people is Scotsman' (OED). The quotation reveals the fact that the corresponding English is *Scotch* (Scotchman, -woman, &c.).

scurfy, scurvy. *Scurfy* is literal, 'full of scurf'; *scurvy* is a metaphorical and archaic term of contempt, exemplified in the Shakespearian 'Thou scurvy knave'.

selvedge, selvage. *Selvedge*, somewhat surprisingly, means what it says —'a self edge'. The first, then, is the natural spelling, with the usual change of *f* to *v*; and *selvage* is a corruption that has the disadvantage of obscuring the true etymology.

semicolon. The semicolon is the 'three-quarter' stop, ranking, that is, between the full stop and the comma. In general, it stands between two related clauses of a sentence that are not actually joined by a conjunction. Thus it is commonly used before a clause beginning with a conjunctive adverb like *therefore, then, however, so*. It often acts as a kind of 'rest' stop, especially in a long sentence where the last clause (following the semicolon) is a summary of what has gone before. Two or three of the following illustrative sentences are from RCR:

'To err is human; to forgive, divine.'
It was raining very hard yesterday; so we shall go into the town this afternoon.
'The temperate man's pleasures are always durable, because they are regular; and all his life is calm and serene, because it is innocent.'
(Here the semicolon is what may be called a 'balance' stop. Notice that it stands between the two parts of the sentence that are exactly balanced. A comma would be correct after *regular* but a semicolon is better, especially as there are already two commas in the sentence.)
'Never speak concerning what you are ignorant of; speak little of what you know; and whether you speak or say not a word, do it with judgement.'
(Three co-ordinate clauses)
'But for all the hurry of his coming, these were not the dews of exertion that he wiped away, but the moisture of some strangling anguish; for his face was white, and his voice, when he spoke, harsh and broken.'

For relation between semicolon and colon see COLON.

sense (< Latin *sentio, sensum*, I feel) has various awkward relatives and derivatives. They are here briefly set out:

sense. (*a*) Physical: any of the bodily faculties by which sensation is aroused (hearing, touch, &c.); (*b*) mental: practical wisdom, judgement, reason; (*c*) meaning.

sensibility. 'Exceptional openness to emotional impressions' (COD). Jane Austen's title *Sense and Sensibility* implies, therefore, the difference between reason and emotion.

sensible: (*a*) of good sense, reasonable; (*b*) perceptible by the senses— 'a sensible difference, alteration'; (*c*) aware, mindful of.

sensitive: easily influenced or affected by outside impressions—'He is sensitive to both praise and blame'; 'sensitive paper' (in photography); *sensible* had once (e.g., in Shakespeare and Milton) the meaning now possessed by *sensitive*.

sensuous: affecting the senses (in a good sense)—'Keats was a sensuous poet.'

sensual: affecting the senses (in a bad sense)—'sensual pleasures'. *Sensuous* is said to have been coined by Milton (in the phrase 'simple, sensuous and passionate', which he applies to great poetry) to avoid the use of *sensual*, which, even in his time, was definitely associated with evil. *Sentiment* and *sentimentality* are distant cousins of *sense*. The first does not, but the second does, convey the idea of excessive and uncontrolled feeling.

sentence.

'Set of words complete in itself, containing subject and predicate and conveying a statement, question, or command' (COD).

The classification of sentences according to construction has never been satisfactorily standardized; but the following is that given in the COD sub-definition: '*simple sentence*, with single subject and predicate; *compound sentence*, with more than one of either or both; *complex sentence*, with subordinate clause or clauses.' The only useful modification of these brief definitions would be to restrict the term *compound* to the sentence with two or more predicates—i.e. the sentence containing two or more co-ordinate clauses. It is obvious that a complex sentence may have two or more co-ordinate main clauses. Such a sentence may be conveniently called Double (or Multiple) Complex. We arrive, then, at the following classifications:

Simple   A

Compound   A —×— B —×— C —×— D

Complex   A \ a

Double Complex   A —×— B \ a

Multiple Complex   A —×— B —×— C —×— D \ a   \ c

Only the simplest forms are shown. A complex sentence may contain any number of subordinate clauses; in a double or multiple complex sentence each co-ordinate main clause may have any number of subordinate clauses. In general, it may be said that every sentence is built up on the following foundation:

Subject	Predicate	
Noun or Noun Equivalent	*Verb* (i) intransitive (ii) transitive —————————→	*Object* (Noun or Noun Equivalent)
	(iii) intransitive, but not completing the predicate (verb of incomplete predication)	*Complement* (Noun or Noun Equivalent; Adjective)

sequence of tenses presents no such difficulty in English as in Latin. The context will always decide what tense is to be used in a subordinate clause. The only special point to call attention to is the use of the present tense in a subordinate clause (expressing a gnomic or universal truth) dependent on a main clause containing a past indefinite. Thus we say: 'We were taught at school that the earth *is* (not *was*) round / that water *boils* (not *boiled*) at 212° F.' &c.

So 'I was informed that you *are* ill' is, we trust, incorrect; but 'I was informed that you *are* near-sighted' may be correct, for it states what may be a fact at all times.

seraph. See CHERUB.

sergeant, serjeant. The first is the military and police title; the second belongs to the law ('Common Serjeant', &c.).

sestet. See SONNET.

sew, sow. *Sew* is the verb used of needle and cotton; *sow* that used of seed. Both verbs are now weak in all forms except the past participle, where the strong form (*sewn, sown*) is still sometimes used. The forms are therefore:

	Past Simple Tense.	Past Participle
to sew	I sewed	sewn, sewed
to sow	I sowed	sown, sowed

It is noteworthy that *sewed* is an older form than *sewn* and (in Mod.E.) is commoner.

Shakespearian. So spelt (not *-ean*). For Shakespearian sonnet see SONNET.

shall and will. (*a*) as auxiliaries: in the Future Simple and the Future in the Past tenses of verbs, *shall* and *should* are used as auxiliaries in the first person, singular and plural, *will* and *would* in the other persons: 'I shall go', 'We should go', but 'He will go', 'You would go'. The first of the following sentences illustrates the common mistake of using *would* for *should* with the verb *like*; in the second sentence the first *will* is misused and the second is correct:

'I *would* like also to register a protest against the too-intellectual kind of parlour games.' / 'Nor *will* we be unduly fantastic if we see in the play Shakespeare's belief that the wise man who by unremitting toil learns to control Ariel and Caliban *will* wield powers that seem to others magical.'

(*b*) as notional verbs: *shall = must* in the second and third persons: 'You shall go, whether you wish to or not', 'He shall do it, in spite of your objections'; and *will = wish, determine,* in the first person: 'Give me my robe, for I will go', where *will* expresses not simple futurity but determination.

(*c*) *Shall* must be used for all persons in all clauses referring to indefinite future time: 'Whatever sum . . *shall* be received from Germany will be shared among the allies' (MEU).

(*d*) After words expressing intention, desire, &c. (but not expectation or hope), the auxiliary verb in a clause introduced by *that* is *shall* or *should*, never *will* or *would*. 'I am anxious that the right site *should* be selected'; 'It is intended that this *shall* be extended to every division.'

share. 'So far as Wagner was concerned Brahms shared similar views to Tchaikovsky.' An example of tautological haziness. If Brahms and Tchaikovsky *shared* views, there is no need to say that the views were *similar*. 'B *held* similar views to T's' (see SIMILAR), or 'B and T shared views.'

sharps. See CONSONANTS.

shears. For number see SINGULAR-PLURAL NOUNS.

shew, show. (i) *Show* is the usual spelling in Mod.E., though *shew* is by no means obsolete. It is common, for instance, at railway station barriers. The old spelling is kept also in *shewbread*. (ii) *Shown* is the usual past participle, though *showed* is sometimes used.

shrink. The forms are:
past tense: *shrank*.
past participle as verb and as predicative adjective: *shrunk*.
past participle as attributive adjective: *shrunken*.

shy. The *y* remains before a suffix: *shyer, shyly, shyness*. Cf. SLY.

sibilant. See CONSONANTS.

signal, single. The phrase is 'to *single* out (a man from a group or number of men)', not 'to *signal* out'.

similar. 'So far as Wagner was concerned Brahms shared similar views to Tchaikovsky.' A common error, in which the two items of the similarity are confused. Brahms's views can be similar only to other views—certainly not to a person (Tchaikovsky). Recast the sentence, correcting also another fault of expression: '. . . Brahms held similar views to those of . . .' or '. . . to Tchaikovsky's'. For a similar error see under LIKE; and for the alteration of *shared* to *held* see SHARE.

simile (Lat. 'like') is a figure of speech in which two things or actions are likened to each other either for clearness and ease of explanation or for rhetorical and poetical effect. There are two kinds of simile: (i) the simple simile, in which the likeness is expressed briefly and directly without enlargement; and (ii) the developed simile (known technically as the 'Homeric simile'), imitated in English from the classical epics of Homer and Virgil, where the likeness is expressed and afterwards developed in a descriptive picture. Both types are shown in the following examples, which illustrate this note without need for further comment:

Simple:

   (i) 'He giveth snow *like wool*; he scattereth the hoar-frost *like ashes*.'
  (ii) '*As the hart panteth after the water-brooks*, so panteth my soul after thee.'
 (iii) 'The leafless trees and every icy crag
        Tinkled *like iron*.'
 (iv) 'His eyen twinkled in his heed aright
        As doon the sterres on a frosty night.'

Developed:

 (i)   Then fly our greetings, fly our speech and smiles!
        As some grave Tyrian trader, from the sea,
        Descried at sunrise an emerging prow
       Lifting the cool-hair'd creepers stealthily,
        The fringes of a southward-facing brow
        Among the Aegean isles:

> And saw the merry Grecian coaster come,
>   Freighted with amber grapes, and Chian wine,
>   Green bursting figs, and tunnies steep'd in brine;
> And knew the intruders on his ancient home,
>
> The young light-hearted Masters of the waves;
>   And snatch'd his rudder, and shook out more sail,
>   And day and night held on indignantly
>   O'er the blue Midland waters with the gale,
>   Betwixt the Syrtes and soft Sicily,
>   To where the Atlantic raves
>   Outside the Western Straits, and unbent sails
>   There, where down cloudy cliffs, through sheets of foam,
>   Shy traffickers, the dark Iberians come;
>   And on the beach undid his corded bales.   (Arnold)

(ii)
> Thus they their doubtful consultations dark
> Ended, rejoicing in their matchless chief:
> *As when from mountain-tops the dusky clouds*
> *Ascending, while the North wind sleeps, o'erspread*
> *Heaven's cheerful face, the louring element*
> *Scowls o'er the darkened landscape snow, or shower;*
> *If chance the radiant Sun with farewell sweet*
> *Extend his evening beam, the fields revive,*
> *The birds their notes renew, and bleating herds*
> *Attest their joy, that hill and valley rings.*   (Milton)

(iii)
> So said he, and the barge with oar and sail
> Moved from the brink, *like some full-breasted swan*
> *That, fluting a wild carol ere her death,*
> *Ruffles her pure cold plume, and takes the flood*
> *With swarthy webs.*
>   (Tennyson)

singular-plural nouns. The nouns *scissors, shears, tongs, trousers,* and *tweezers* are all plural by etymology. If their singular aspect (as being *one* tool, *one* garment, &c.) is to be emphasized, the phrase 'a pair of scissors, shears, &c.', may be used, and the verb made singular, agreeing with *pair*: 'A pair of trousers was hanging in the shop'.

Four words with a plural-looking form, *lens, forceps, riches, biceps,* are etymologically singular. Of these, *lens* is always treated as singular (plural *lenses*), *riches* always as plural; *forceps* may be treated as either, but is usually singular; *biceps* is treated as a singular (plural *bicepses*). *Gallows* is very odd; it is really plural, but is now always treated as singular. On the other hand, *wages* is now always plural, though 'The wages of sin *is* death' (AV) reminds us that it was once singular.

slough. When this word means a marsh or bog, pronounce it *slau* (to rhyme with *cow*); when it means a skin or, as a verb, 'to cast off (a skin)', pronounce it *sluff*: 'the *Slau* of Despond', but 'the *sluff* of a snake'. See ARTIFICIAL DISTINCTION.

sly. The *y* remains before a suffix: *slyer, slyly* (not *slier, slily*). Cf. SHY.

smell.
> 'The roses smell *sweet*.'
> 'The room smells *sweetly* of violets.'

The adjective, not the adverb, follows *smell*, when there is no explanatory *of* phrase.

so. (i) When *so* is an adverb standing alone—that is, neither modifying

SONNET

an adjective or another adverb (as in 'so cold', 'so pleasantly') nor correlated with a conjunction (as in *so . . . that, so . . . as*)—it is the equivalent of *therefore,* and the best punctuation before it is a semicolon. Thus: 'It was raining hard; so we did not go out' (not 'hard, so'). Notice that in the sentence 'We could not go out, it was raining so hard' the comma stands, since the *so* gives the effect of a conjunction *for*; or the sentence is recast mentally: 'It was raining so hard that we could not go out.'

(ii) *do so.* The expression *do so*, where *so* is the equivalent of a demonstrative pronoun (= it, this, that), is a legitimate substitute for a verb already mentioned, but it should have the same form as the original verb—i.e. finite verb should stand with finite verb (not necessarily the same tense of the verb), participle with participle, active voice with active voice. Thus 'I did not go to the Baths this morning, but I shall do so to-morrow' is idiomatically and grammatically correct. The sentence 'You are warned not to trespass; anybody doing so will be prosecuted', while breaking the above rule may be defended for grammar, though not for idiom, on the ground that 'do so' = 'act thus'. But 'This book is not to be taken away; anybody doing so will be fined' is neither grammatical nor idiomatic. The moral is, abstain from using 'do so' except in the form (finite verb, infinite part, voice) of the original verb.

so far. There are two constructions:

(*a*) 'so far (successful, a success, a failure) *as* . . .' (where *as* = 'in proportion as');

(*b*) so far (i) as + infinitive ⎱ introducing a phrase or clause of conse
        (ii) that   ⎰ quence.

Examples:

(*a*) He was so far successful as he kept the batsman on the defensive (i.e. 'in proportion as he kept . . .'. If he did not keep the batsman on the defensive he was a failure; but if he did keep the batsman on the defensive all the time he was completely successful.)

(*b*) He was so far afraid of the consequences as to withdraw / that he withdrew his support.

solecism. Ancient writers tell us that the Greek language was barbarously corrupted among the Athenian colonists of Soloi in Cilicia. Hence a *solecism* (< Soloi) is an impropriety or irregularity in grammar, idiom, pronunciation, or manners.

somewhat. *Somewhat* should not be used to modify a word that is absolute or superlative in sense—'*somewhat* UNIQUE, amazing, extraordinary, pre-eminent'. Such usage reveals an illogical mind and the fact that the writer has not the courage of his convictions.

sonnet. The technical name for the fourteen-lined poem in rhymed iambic pentameters introduced into England by Wyatt and Surrey in the early 16th century. Its original form was imitated from the sonnet of Petrarch the Italian poet. This sonnet had two parts of eight lines and six lines respectively—the *octave* or *octet*, representing the 'flow' of the thought, followed after a definite break by the *sestet*, representing the 'ebb'. The rhyme scheme of the octet was abbaabba, and of the sestet usually cdcdcd or cdecde. Owing to the difficulty of rhyming, the strict Petrarchan form of the sonnet never became popular in

English. Milton used it, and Wordsworth and Keats after him; but none of these poets observed strictly the rule of the break between octet and sestet. The Elizabethan poets took the fourteen-lined stanza and adapted it to their own language and style. In the numerous sonnet sequences of the period all kinds of rhyme arrangements may be traced. Two are especially interesting:

(i) the arrangement used by Spenser in his *Amoretti*, in which the rhymes are delicately and ingeniously interlinked in the scheme ababbcbccdcdee, and

(ii) the arrangement which has since been recognized as the standard 'English' form, used by Shakespeare in his sonnet sequence. It consists of three quatrains rhyming abab, cdcd, efef, rounded off with a couplet, gg. The thought or argument is developed through the quatrains and finally clinched in the couplet.

(a) Petrarchan or Italian:

> Cyriack, whose grandsire, on the royal bench
>   Of British Themis, with no mean applause
>   Pronounced, and in his volumes taught, our laws,
> Which others at their bar so often wrench;
> To-day deep thoughts resolve with me to drench
>   In mirth, that after no repenting draws;
>   Let Euclid rest, and Archimedes pause,
> And what the Swede intend, and what the French.
> To measure life learn thou betimes, and know
>   Toward solid good what leads the nearest way;
>   For other things mild Heaven a time ordains,
> And disapproves that care, though wise in show,
>   That with superfluous burden loads the day,
>   And, when God sends a cheerful hour, refrains.

(Milton)

(Here Milton observes the break between octet and sestet. In other sonnets, including the famous 'On His Blindness', he does not.)

(b) Spenserian:

> One day I wrote her name upon the strand;
> But came the waves, and washed it away:
> Again, I wrote it with a second hand;
> But came the tide, and made my pains his prey.
> Vain man, said she, that dost in vain assay
> A mortal thing so to immortalize;
> For I myself shall like to this decay,
> And eek my name be wiped out likewise.
> Not so, quoth I: let baser things devise
> To die in dust, but you shall live by fame:
> My verse your virtues rare shall éternise,
> And in the heavens write your glorious name.
>   Where, whenas death shall all the world subdue,
>   Our love shall live, and later life renew.

(Spenser)

(c) Shakespearian or English:

> That time of year thou may'st in me behold
>   When yellow leaves, or none, or few, do hang
> Upon those boughs which shake against the cold,
>   Bare ruin'd choirs, where late the sweet birds sang.

In me thou see'st the twilight of such day
  As after sunset fadeth in the west,
Which by and by black night doth take away,
  Death's second self, that seals up all in rest.

In me thou see'st the glowing of such fire
  That on the ashes of his youth doth lie
As the death-bed whereon it must expire,
  Consumed with that which it was nourish'd by:

—This thou perceiv'st, which makes thy love more strong,
To love that well which thou must leave ere long.

(Shakespeare)

sort. (i) 'These sort of —'. Of the following sentences

> (*a*) These sort of things interest me
> (*b*) This sort of things interests me
> (*c*) This sort of thing interests me

(*a*) is definitely ungrammatical, since a singular noun is qualified by a plural demonstrative adjective, and, as subject, is yoked with a plural verb;

(*b*) is awkward and unidiomatic, but is at least grammatical;

(*c*) is grammatical and idiomatic, and is strongly recommended together with the alternative form 'Things of this sort'. But both OED and MEU deal leniently with the fault perpetrated in (*a*) and even more leniently with that in (*b*).

(ii) 'Sort of', in 'I sort of saw the ghost flit by', is a colloquialism which has been tolerated too long and does not deserve even the lenient treatment given it by OED and MEU. The remarks applied to *sort* throughout this note apply equally to *kind*.

specially. See ESPECIALLY.

spelling. Various rules for spelling are given under their appropriate headings (DOUBLE CONSONANTS, Y > I, IE AND EI, &c.). In general, English spelling may be said to be difficult for the following main reasons:

(i) The alphabet is

(*a*) defective, in that its twenty-six letters have to represent over forty different sounds. Thus all five vowels have widely different 'qualities' of pronunciation; and consonants may have distinct sounds—e.g., *c* and *g*, which may be hard or soft; *s*, which may be voiceless (*s*) or voiced (*z*); *t*, which may have the different sounds represented in *to*, *nature*, *admiration*;

(*b*) redundant, in the consonants *c* (soft = *s*; hard = *k*), *j* (= *g*, soft), *q* (= *k*), *x* (= *ks*).

(ii) English spelling is etymological rather than phonetic. Thus sounds are often represented in spelling that have long dropped out of pronunciation. *Gh* is the best example; it stands for an OE. guttural sound which has not survived in Mod.E. It is often mute (as in *plough*, *dough*), sometimes pronounced ff (as in *cough*, *rough*), once pronounced p (in *hiccough*) and once k (in *hough*).

In the same way we get 'silent' consonants that are (*a*) the survivals in spelling of OE. sounds—*g*nat, *k*now, *g*narled, or (*b*) Greek in origin—*p*salm, *p*neumatic, *p*sychology. Initial *ph* (= Greek φ), as in words compounded with *phil*(o)-, -*pho*be, *phono*-, -*pho*re, always indicates Greek origin.

A few words are deliberate etymological spellings of Latin derivatives—e.g., *debt* (<Latin *debitum*), *doubt* (<Latin *dubitare*, through O.F. *douter*), where the *b* was inserted deliberately about the 16th century in order to emphasize the Latin origin of the words. Their true form in Mod.E. should be *dette* (or *det*) and *dout*.

Spenserian stanza. The stanza invented by Spenser for *The Faerie Queene*, and used afterwards by various poets, especially Keats in *The Eve of Saint Agnes* and Byron in *Childe Harold's Pilgrimage*. It consists of nine lines, the first eight being iambic pentameters and the last an alexandrine, rounding off the stanza. The rhyme scheme is ababbcbcc. The following stanza is from *The Eve of Saint Agnes*:

> She hurried at his words, beset with fears,
> For there were sleeping dragons all around,
> At glaring watch, perhaps, with ready spears—
> Down the wide stairs a darkling way they found—.
> In all the house was heard no human sound.
> A chain-droop'd lamp was flickering by each door;
> The arras, rich with horseman, hawk, and hound,
> Fluttered in the besieging wind's uproar;
> And the long carpets rose along the gusty floor.

spirants. See CONSONANTS.

split infinitive. The intrusion of an adverb or an adverb phrase between the *to* and the verb of the infinitive: '*to* hastily *speak*', '*to* at least *take* notice'. MEU defends the construction when the avoidance of it would lead to stilted or self-conscious awkwardness or actual ambiguity. Thus—

> (*a*) It is difficult always to tell the truth.
> (*b*) It is difficult to tell the truth always.
> (*c*) It is difficult to tell always the truth.

Avoiding the split infinitive has led in (*a*) and (*b*) to definite ambiguity (does *always* modify the predicate *is difficult* or the infinitive *to tell*?) and in (*c*) to an intolerable awkwardness. Unless, therefore, the sentence is entirely recast the infinitive must be split: 'It is difficult to always tell the truth.' As if in support of his argument Fowler now and then splits an infinitive in MEU itself: 'Those who scorn grammar are apt to wrongly give the first the question mark they fail to give the second.' When anything more than a single adverb or a short adverb phrase comes between the *to* and the verb the construction is indefensible. Fowler quotes an almost unbelievable example: 'Its main idea is to historically, even while events are maturing, and divinely—from the Divine point of view—impeach the European system of Church and States.' Guiding rule: Do not split an infinitive unless to refrain would make your sentence awkward or ambiguous; never split an infinitive with a long phrase. Notice that 'to have often asked', 'to be idly scanning' are not examples of the split infinitive. The adverb falls between the auxiliary and the infinitive verb, not between the preposition and the verb.

spoiled, spoilt. *spoiled* = stripped, took away the possessions of; *spoilt* = damaged: The Israelites *spoiled* the Egyptians; A new hat is *spoilt* by rain.

spondee. See FOOT.

spry. Adverb *spryly*; the *y* does not >*i* before a suffix. Cf. SHY, SLY.

staffs, staves. In the metaphorical sense the plural of *staff* is *staffs*—especially in the meaning of personnel of a firm, office, school, &c. *Staves* is the plural in music, where there is even a back-formation *stave* for the singular. MEU gives *staves* as the plural 'in music and in archaic senses'. It is noteworthy that the word *staff* with the literal meaning of 'rod' or 'stick' is archaic; its plural is therefore *staves*.

stanza. A passage in *As You Like It* reminds us that the word *stanza* (or *stanzo*) was a new one in Shakespeare's time:

'*Jaques* I do not desire you to please me; I do desire you to sing. Come, more; another stanzo; call you them stanzos?

Amiens What you will, Monsieur Jaques.'

The word came from Italy, on the tide of the Renaissance, and was applied to the group of lines into which verse was sometimes divided. A poem like *Paradise Lost* has no stanza division metrically. But most lyrical poems, and some long narrative poems (e.g. Byron's *Don Juan*) are written in stanzas. Stanzas may be of all types in length and metrical structure. The three quoted below illustrate the variety in form:

(a)   We have short time to stay, as you,
            We have as short a Spring;
        As quick a growth to meet decay
            As you, or any thing.
                We die,
            As your hours do, and dry
                Away
        Like to the Summer's rain;
        Or as the pearls of morning's dew,
            Ne'er to be found again.
                (From *To Daffodils*, Herrick)

(b) Ye blessèd Creatures, I have heard the call
        Ye to each other make; I see
    The heavens laugh with you in your jubilee:
        My heart is at your festival,
        My head hath its coronal,
    The fullness of your bliss, I feel—I feel it all.
            O evil day! if I were sullen
            While Earth herself is adorning
                This sweet May-morning:
            And the children are culling
                On every side
        In a thousand valleys far and wide
        Fresh flowers; while the sun shines warm,
    And the babe leaps up on his mother's arm:—
            I hear, I hear, with joy I hear!
            —But there's a tree, of many, one,
    A single field which I have look'd upon,
    Both of them speak of something that is gone:
                The pansy at my feet
                Doth the same tale repeat:
    Whither is fled the visionary gleam?
    Where is it now, the glory and the dream?
                (A 'free' stanza, from *Ode on
                Intimations of Immortality*, Wordsworth)

(c) I cannot see what flowers are at my feet,
 Nor what soft incense hangs upon the boughs,
But, in embalmèd darkness, guess each sweet
 Wherewith the seasonable month endows
The grass, the thicket, and the fruit-tree wild;
 White hawthorn, and the pastoral eglantine;
 Fast-fading violets cover'd up in leaves;
  And mid-May's eldest child
The coming musk-rose, full of dewy wine,
 The murmurous haunt of flies on summer eves.

(From the *Ode to a Nightingale*, Keats)

Generally the stanzas of a poem are uniform, but not always. Thus *Lycidas* and *The Pied Piper of Hamelin* are examples of poems in which the stanzas are cunningly varied in form to suit the sense and 'atmosphere' of the verse.

See also QUATRAIN and SPENSERIAN STANZA; for the common use of 'verse' for 'stanza' see VERSE.

start. See BEGIN.

stationary, stationery. *Stationary* is an adjective, 'standing still': *stationery* a noun, meaning paper, envelopes, and other similar articles. A *stationer* was originally a man who had a fixed or 'standing' stall or booth from which to sell his wares, i.e. a 'shop-keeper', not a pedlar. The Latin root is *sto*, 'stand': *statio*, 'a standing place'.

step. For stepfather, -mother, &c. see IN-LAW.

stimulant, stimulus. *Stimulant* has a restricted meaning. Spirits and tonics calculated to excite the body or mind are *stimulants*; anything that urges a man on, 'stimulates' him, is a *stimulus* (Lat. 'a goad'). The schoolboy may think of an approaching examination as a *stimulus* to greater effort.

stoic, stoical. The COD definition of the noun *stoic* is: 'Philosopher of the school founded at Athens *c.* 308 B.C. by Zeno, making virtue the highest good, concentrating attention on ethics, and inculcating control of the passions and indifference to pleasure and pain'. When this philosophy is actually or by implication referred to, the adjective used is *stoic*: 'stoic indifference' is the indifference of a 'stoic philosopher'. *Stoical* is used in the more general sense: *stoical* indifference (e.g., to pain) is determined courageous indifference. The form *stoical*, not *stoic*, always qualifies persons: 'a *stoical* sufferer, soldier, batsman'.

stops. See CONSONANTS.

storey, story. The differentiation between the two words in spelling is not yet established and seems to be definitely losing ground, especially in the plural; but the word for a tale is always spelt without and the word for the floor is usually spelt with the *e*. The plural of *storey* is *storeys*, and the adjective *storeyed*. Milton's 'storied windows' were windows with Bible *stories* depicted on them.

stress. See ACCENT, RHYTHM.

stringed, strung. *Stringed* means 'furnished with a string or strings', and is formed from the noun *string*; *strung* is the past participle of the verb. Hence:

> *stringed* instruments; gut-*stringed* racket;
> highly *strung* nerves; over-*strung* piano.

strong and weak verbs. Strong verbs are those that survive from the OE. 'strong' conjugation which made its past tense and past participle by 'ABLAUT' or 'GRADATION', i.e. changes in the vowel change of the stem. In OE. there were seven variations of this vowel change or gradation, most of which survive in modern forms. The other main characteristic of the strong verb was its past participle ending in *-n*. In Modern English survivals there have been two main tendencies: (*a*) to retain only one vowel for the past tense and past participle where there were originally two; (*b*) to drop the *-n* ending of the participle. Typical modern strong verbs are: to sp*ea*k, I sp*o*ke, sp*o*ken; to dr*i*nk, I dr*a*nk, dr*u*nk; to kn*o*w, I kn*e*w, kn*o*wn.

Weak verbs form their past tense and past participle by the addition of a dental ending (-*d*, -*t*) to their present form: to talk, I talk*ed*, talk*ed*; to kill, I kill*ed*, kill*ed*; to lay, I lai*d*, lai*d*; to seek, I sough*t*, sough*t*; to keep, I kep*t*, kep*t*. The forms quoted illustrate certain orthographical and etymological peculiarities in weak verbs. Thus the vowel in *kept* is simply a shortening of the original vowel owing to the influence of the dental; *laid* exemplifies the orthographical vocalization of *y* (see Y>I); and the vowel of *seek* is an *i*-mutation form of the vowel in *sought* (see I-MUTATION). Most English verbs are weak: they comprise

(*a*) all OE. original weak verbs together with strong verbs that have become weak, of which *sleep* is an example. Chaucer has

> 'He slep namore than dooth a nightingale,'

where *slep* is the strong past tense. So also *help* and *climb* were once strong verbs, as we are reminded by the form *holpen* (in AV) and *clomb* (in, e.g., *The Ancient Mariner*);

(*b*) all newly formed verbs, and those of other than OE. origin (i.e. verbs derived from French, &c.); e.g., to arrive, arrived; to postpone, postponed; to telegraph, telegraphed.

strophe. See ODE.

subjunctive mood. 1. *Form*. The subjunctive inflexion reveals itself in Mod.E. only in (*a*) the 3rd singular present: '(if) he go'; '(if) he have'; and (*b*) in the present and past singular of the verb *to be*, '(if) I be', '(if) I were'. It follows that those compound tenses of a verb in which *to be* is an auxiliary have the subjunctive inflexion.

2. *Syntax*. The subjunctive is used in English

(*a*) in main clauses to express a wish (optative subjunctive): 'God *save* the King'; 'Far *be* it from me', or an exhortation (jussive subjunctive)—a very rare use, even in poetry: '*Wind* we up the height.'

(*b*) in subordinate clauses expressing (i) purpose, 'Work lest thou *fail*'; (ii) condition, 'If he *die* . . .'; or (iii) concession, 'Though he *kill* me . . .' But these examples point to the fact that even in such clauses the use of the subjunctive has almost died out. It is consistently used only when the verb *to be* is concerned. Indeed the verb *to be* is the last stronghold of the English subjunctive, at any rate in subordinate clauses. The sense of the subjunctive is often expressed by the auxiliaries *may* and *should*; but as an actual mood, with a special syntax such as it has in Latin and French, the subjunctive scarcely exists in English.

substitute, replace. When A is *substituted for* B, B is *replaced by* A.

such. Like SAME, *such* is followed not by the relative pronoun itself, but by *as* with the function of the relative: 'It was such a day as we rarely see in England' (not 'such a day which . . .'); 'Unto bad causes swear such creatures as men doubt'. In the second of the two sentences *such* is the equivalent of a demonstrative pronoun (such as = those whom).

For difficulties and dangers see SAME and ELLIPSIS.

suddenness. So spelt. Cf. GREENNESS and WITHHOLD.

suffix. See AFFIXES.

suit, suite. *Suit* is the original word (<OF. *suitte* 'a following') and is used in most senses: a suit to the King, lawsuit, a suit of clothes, a suit in cards; *suite* is a late (17th-century) borrowing from the same French source, and is distinguished from *suit* by pronunciation (swēt) as well as spelling. It has three main senses: (*a*) retinue of persons, (*b*) set of, e.g., rooms, furniture, (*c*) series of tunes in music.

summon. The verb is *summon* except in the special sense of 'serve with a legal summons', for which either *summon* or *summons* is correct. The noun is *summons* ('I received a *summons* from the Head Master to go to his study'), plural *summonses*.

superior. Superior *to*, not *than*. The important and interesting point is that *superior* is a Latin comparative which does not conform to the syntax of the English comparative. So also *inferior*, *exterior*.

superlative with any.

(*a*) The biggest circulation of any morning paper.
(*b*) The English have the ugliest towns and the most beautiful country of any nation in the world.
(*c*) Sir Thomas Barlow, the Physician Extraordinary to the King, has the most imposing list of degrees of any of his fellow recipients.

The idiom illustrated in these sentences, though illogical, is well established. It probably arises from a confusion of two logically and grammatically correct constructions: 'The morning paper with the biggest circulation of any [morning papers' circulations]' and 'The biggest circulation of [the circulations of] all the morning papers'. The use of *any* as a plural adjective or pronoun is quite grammatical, and the ellipses in these two examples are in accordance with usage and idiom.

But the fact that the usage is well established does not justify it; especially as it may be avoided in at least two ways: (i) by using one of the constructions illustrated above or (ii) by using a comparative instead of a superlative:

(*a*) 'A bigger circulation than that of any other morning paper.'
(*b*) 'The English have uglier towns and more beautiful country than any other nation in the world [has].'
(*c*) 'Sir Thomas Barlow, the Physician Extraordinary to the King, has a more imposing list of degrees than any of his fellow recipients [has].'

For the syntax of sentences (*b*) and (*c*) see ELLIPSIS.

swell. The past simple tense is *swelled*; the past participle *swollen*; '*swelled* head' is the only phrase which has the weak form for the participle.

syllepsis (Greek = 'taking together') is a rhetorical figure in which we have the application of a word to two others in different senses, or to two of which it grammatically suits one only. It is common in Latin. An adjective intended to qualify more than one noun is frequently expressed once only and is then put in the case and number of the noun nearest itself in the sentence: thus 'Omnes agri et maria', or 'Agri et maria omnia'.

'She was seen washing clothes with happiness and Pears' soap.'
'She swallowed bread and butter and a spasm of emotion' (from a recent novel).
'Kent beat the clock and Glamorgan' (from the Press).

Note that syllepsis is often confused with ZEUGMA. The difference is that syllepsis merely requires the single word to be understood in a different sense with each of its pair (*with, swallowed, beat* in the examples quoted). In zeugma the single word actually fails to give sense with one of its pair, and from it the appropriate word has to be supplied.

synecdoche (Greek = 'understood along with') is the figure in which a part is used for the whole, or the whole is used for the part, e.g., 'bread' (for food in general), 'brains' (for brainy people), 'sail' (for ship), all 'hands' on deck (for crew), 'England' (for the English Rugby XV or Cricket XI). Cf. METONYMY.

synesis (Greek = 'meaning'): a grammatical construction in accordance with the 'meaning' rather than with strict syntax—a 'constructio ad sensum'. A plural verb is frequently used with a noun of multitude as subject, e.g. 'A large number (= many) were present'. Milton gives us a strange example: 'minded Not to be absent at that spectacle', where 'not to be absent' is equivalent in sense to 'to be present'.

This construction is commoner in Latin than in English. Thus, a verb may agree only in sense with its subject:

pars (= alii) epulis *onerant* mensas.

Similarly an adjective may agree only in sense with its noun:

capita (= principes) coniurationis *caesi* sunt;

and a relative may agree only in sense with its antecedent:

otium atque divitiae—*quae* prima mortales putant.

synonym. Synonyms are words which have approximately the same meaning and use. If two words exactly coincide in meaning and use, the natural tendency is for one of them to drop out of the language. A simple example is the word *an*, which in Shakespeare's time had the same function and sense as *if*; in the fight for survival *if* won. Many other words now marked 'archaic' in dictionaries have dropped out in the same kind of battle of synonyms; others have run away and live to fight again with a meaning more or less far removed from their original one. *Wench, knave,* and *churl* are good examples of these; they have all forsaken their old dignity—*girl, boy,* and *peasant* or *labourer*—because there were so many synonymous terms to hand. English is peculiarly rich in synonyms because its vocabulary is derived from so many different sources.

True synonyms (i.e. words which are synonymous in every sense) are very rare: *gorse* and *furze*, two distinct names for the same plant, are completely synonymous. But usually 'synonyms' travel only part of the way together, and then their roads divide. MEU illustrates with the words *sense* and *meaning*. 'Two phrases may have the same sense or meaning'—here *sense* and *meaning* are synonyms; but 'a man of sense is not a man of meaning'—here *sense* and *meaning* are not synonyms.

-t. For *-t* as ending of past tense and past participle of weak verbs see -ED, -T.

tautology. Tautology is exactly what its etymology (Greek *tauto*, 'the same'+*logia*, meaning 'speech', 'way of speaking') connotes, 'saying the same kind of thing as one has already said'. It is one form of PLEONASM. Examples are rife in current speech and writing; e.g., 'very (most or quite) equal, perfect, ideal, complete, unique'; 'joint partnership'; 'surrounding circumstances'. MEU gives the example 'It is sheer pretence to suppose that speed and speed alone is the only thing that counts', where the tautology consists in repeating in *only* the idea that has already been expressed in *alone*. A few tautological idioms are well established: such are 'goods and chattels', 'pray and beseech', 'might and main', 'lord and master', 'last will and testament'.

tense. The action expressed in the verb may be thought of as taking place in three different *times*—Past, Present, Future—and may be of three different *types*—Simple, Continuous, Perfect. Simple action is expressed directly: *I go, I shall go*; continuous action is that which is incomplete: *I am going, I was going*; perfect action is that which is rounded off or complete: *I have gone, I had gone*. The following table represents the basic tenses of the verb in the indicative mood, active voice:

	Past	*Present*	*Future*
Simple	Strong: I saw Weak: I walked	I see I walk	I shall see I shall walk
Continuous	Strong: I was seeing Weak: I was walking	I am seeing I am walking	I shall be seeing I shall be walking
Perfect	Strong: I had seen Weak: I had walked	I have seen I have walked	I shall have seen I shall have walked

In addition there is the Future tense of indirect speech called *Future in the Past*: *Simple*: I should see; *Continuous*: I should be seeing; *Perfect*: I should have seen.

The auxiliary *do* makes special emphatic tenses in the present and the past: I do see; I did see. This is also the construction normally used in questions: 'Do you see?', not 'See you?'; 'Did he go?', not 'Went he?' and in negative sentences: 'I do not see', not 'I see not'.

See also SUBJUNCTIVE MOOD, PASSIVE VOICE, SEQUENCE OF TENSES, and DO.

tercet. See TERZA RIMA.

terza rima. In English verse, iambic pentameters arranged in groups of three, called *tercets*, to build up a stanza, 'so rhymed that every rhyme occurs thrice in alternate lines, except the rhymes of the first and last lines of a canto, which occur twice only'. It is the stanza of Dante's *Divina Commedia*: hence, perhaps, the retention of the Italian name in English. The most familiar example of *terza rima* in English is Shelley's 'Ode to the West Wind'. One stanza is here given to illustrate the definition above. It will be noted that Shelley has added a line to the usual scheme of the terza rima. According to the definition given above he should have stopped at the thirteenth line; but he adds a line and ends with a couplet—a slight departure from the scheme of true *terza rima*. The general mechanism of the verse form and the 'effect of unending continuity' (suggesting in this particular poem the rush of the wind) are clear in the passage quoted:

> If I were a dead leaf thou mightest bear,   *a*
>   If I were a swift cloud to fly with thee,   *b*
> A wave to pant beneath thy power, and share *a*
> The impulse of thy strength, only less free   *b*
>   Than thou, O uncontrollable! If even   *c*
> I were as in my boyhood, and could be   *b*
> The comrade of thy wanderings over Heaven, *c*
>   As then, when to outstrip thy skyey speed *d*
> Scarce seemed a vision, I would ne'er have striven *c*
> As thus with thee in prayer in my sore need. *d*
>   Oh, lift me as a wave, a leaf, a cloud!   *e*
> I fall upon the thorns of life! I bleed!   *d*
> A heavy weight of hours has chained and bowed *e*
> One too like thee: tameless, and swift, and proud. *e*

than. (i) *Than* is normally a conjunction, and follows only a comparative adjective or adverb. That is the safe guiding rule. Remember that *than* should not follow HARDLY, SCARCELY, PREFER, but should follow OTHER, RATHER, which are disguised comparatives, and *sooner* in the idiom *no sooner . . . than*. ELSE is the one true non-comparative to be followed by *than*.

(ii) For case after *than* see CASE. In one construction and one only is *than* admitted by the OED to be a preposition—that is, when it governs a relative pronoun. The *whom* in the following sentence is therefore correct: 'Now I hope you have noticed how I quietly inserted into that list of distinguished pianists *than whom* Mr. Horowitz is said to be greater one name which is, or was until quite recently, unfamiliar in London.'

that. *That* may be:

(i) a demonstrative adjective or a demonstrative pronoun (pl. *those*).

(ii) a relative pronoun, used mainly for introducing defining adjective clauses. It is important to note that as a relative pronoun it cannot be preceded by a preposition. In the following sentence the first adjective clause is defining and correctly introduced by *that*; the second adjective clause is non-defining and should be introduced by *which*: 'Sir Edward Elgar's work includes much *that* was definitely written for children, finishing with the Nursery Suite *that* was almost the last thing he composed.' Fowler deplores the fact that this distinction between *that* and *which* is not widely recognized in written English. See note under RELATIVE PRONOUN.

(iii) a conjunction introducing a noun clause.

(iv) a conjunction introducing an adverb clause of purpose, consequence ; often compounded with *so, in order*.

(v) in older English sometimes = *what, that which*:

> 'All the conspirators, save only he,
> Did *that* they did in envy of great Caesar.'

the. In the expressions '*the* more *the* merrier' and 'We are none *the* better', *the* is adverbial, representing an older instrumental demonstrative (= 'by this', 'by that'); the first expression means 'by what (= how much) more, by that (= so much) the merrier' and the second 'We are not by any amount better' (Lat. *quo . . . eo*; *quanto . . . tanto*).

The hideous syntactical traps into which this adverbial *the* may lead the unwary writer are discussed in eight or nine columns of MEU ; and the curious or timid reader is referred to them. One or two simple hints follow.

In the single type (i.e. where *the* occurs once) *the* is

(a) most idiomatic where (as in 'we are none the better') it is 'self-explanatory'; i.e. when no phrase or clause is added to represent the *that* in the hypothetical 'by that';

(b) less idiomatic, but common and defensible, where the *the* is supplemented by an explaining phrase: 'I am none the better for the change'. Here 'I am no better for the change' is a good alternative form ;

(c) not idiomatic where the comparative is followed by *than*: 'I am none the better than if I had had no change.'

In the double (*the . . . the*) type, the comparative of the first, or 'measure', clause should not be followed by a relative pronoun:

'The more limpets can be kept out of the sea, the better are the prospects of the oyster' (not 'limpets *that* can be kept').

'The less is said, the easier will be the settlement' (not 'the less *that* is said').

their, theirs. Both are plural, and cannot stand as possessives to singular indefinite pronouns like *one, anyone, everybody, nobody*, or distributives like *each*. The following sentences illustrate the error:

> 'Nobody has forgotten *their* books.'
> 'I have not taken mine; each of them has taken *theirs*.'

See also AGREEMENT and ATTRACTION, and for spelling of *theirs* see OURS.

there. In its use before verbs like *be* and *exist*, *there* is an anticipatory adverb, 'accompanying and announcing inversion of verb and subject' (MEU). The number of the verb is, of course, determined by the number of the subject, not by *there*. But *there* is always apt to attract the verb into the singular, especially in speech: 'There's two of them', instead of 'There are . . .'. Such colloquial usage should not creep into writing. Perhaps Shakespeare's 'There is pansies, that's for thoughts' has something to answer for.

thus. 'Smith was bowled by the last ball of the match, *thus* giving us the victory by ten runs.' The sentence illustrates a slovenly use of *thus* in an attempt to disguise an UNATTACHED PARTICIPLE. Two questions arise:

(a) What does *giving* qualify? Obviously not *Smith* or *ball* or *match*, but the general idea in the clause. The participle is so loosely attached as to offend against the laws of syntax; so *thus* is introduced to throw dust in the eyes of the reader. But (*b*) what does *thus* mean? 'By that'? By what? The *that* is just as undefined as the noun which the participle should qualify.

titles. In writing, when quoting the titles of books, &c., (*a*) main titles should be underlined (= italicized in print); titles of chapters, poems, &c., inside a book should be set in inverted commas. Thus: 'To Daffodils' is one of the best-known poems in Herrick's *Hesperides*. Names of battleships and liners also should be underlined: The *Bellerophon* sailed to-day for China; I have booked a passage to Sydney on the *Orontes*.

(*b*) Special care must be taken in indicating titles that begin with an article, indefinite or definite. In the sentence '*The Daily Telegraph* is a famous morning newspaper' the article is part of the title, and is therefore italicized; but in the sentences 'The *Daily Telegraph* was lying on the table' and 'Have you seen the *Daily Telegraph*?' the article is used in the ordinary way, and is not part of the title. The *Daily Telegraph* = the copy of *The Daily Telegraph*; i.e. the ordinary (un-italicized) article has swallowed up the title-article. But *The Times* insists upon being always *The Times*. So, 'Dickens wrote *A Tale of Two Cities*' but 'The/A *Tale of Two Cities* was on the second shelf of the bookcase'. The title *A Tale of Two Cities* is a reminder that special care should be taken to quote a title correctly. Dickens did not write *The Tale of Two Cities*. A. E. Housman wrote *A Shropshire Lad*, though the University of London Regulations for the Higher School Certificate quoted it as *The Shropshire Lad* for two or three years on end.

(*c*) A title is always singular. '*Loyalties* is Mr. Galsworthy's most famous play' not '*Loyalties* are'; '*Poems of To-day* is a familiar anthology of modern verse', not 'are'.

(*d*) For capital letters in titles see CAPITAL LETTERS.

ton, tun. *Ton* is the word for the measure of weight, *tun* for the measure of capacity: a *ton* of coals; a *tun* cask, vat; a *tun* of wine.

tongs. For number see SINGULAR-PLURAL NOUNS.

transferred epithet. See HYPALLAGE.

transient, transitional, transitive, transitory. All four adjectives are derived from the Latin words *trans*, 'across'+*eo*, 'I go'. *Transitional* = at the 'going across' from one thing (e.g. period, style, régime) to another. We talk of a *transitional* period in history; i.e. one that stands between two defined and generally contrasted periods. TRANSITIVE has a grammatical meaning only. *Transitory* and *transient* are as nearly synonymous as any two words may well be, but each has meanings it does not share with the other. *Transient* refers to the affairs and feelings of man—*transient* greatness, hopes, fears; the Prayer Book speaks of life itself as *transitory*.

transitive. A verb is said to be used transitively (Lat. *transire*, to go across) when the action or state that it denotes is regarded as *going over* to, i.e. as directed towards, an object. When the action or state is regarded as affecting only the subject, i.e. as not directed towards an object, the verb is called *intransitive*. In 'Birds *fly*', the verb is intransitive; in 'Boys *fly* kites' it is transitive. Many verbs can thus be used either transitively or intransitively, but of course with a difference in meaning, as is illustrated in the above two sentences. A verb that would normally be intransitive may be followed by an object of kindred meaning with that expressed by the verb, i.e. a cognate object, or by *it* as an impersonal object: e.g.,

Fight the good *fight*; He has *slept* the *sleep* of the just; to trip *it* lightly; to fight *it* out.

Note: (*a*) that an accusative of extent (of distance, time, cost) may follow intransitive verbs, e.g.,

He *swam* a hundred *yards*; He *lived* five *years* in London; This book *cost* five *shillings*.

(*b*) that idiomatically some intransitive verbs have a semi-passive sense (cf. Lat. *exulo* = I am banished; *vapulo* = I am beaten): e.g.,

The house *sells / lets* well; This cake *eats* short; The air *smells* fresh; Honey *tastes* sweet.

An intransitive verb may be made transitive in one of two ways:

(i) by the addition to it of a preposition which acquires an adverbial force: 'I *laugh*' (intrans.); 'I *laugh at* (trans.) you', which becomes in the passive 'You *are laughed at* by me'. Such a transitive formation is sometimes called a Prepositional Verb. It is simplest to analyse such a sentence as 'They tell us of an Indian tree' thus: They (subject), tell of (finite verb), an Indian tree (direct object), us (indirect object).

(ii) by combining the preposition with the verb, thus:

$$\textit{Intrans.} \left.\begin{array}{l} \text{run} \\ \text{go} \\ \text{come} \end{array}\right\} > \textit{trans.} \left\{\begin{array}{l} \text{outrun, overrun} \\ \text{undergo} \\ \text{overcome} \end{array}\right.$$

transpire does not mean 'occur', 'turn out', except in penny-a-line journalese. The etymological meaning is 'breathe through'; hence in the sense 'to leak out', 'to become known by degrees' the verb is used quite legitimately and correctly:

Cabinet secrets must not be allowed to *transpire* (correct).
It *transpired* that the day fixed for the excursion was wet (incorrect).

travel makes trave*ll*er, trave*ll*ing, trave*ll*ed.

triolet. A poem of eight lines in which the first, fourth, and seventh lines are the same, and the second and the eighth. The other three lines rhyme with these, thus: abaaabab. The great art of the triolet—as the *Encyclopaedia Britannica* reminds us—consists in using the refrain lines with a seeming inevitableness, and yet in each repetition slightly altering the meaning. Example (from Robert Bridges):

'When first we met we did not guess
That Love would prove so hard a master;
Of more than common friendliness
When first we met we did not guess.
Who could foretell this sore distress,
This irretrievable disaster
When first we met?—We did not guess
That Love would prove so hard a master.'

trochee. See FOOT.

trousers. For number see SINGULAR-PLURAL NOUNS.

try and. The correction 'try to [do, be,' &c.] is unnecessary; 'try and do' is an example of HENDIADYS.

tweezers. For number see SINGULAR-PLURAL NOUNS.

umlaut. Same as I-MUTATION.

un-. See IN-, UN-.

unattached participle. The participle which is so placed in the sentence as either to have no noun to qualify or to qualify the wrong noun. For further notes see ADJECTIVE PHRASE. One or two examples are given:

Knowing he was ill, there was nothing to be done.
  [Is the participle qualifying *nothing*? Correct: 'Knowing he was ill, I felt there was nothing &c.' *or* 'Since he was ill, there was nothing &c.'.]
Being a great philosopher, all honour is due to Pythagoras.
  [Is honour, then, a great philosopher? Correct: 'Being a great philosopher, Pythagoras is worthy of all honour.']
Worn out with the journey, the town seemed to the traveller miles away.
  [A worn-out town?]

But certain participles have attained to a state of independence in which they do not demand or require attachment to a noun; they take on instead a prepositional or adverbial quality. Such are: *considering, speaking, talking (of), coming (to), granting, failing, counting, allowing (for)*. The following sentences, taken from MEU, exemplify their use:

> Failing you, there is no chance left.
> Allowing for exceptions, the rule may stand.
> Twelve were saved, not counting the dog.
> Considering the circumstances, you were justified.

uninterested. See DISINTERESTED.

unique is a much misused epithet. Strictly speaking, it can be applied only to what is in some respect the sole existing specimen. The Sphinx, the Codex Sinaiticus, the Rock of Gibraltar, the Leaning Tower of Pisa are all unique, and of course we can correctly say 'This vase is so far as is known unique'. MEU allows *quite, almost, nearly, really, surely, perhaps, absolutely, in some respects* to modify unique. But nothing can be *rather, somewhat, more, most, very, comparatively* unique: there can be no degrees of uniqueness. See also QUITE and SOMEWHAT.

unities. See DRAMATIC UNITIES.

urban, urbane. *Urban* means 'of the city' in the literal sense: 'an urban district council'; 'urban (as opposed to *rural*) conditions': *urbane* is artificially distinguished by its spelling from *urban*, and means metaphorically 'of the city', i.e. 'of town manners', as opposed to *rustic*, 'of country manners'. The COD definition is 'courteous, suave, elegant, or refined in manner'.

use (noun).
        (*a*) What is the use of complaining?
        (*b*) There is no use in complaining.
        (*c*) It is no use complaining.
        (*d*) Complaining is no use.

MEU admits the idioms in (a) and (b) without question. Of (c) and (d) it says 'Critics would have us correct them by inserting *of*'. However, it attempted to justify the idioms without *of* partly on the admittedly imperfect analogy of 'It is no good', 'It is no harm', and partly as 'sturdy indefensibles'; and it awaited the OED's pronouncement. The OED is now complete; it gives the construction illustrated in (a) and (b), with quotations dating from 1382; and for the doubtful construction in (c) and (d) says merely 'with ellipse of prep.', giving as its first example a quotation from one of Shelley's letters (1820).

used. Ordinarily pronounced *ūzd*; but in the senses 'accustomed' and 'was accustomed' ('He used to be a good fellow'; 'He is used to disappointments') the consonants are unvoiced: *ūst*.

v. See F AND V.

valueless. See INVALUABLE.

venal, venial. *Venal* (Lat. *venum* = sale) means 'capable of being bought or sold, mercenary', and may be applied either to a person or to his conduct. *Venial* (Lat. *venia* = pardon) means 'pardonable' and therefore 'trivial'. A *venial* fault is one that has not much wrong in it.

verbal noun. The term verbal noun is applied to the infinite parts of the verb that act as nouns: i.e. the INFINITIVE MOOD and the GERUND. By some grammarians it is used particularly of the infinite part in *-ing* that has no verbal force. See GERUND (4).

verse. The difference between prose and verse is one of form, and may be tabulated thus:

Prose	Verse
no METRE	METRE
irregular RHYTHM	regular RHYTHM
no RHYME	(sometimes) RHYME

In effect, prose [<Latin *prosa*, i.e. *prorsa* (oratio) = straightforward speech] runs on, without any divisions into lines dependent upon metre and regular rhythm. Verse (<Lat. *versus* 'turn'), however, has such divisions. It is noteworthy that in strict terminology the term *verse* itself means a line (cf. its derivation); thus a quatrain consists of four 'verses'. But in popular terminology the term *verse* is applied to what should strictly be called a STANZA. There is no essential connexion of verse with poetry; it merely happens that in English most poetry is written in verse form. Written poetry may be, and often is, cast in the form of prose, e.g. in the Bible.

very. Should 'I was *very* pleased' be corrected to 'I was *much* (or *very much*) pleased'?

The question stated in more general terms is: Should *very* modify a past participle?; and the answer depends on the function of the participle. If the participle retains its verbal force the modifying word should be *much*, not *very*, since *very*, being a pure adverb of degree, cannot modify a verb. But if the past participle has become an adjective (having, that is, lost its verbal force) *very* may legitimately modify it. Thus:

I am *much* (or *very much*) concerned about it.
The Labour Opposition was *much* (or *very much*) disgusted with the Prime Minister.
We were *much* (or *very much*) surprised at your attitude.

where *concerned*, *disgusted*, and *surprised* are true participles, but

I am *very* tired.
He was *very* drunk.
The seating accommodation was *very* limited.

where *tired*, *drunk*, and *limited* are adjectives.

To return to the example given in the first sentence of this note, if *pleased* is considered as a pure adjective (= *glad*, *happy*) *very* may stand; but should *pleased* take upon itself verbal force as in the sentence 'I was pleased with your letter' (in which *glad*, *happy* cannot be substituted for *pleased*) the modifying word is *much*: 'I was *much* pleased with your letter'.

MEU notes that *afraid* and one or two other adjectives (e.g. *awake*, *aghast*) that are used only predicatively are under the same limitation as past participles in regard to modification by *very*, and *much*: 'I was *much* (not *very*) afraid of being ill'.

view. Three idiomatic constructions are tabulated below, with examples:

Idiom	Meaning	Example
(a) *in view of* (+noun)	'taking into account', 'considering'.	In view of the state of the ground, the match will not be played.
(b) *with a view to* (+noun, gerund, or less idiomatically infinitive)	'calculating upon or contemplating as a desired result'.	With a view to { the study of / studying / study } the most modern books, he joined the local Library.
(c) *with the view of* (+gerund)	same meaning as *with a view to*	With the view of studying the most modern books, &c.

The following sentences, quoted from MEU, are a reminder of the fact that it is possible to confuse the idioms:

'The Sultan will seek to obtain money *in view of* beginning for himself the preliminary reforms' ('with a view to');
'Dr. Keane was educated *with a view of* becoming a priest' (for *of* read *to*).

violoncello. So spelt (not 'vio*l*ncello'). The contraction is *'cello*. The *c* is pronounced *ch*.

virtual, virtuous. *Virtual* = in effect, but not in form. A *virtual* promise is one that is such for practical purposes, though not formally given; *virtuous* = possessing moral goodness, blameless.

vogue-words. Under this heading MEU tabulates and discusses certain words which, at various periods of the language, have become 'fashionable', and have usually taken some harm from their popularity. NICE, INDIVIDUAL, PROTAGONIST, METICULOUS are among the examples dealt with in this book. It is worth while remembering Feste's observation in *Twelfth Night*: 'Who you are and what you would are out of my welkin, I might say *element*, but the word is over-worn.' That is, *element* was a vogue-word in the time of Shakespeare.

voice. See PASSIVE VOICE.

wait. The constructions with *lie*, *lay* are '*lie* in wait for' and '*lay* wait for'. See also AWAIT.

waive, wave. You *wave* a thing, a person, aside; but you *waive* (= abandon) your claim.

wake, waken. See AWAKE.

was when. 'The last time I saw you was when we were standing on Victoria Station together.' An ellipsis for 'was the time when', which offends both idiom and grammar. Recast: 'I saw you last when we were standing . . .'; and always avoid *was when* if *when* is introducing a clause that grammatically would be complement of *was*.

way, weigh. 'Under *way*' or 'under *weigh*'? OED says '*under weigh* is a common variant of *under way*, from erroneous association with the phrase "to weigh anchor"'. Its earliest quotation for *under weigh* is dated 1785, and for *under way* 1743.

weak ending. See BLANK VERSE.

weak verb. See STRONG AND WEAK VERBS.

weights. See NUMBERS.

wharfs, wharves. *Wharfs* is the English and *wharves* the American plural; but the American plural is steadily gaining ground in England.

what. *What* is

(i) an interrogative pronoun and adjective:

> '*What* should I say to you?'
> '*What* pleasure have great princes?' } in direct question.

> 'I know not, gentlemen, *what* you intend' } in indirect question.
> 'I asked *what* book you were reading' }

(ii) what MEU calls an 'antecedent-relative'; i.e. a relative pronoun which has its antecedent contained in itself (= 'that/those which'):

> I appreciate *what* you say.
> '*What* follows is pure innocence.'
> There is something in *what* he says.

It follows that

(*a*) since *what* is itself a relative, a relative pronoun should not follow it in a co-ordinate clause or phrase. The example is from MEU: 'Francis Turner Palgrave, whose name is inseparably connected with *what* is probably the best, and *which* has certainly proved the most popular, of English anthologies.' *What* is the subject of the two co-ordinate clauses governed by *with*; the actual relative *which* is therefore an intrusion in the second clause. Correct: 'with what is probably the best, and has certainly proved—';

(*b*) since *what* as 'antecedent relative' can always be resolved into two parts (noun or demonstrative+relative) both parts must be taken care of in the sentence. Thus if the demonstrative part is plural—i.e. if *what* = 'those which'—*what* itself must be considered plural: 'What *seem* to be good reasons' (not *seems*, since *what* = 'reasons which'). In cases of doubt, it is always wise to resolve *what* into its parts and arrange for its government and agreement before dealing with it as a single word. That is the price we have to pay for what MEU calls its 'beautiful conciseness'.

whatever. For *whatever* and kindred forms (*whoever*, &c.), see -EVER.

when. 1. *When* has the following main uses in English:

    (*a*) as interrogative particle (adverb): '*When* does the play begin?'

    (*b*) as conjunction introducing a noun clause (indirect question): 'I asked him *when* the play began.'

    (*c*) as conjunction introducing an adverb clause of time: '*When* he left us, our conversation naturally turned upon so extraordinary a character.'

    (*d*) as relative conjunction (= at, during, in which time) introducing an adjective clause: 'During the first day or so of any tour there are moments of bitterness, *when* the traveller feels more than coldly towards his knapsack' (*when* = 'during which': antecedent, *moments*). See also WHERE, WHY.

    2. For *when* after *hardly* and *scarcely* see BUT, THAN, WHEN.

    3. *That* for *when*. The following sentence illustrates a familiar error: 'He may construct a picture in his mind of Cornwall in the year *that* the Lord-General came down with his army to meet its fate on the narrow neck of land between Lostwithiel and the sea.' *That* is used incorrectly for *in which* or *when*. The writer did not think of *when* and hesitated at the awkwardness of 'in the year in which'. So 'during the time that' is an ellipsis for 'during the time during which'. Usually the awkwardness of construction can be avoided by the use of *when*: 'during the time when'.

where. *Where* has the following main uses in English:

    (*a*) as interrogative particle (adverb); '*Where* are you going to, my pretty maid?'

    (*b*) as conjunction introducing a noun clause (indirect question): 'I don't know *where* he lives'.

    (*c*) as conjunction introducing an adverb clause of place: 'You turn to the right *where* the white house faces the road'.

    (*d*) as relative conjunction (= at, on, in, &c., which) introducing an adjective clause: 'I know a bank *where* the wild thyme blows'. See also under WHEN, WHY.

whether. *Whether* is a correlative conjunction (*whether . . . or*) introducing an indirect question or condition. The alternative which it infers may be (*a*) unexpressed, (*b*) elliptically expressed, (*c*) fully expressed:

    (*a*) I don't know whether he is here.
    (*b*) I don't know whether he is here or not.
    (*c*) I don't know whether he is here or is not here.

In (*a*) *if* is substituted for *whether* when the notion of an alternative is not to be emphasized. In (*b*) the idiom 'whether or no' alternates with the 'whether or not', especially when the *or* immediately follows *whether*. For *whether* following a noun or adjective see DOUBT.

while. (*a*) *While* is a subordinating conjunction, usually of time, but sometimes of contrast: 'While I was busy here and there, he was gone.' 'While you may be right, I cannot altogether agree with you.'

It is not a co-ordinating conjunction (= *and*) except in the modern journalistic and colloquial use which the OED terms 'colourless'. In the sentence 'Walters made 52 while Sutcliffe was making 16' *while* is a true subordinate conjunction of time; but in 'Walters made 52, *while* Sutcliffe made 16' *while* is 'colourless' (= *and*).

(*b*) *While* with the present participle in ellipsis sometimes introduces an UNATTACHED PARTICIPLE phrase: 'While waiting for them at the station, they were already on the way home by another road.'

The elliptical phrase with *while* is grammatically related to *they*; the sense, however, requires not *they* but *we*: correct to 'While we were waiting, they were . . .'

See also WORTH WHILE.

whoever. See -EVER.

whom.

'There is probably no word in the language more misused than *whom*, and it would not be a bad thing, as Sir Richard Paget suggests, if it were to disappear altogether. One can hardly look into a novel without finding it masquerading as a nominative ('Whom he understood was a Fascist', &c.). The converse error ('Who am I to believe') is more in the nature of a colloquialism, and does not offend in quite the same way. But we could very well get along without *whom* as we do without *thou* and *hath*. To-day it merely serves as a hurdle over which two people out of ten trip.'

The quotation is from a reputable newspaper. With such a specious argument as this to help us, however, we should soon rid our language of all the words that give us a little syntactical trouble. After all, the case of the interrogative and relative pronoun should not be difficult to decide. True, the colloquial use of the interrogative nominative *who* for accusative *whom* illustrated in the quotation is well established; it is common, for example, in Shakespeare. But there is no reason why what is permitted in the hurry of speech should also be permitted in writing, when a moment's mental analysis of the sentence concerned would decide the correct case to be used. For a treatment of the main (largely imaginary) difficulties, see CASE (in grammar).

why. 1. *Why* may be either (*a*) an interrogative or (*b*) a relative particle. As (*a*) it is used in a direct question ('*Why* did you do it?') or as the conjunction introducing a noun clause as indirect question ('I asked him *why* he did it'); as (*b*) it introduces an adjective clause qualifying *reason* ('The reason *why* I did it . . .').

2. 'He perceives that *why* Clare was not a poet of the first rank was that his attention was hampered by incessant beauties.' This is a muddle of two constructions, in which the *why* clause is wrongly burdened with the responsibility of being subject. The following corrections will make the matter clear:

(*a*) 'He perceives that the reason why Clare &c. was that . . .'
(*b*) 'He perceives that Clare was not a poet of the first rank because his attention . . .'

For a similar confusion see REASON.

will. (i) For difference between *shall* and *will* see SHALL AND WILL.

(ii) *Will*, like *shall*, is often used as a notional verb. Thus when Caesar says 'Give me my robe, for I will go' *will* has the definite meaning 'desire', 'am determined'. But, unlike *shall*, it has special notional forms of its own—*I will, thou willest, he wills, I willed*. Its chief use as a notional verb with these forms is in the special meaning 'leave by will': 'I willed him ten pounds.'

wit is an obsolete verb = to know. The present tense is *wot* and the past *wist*. The present participle survives in [un]*witting*ly. The infinitive *to wit* (= that is to say, namely) is used in legal documents.

> 'The slave . . . little *wots*
> What watch the King keeps to maintain the peace.'
> (Shakespeare)

> 'And Samson *wist* not that the Lord had departed from him.'
> (AV)

Some poets (e.g. Macaulay in *Horatius*) use *I wis* as though it were 1st person singular of a verb. It is really an adverb (one word) = certainly (OE. *gewis*, cf. Germ. *gewiss*).

> 'A right good knight, and trew of word *ywis*.'
> (Spenser)

withal. See PREPOSITION AT END.

withhold. Not *withold*. Cf. GREENNESS.

wont is the past participle of an obsolete verb *wonen* = to dwell, to be accustomed. The original past participle *woned* developed into *wont*, to which in course of time the past participle suffix -*ed* was again added, producing *wonted* (= accustomed).

word-confusion. Word-confusion may be due to

(*a*) what Doctor Johnson called 'ignorance, pure ignorance'. It is the besetting sin of such as overreach themselves in their use of what vocabulary they have, and fondly think they can correctly use unfamiliar words. Most of us are guilty at some time or other. See MALAPROPISM.

(*b*) a more pardonable mental (or even optical) confusion of words that look alike, as PRINCIPAL, PRINCIPLE; *statue, statute*; *alligator, allegory*. The result again is a MALAPROPISM.

(*c*) the even commoner confusion of words (particularly Latin derivatives) that have the same stem but different suffixes or (more rarely) prefixes, or that have subtle distinctions of meaning without any likeness of form.

A list of words liable to be so confused, adapted from a list in MEU, follows. Some of the more important groups are treated in their alphabetical place.

acceptance	acceptation
affect	effect
alternate	alternative
ascendancy	ascendant
ceremonial	ceremonious
complaisant	complacent
compose	comprise
consequent	consequential
contemptible	contemptuous

contend	contest	
continual	continuous	
continuance	continuation	
council	counsel	
definite	definitive	
deprecate	depreciate	
derisive	derisory	
distinct	distinctive	
euphemism	euphuism	euphony
expedient	expeditious	
factitious	fictitious	
imperial	imperious	
inflammable	inflammatory	
ingenious	ingenuous	
judicial	judicious	
laudable	laudatory	
luxuriant	luxurious	
masterful	masterly	
mutual	common	reciprocal
oblivious	unconscious	
observance	observation	
perspicacity	perspicuity	
precipitate	precipitous	
predicate	predict	
preface	prefix	
purport	purpose	
repel	repulse	
resource	recourse	resort
respective	respectable	respectful
reverend	reverent	
reversal	reversion	
transcendent	transcendental	
triumphal	triumphant	
unexceptionable	unexceptional	

worth. There is an obsolete verb *worth* (<OE *weorthen*, to come to pass, to happen, to become. Cf. Germ. *werden*) surviving only in 3rd sing. pres. subj. (used optatively):

> Woe *worth* (= be to) the day.

worth while. The chief point to remember is that the verb 'is worth' demands an object (see ACCUSATIVE CASE), and that *while*, as a noun (= time), acts as its object in certain idiomatic expressions. And out of this the question arises 'When does *worth* require *while* and when is it able to stand alone?' The simple answer is that it requires *while* only when it has no other object, and does not require *while* when it has another object. Of the following sentences those italicized are wrong:

(*a*) That was worth doing.
(*b*) *That was worth while doing.*
    (*doing* is object; *while* is therefore superfluous).
(*c*) It was worth doing.
(*d*) *It was worth doing the extra work.*
(*e*) It was worth while doing the extra work.
    (In (*c*) *doing* is the object; in (*d*) *doing* is not the object, but the real subject of the sentence, the *it* being anticipatory. 'Doing the extra work was worth (while).' It is obvious that *while* must be introduced as object.)

wry. Adverb *wryly*. As in SLY and SHY the *y* does not >*i* before a suffix.

y>i. General Rule. Final *y* becomes *i* before a suffix if the *y* is immediately preceded by a consonant. Representative examples: *lady—lad i es* (but *valley—valleys, boy—boys*), *happy—happ i ly, beauty—beaut i ful, pity—pit i less, lonely—lonel i ness, deny—den i al, marry—marr i age,*.

There are a few exceptions:

(*a*) *beauty, pity, bounty+ous>* beauteous, piteous, bounteous; the *e* has the effect of keeping the *t* hard.

(*b*) *y* does not change to *i* before a suffix beginning with *i*: *hurry-ing, worry-ing*.

(*c*) in certain monosyllables the final *y* is kept before the adverb suffix -ly and other suffixes; e.g., *shyness, shyer, shyest, shyly, slyly, slyness*. *Dry*, however, makes *dri-ly*, especially in the metaphorical sense.

(*d*) *flies* is the plural of *fly*, the insect; *flys* the plural of *fly*, the carriage.

(*e*) the three verbs *pay, say, lay*, make their past simple tense and past participle *paid, said, laid*.

(*f*) in the participle *dyeing* (from *to dye*) the *e* is kept to distinguish it from *dying* (from *to die*).

(*g*) *ga i ety*, not *gayety*, is the noun from the adjective *gay*.

yclept, the past participle of an obsolete verb (AS. *clipian*, to call) = called.

The *y* (OE. *ge-*, ME. *y, i*) is the past participle prefix, traces of which still survive as in *a-go* = *agone, ygoe, ygone*, past participle of 'to go'. Milton uses it incorrectly with the present participle in

> Under a star-*ypointing* pyramid,

but correctly in

> Yet first to those *ychain'd* in sleep.

your. In the sentence '*Your* worm is *your* only emperor for diet' the *your* is an idiomatic possessive corresponding with the ethic dative—possessive of familiar address. The idiom survives, perhaps with some twist of meaning towards sarcasm: 'There's *your* efficient BBC.'—the *your* inferring that the BBC. is the reverse of efficient.

yours. See OURS.

z. See -ISE, -IZE.

zeugma (Greek = yoking). In this figure a verb or adjective belongs to two or more nouns to only one of which it is strictly applicable. The word applicable to the other noun is suppressed. Horace supplies an excellent example in Latin:

> Te greges centum Siculaeque circum *mugiunt* vaccae,

where *mugiunt* is appropriate with *vaccae*, but not with *greges*, i.e. *oves*. Examples in English are:

> '*Kill* the boys and (*sc.* destroy) the luggage.'
> 'See Pan with flocks (*sc.* surrounded), with fruits Pomona *crowned*.'

See SYLLEPSIS.

WORDS DERIVED FROM NAMES OF PERSONS AND PLACES

abigail: a lady's-maid. The name originates in 1 Samuel xxv. 24–31, but its sense derives (probably) from a 'waiting gentlewoman' of that name in Beaumont and Fletcher's play, *The Scornful Lady* (1610).

academy: a place of study, < *Academus*, who gave his name to a grove near Athens in which the philosopher Plato taught.

argosy: a large merchant-vessel (earlier form *ragusye*), < *Ragusa* in Dalmatia.

arras: rich tapestry, < *Arras*, a town in Artois famous for the fabric.

artesian: an epithet for wells resembling those made in *Artois* in the eighteenth century.

assassin: the word derives from *hashashin* (= hashish eaters), the name of a tribe of fanatical Moslems at the time of the Crusades.

atlas: < *Atlas*, the Titan who held on his shoulders the pillars of the universe. Its use to denote a book of maps is probably due to a drawing of the Titan used as a frontispiece in a book of this kind by Mercator in the sixteenth century.

attic: < *Attica* in Greece. The small top storeys of large seventeenth-century buildings in the classical style were generally built in what was called the 'Attic order' (the columns of the main façade being Ionic, Corinthian, etc.). Hence *attic* came to mean the top storey of any tall house or building.

babel: a medley of sounds, < *Babel*, Genesis ix.

bakelite: an insulating material, named after its inventor, L.H. Baekeland, a Belgian professor (born 1863).

bantam: supposed to derive from *Bantam* in the north-west of Java.

bayonet: the weapon was first made or used in *Bayonne*.

bedlam: a lunatic asylum, < St. Mary of *Bethlehem*, the name of a hospital in London, which, founded as a priory, became a lunatic asylum in the fourteenth century.

beggar: probably from the French *beghard* or *beguin*, a lay mendicant order of the Middle Ages, called after Lambert *Bègue*.

Bessemer (steel): named after its inventor, Sir Henry *Bessemer* (d. 1898).

bohemian: < Fr. *bohémien*, meaning a gypsy (a native of Bohemia). The meaning of the English adjective and noun (socially unconventional, a socially unconventional person) was introduced by Thackeray.

bowdlerize: to expurgate and remove improper passages from a book, < Dr. Thomas *Bowdler* (d. 1825), who published an expurgated Shakespeare in 1818.

boycott: to isolate, cut off from social relations. Charles *Boycott* (d. 1897) suffered in this way at the hands of the Irish Land League about 1880.

brougham: a type of carriage called after Lord *Brougham* (d. 1868).

bunkum : nonsense, < the county of *Buncombe* in N. Carolina, whose member made a foolish speech in Congress.

burke: to 'strangle' or smother inquiry, < William *Burke*, a notorious strangler executed at Edinburgh in 1829.

calico: linen cloth, < *Calicut* on the coast of India.

cambric: a fabric, < *Cambrai* in France.

canter : < *Canterbury*; a 'Canterbury' gallop.

cardigan: named after the Earl of *Cardigan*, a distinguished figure in the Crimean War.

cereal: corn or corn-food, < *Ceres*, the goddess of corn.

champagne: the wine called after *Champagne*, a district in France; cf. also *port* (< *Oporto*), *madeira*, &c.

chesterfield: a couch, probably from the name of a nineteenth-century Earl of *Chesterfield*.

chimera : a bogy, fanciful conception, < *chimaera*, the fire-breathing monster killed by Bellerophon.

cicerone: a guide who makes explanations and comments to visitors, < *Cicero*, the famous Roman orator.

coach: named after *Kocs* in Hungary.

copper : < Lat. *Cyprium* aes, metal of Cyprus. Cf. *crape, cypress*.

cravat: a neck-tie, from a French form of *Croat*.

currant: dried grapes of *Corinth* in Greece.

dahlia: named after a Swedish botanist, *Dahl*, in 1791.

damask: figured woven material, < *Damascus*. Cf. *damascene* and *damson*.

davit : formerly also *davit*, the crane used to lower a ship's boats, probably < David. Cf. *jemmy*, < James.

dollar: named after the silver coin (*thaler*) first minted in Joachims*thal* (*dale* of St. Joachim) in the sixteenth century.

draconian : harsh (of laws), < *Dracon*, the rigorous Athenian legislator, B.C. 621.

dunce: a name originally applied, by their opponents, to the followers of John *Duns* Scotus, the celebrated Oxford philosopher (d. 1308).

epicure: one who cultivates a refined taste in food and drink, < *Epicurus*, the Athenian philosopher who believed that the highest good is pleasure.

euphuism: an elaborate prose style, which took its name from the romance, *Euphues, the Anatomy of Wit*, by John Lyly, 1578.

filbert: the nut which ripens about St. *Philbert's* day (August 22).

florin: (perhaps) named after the coins of *Florence*.

frank: straightforward, free, open, < the *Franks* (French) who in medieval times were the free people in their kingdom.

fuchsia: named after *Fuchs*, a German botanist of the sixteenth century.

galvanism: < *Galvani*, who first described the phenomenon in 1792.

gin: the spirit, an abbreviation of *Geneva*.

grog: the drink, so called because Admiral Vernon, who in 1740 ordered it to be served to the sailors, regularly wore a *grogram* cloak.

guillotine: instrument of execution, designed by *Guillotin* at the beginning of the French revolution (1789).

guinea: a coin first minted in 1663 for use in the *Guinea* trade.

gypsy: a corruption of *Egyptian*.

hansom (cab): named after its inventor, Joseph *Hansom* (1803–82).

hector: to bluster, bully, after *Hector* in Homer.

hermetically (sealed): < *Hermes*, god of secrets.

homeric (laughter): like that of the gods in Homer, as they watched lame Hephaestus hobbling.

indigo: the dye, < the Greek form for *India*.

jeremiad: a doleful complaining, < *Jeremiah*, the reputed author of the Lamentations, in O.T.

jersey: after *Jersey* in the Channel Islands, where knitting of this garment was long a staple industry.

jovial: light-hearted, after the planet of *Jove* (Jupiter), which was said to effect good-humour.

knickerbocker: the garment named after the pretended author of Washington Irving's *History of New York*.

laconic: terse. The people of *Laconia* (i.e. Sparta) were noted for their conciseness of speech.

lazaret: a hospital for the diseased poor, < *Lazarus*, Luke xvi. 20.

lumber: probably a variant of *Lombard*, < Lombard St., famous for its pawnbroking establishments.

lynch: illegal punishment or execution, named after Charles *Lynch*, a J.P. in Virginia, who in 1782 was exonerated for having illegally fined his opponents, or perhaps after Lynche's Creek in Carolina, a meeting place of the Vigilantes.

macadam: a material for repairing roads, invented by J. L. *McAdam* (d. 1836). The verb is *macadamize*.

magnet: the stone of Magnesia in Thessaly; cf. also *magnesia, manganese*.

malapropism: a ludicrous misuse of words, < Mrs. *Malaprop*, a character in Sheridan's play *The Rivals*.

martinet: a strict disciplinarian, from the name of General *Martinet*, a French drill-master of the reign of Louis XIV.

maudlin: weeping, tearful, sentimental, < St. Mary Magdalene, who was often represented in medieval pictures as weeping.

mausoleum: after *Mausolus*, King of Caria, for whom his wife Artemisia erected a magnificent tomb.

meander: after the river *Maeander* in Asia Minor, which winds unusually in its course.

mendelism : a theory of heredity, < G. J. *Mendel*, 1822–84.

mentor: adviser, < *Mentor*, the adviser of Ulysses' son Telemachus.

mercurial: sprightly, ready-witted, born under the influence of the planet *Mercury*.

milliner: a vendor of goods, < *Milan*.

muslin: ware, < *Mosul*, a town on the Tigris.

palace: < *Palatium*, the hill in Rome on which the Emperor Augustus built his home.

panic: < *Pan*, god of shepherds.

parchment: < *Pergamum* in Asia Minor.

parrot: a diminutive of *Pierre* (Peter).

pasteurization: the process invented by Louis *Pasteur* (d. 1895). The verb is *pasteurize*.

peach: Lat. *persicum* (*malum*) = Persian apple.

petrel: the sea-bird, named after St. *Peter*. Cf. cuddy, a donkey, from *Cuthbert*.

phaeton: a type of carriage, named after *Phaethon*, who drove the chariot of the sun so that it struck the earth.

pheasant: called after the river *Phasis* in Asia Minor.

pinchbeck: an alloy named after Christopher *Pinchbeck*, a watchmaker (d. 1732).

pistol: < *Pistoia*, a small town in Tuscany.

Plimsoll (line): named after Samuel *Plimsoll*, a supporter of the Merchant Shipping Act of 1876, which instituted the Plimsoll line.

quince: derived from *Cydonia* in Crete.

sandwich: said to derive from the Earl of *Sandwich* (d. 1792), who ate slices of meat and cold toast at the gaming-table.

saturnine: those born under the influence of the planet *Saturn* were credited with a gloomy disposition.

shrapnel: named after Gen. H. *Shrapnel*, who invented the shell during the Peninsular War.

silhouette: after Etienne de *Silhouette* (1709–67).

silk: ultimately from *Sericus* (Lat. = of *Seres*), the Oriental people from whom silk was obtained.

simony: < *Simon* Magus, *v.* Acts viii. 9–13.

solecism: < *Soloi*, a Greek colony in Cilicia.

spaniel: the *Spanish* dog.

spoonerism: accidental confusion of words, named after Rev. W. A. *Spooner*, Warden of New College, Oxford (died 1930), who was famous for such transpositions as 'half-warmed fish' for 'half-formed wish', &c.

stentorian: derived from *Stentor*, the powerful-voiced herald in Homer's *Iliad*.

stoic: < Greek *stoa* = porch. The philosopher Zeno founded his school in the Stoa Poicīlē (Painted Porch) at Athens.

tantalize: to exasperate. Tantalus was condemned by Zeus to stand up to the chin in water which always receded as he stooped to drink.

tawdry: originally applied to lace bought at (Sain)t *Audrey's* (or Etheldrida's) fair.

turkey: this bird, although introduced from America, took its name from *Turkey* by confusion with the African guinea-fowl; cf. also *turquoise*, a precious stone.

tweed: this cloth took its name from a confusion of *twill* (woven cloth) with *Tweed*, the name of the river.

volcano: < *Vulcan*, god of fire. Cf. *vulcanite*, *-ize*.

voltaic, volt: < *Volta*, the Italian physicist (d. 1827); cf. also *watt, ohm, ampere*.

worsted: the cloth called after *Worstead*, a parish in Norfolk.

PRINTED IN GREAT BRITAIN
AT THE UNIVERSITY PRESS, OXFORD
BY CHARLES BATEY, PRINTER TO THE UNIVERSITY